Customer Encounters on Twitter

Anna Tereszkiewicz

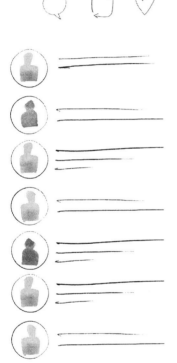

Customer Encounters on Twitter

A Study of Positive Evaluation and Complaint Management on English Corporate Profiles

JAGIELLONIAN UNIVERSITY PRESS

Reviewer
Prof. dr hab. Andrzej Łyda

Cover design
Małgorzata Flis

With the financial support of the Faculty of Philology of the Jagiellonian University

ISBN 978-83-233-4657-9
ISBN 978-83-233-9997-1 (e-book)

www.wuj.pl

Jagiellonian University Press
Editorial Offices: ul. Michałowskiego 9/2, 31-126 Kraków
Phone: +48 12 663 23 80, +48 12 663 23 82, Fax: +48 12 663 23 83
Distribution: Phone: +48 12 631 01 97, Fax: +48 12 631 01 98
Cell Phone: +48 506 006 674, e-mail: sprzedaz@wuj.pl
Bank: PEKAO SA, IBAN PL80 1240 4722 1111 0000 4856 3325

Table of contents

Acknowledgements

First and foremost, I would like to acknowledge the tremendous help provided by Professor Elżbieta Mańczak-Wohlfeld. I am truly grateful for her guidance, constant support and encouragement. Her advice and valuable comments concerning my research and the content of this work have been priceless. I am also truly indebted to Professor Andrzej Łyda for his insightful comments on the manuscript of the book and suggestions on the final shape of the work. I am grateful to Professor Marta Dąbrowska and Professor Grzegorz Szpila for the time they devoted to discussing the various components of my research. I would also like to thank all of my colleagues at the Jagiellonian University for their interest in this topic and my work in general. I wish to express my gratitude to the Faculty of Philology at the Jagiellonian University in Kraków for the financial assistance which made this publication possible.

Introduction

The analysis which follows focuses on customer encounters in social media. Owing to the widespread popularity of social media as a channel of corporate interaction, their extensive use among consumers as a means of electronic word-of-mouth communication and the role they play as corporate reputation management tools, it was considered interesting and important to investigate company practices in the management of online encounters. The analysis concentrates on two areas of customer interaction which are significant and/or critical for the company's reputation, i.e. positive and negative evaluation management, and aims to investigate strategies employed by English companies in the management of consumer reviews. The manner in which a company approaches such an evaluation is an important factor in determining the perception of the company by clients and may have consequences for the company's image and future relations with consumers.

More specifically, the study is devoted to customer encounters on Twitter, a microblogging platform. Twitter has been selected for analysis due to the characteristics of the medium, which may significantly impact the shape of customer encounters. The technological and medium-related factors which may influence the interaction comprise the following, among others:
- Twitter offers access to naturally occurring exchanges;
- Twitter, in contrast to other social media, places more emphasis on distributed content than on profile construction and people (Thelwall et al. 2011). The posts published by consumers, due to their rapid and real-time nature, are said to reflect the real-time interests of users. Consumers' messages are dynamic, spontaneous and usually genuine;
- interaction on Twitter is primarily text-based. The company's image is created mainly through the written message. The language and strategies used in the encounters, therefore, have a special commercial and strategic importance, since they are the primary determinants of the quality of service (cf. Cameron 2000b: 327-328, Jagodziński and Archer 2018);
- Twitter imposes constraints on the length of the message (140 words). Each message has to be brief or divided into several tweets;
- interactions can be conducted in synchronous and asynchronous forms. Twitter allows for both real-time and delayed communication;

– interaction is public by default. A large part of customer-encounters takes place on public profiles of the companies, in which case the interaction is open to other users. Since the impact of both positive and negative evaluation expressed in public can be significant for the company's image, companies need to undertake effective strategies to handle the comments;

– users may retain full or partial anonymity. Verification of the authenticity of the profiles is not required and users do not have to reveal their true identity. The anonymity of the users may influence customer interaction as it creates a favourable environment for trolling, uninhibited behaviour and aggressiveness, for the expression of severe and unfounded criticism of the company, as well as for the expression of fake and unfounded positive evaluation. Research has indicated that it is negative, critical and neutral rather than positive brand related content that tends to be published on Twitter more frequently, indicating that brands are particularly vulnerable in this channel of interaction (Smith et al. 2012: 111) and need to implement careful interaction strategies in these encounters.

In light of the above-mentioned factors, the objective of the study was to investigate the following aspects of the encounters:

– the structure of customer encounters on Twitter on British profiles;

– pragmatic strategies applied by companies in their interactions in the areas of positive evaluation, complaint and negative evaluation management;

– the structural complexity of companies' responses – the structure of specific acts, compositional units of the tweets, the presence of speech act sets in the tweets and the pragmatic function of the sets;

– the use of conventional politeness acts in companies' tweets, the presence of informal language and non-standard structures, the use of emoticons, emojis and hashtags.

The analysis aimed to verify the following hypotheses:

– company responses will reveal an emphasis placed on customer-orientation, on enhancing customer relations and creating or maintaining a positive image of the company owing to the public character of the interaction;

– in the case of complaint management strategies, a frequent use of apology strategies and a low occurrence of denials is expected;

– in the context of positive evaluation management, a high number and variety of promotional and self-praise strategies is hypothesized;

– company responses will reveal a relational orientation;

– company representatives will not be constrained by their institutional and social roles, and a tendency towards a diminishing of distance will be observed, reflecting the influence of the medium and the conventions typical of social media;

- a reduction in conventional politeness will be visible in company tweets owing to technological constraints and contextual features influencing the mode of interaction;
- a preference for the casual style of communication and informality will be observed in the language of companies' tweets.

Twitter has relatively recently been adapted for use as a channel of customer encounters. Therefore, the investigation of customer encounters in this channel may provide insights into emergent practices and reveal whether the medium and the context of the interaction influence the conventions associated with customer-provider interaction.

Overview of the content of the book

The book is divided into two major parts. The first part, comprising the first two chapters, was designed to provide a theoretical background to the analysis. The chapters are devoted to the phenomenon of social media interactions and the genre of customer encounters, respectively. The second part of the book focuses on corporate profiles on Twitter and investigates the management of positive evaluations and complaints.

More specifically, the respective chapters are devoted to the following themes.

Chapter 1 provides a definition of social media as a channel of interaction and proceeds to a discussion of the use of social media in corporate communication. The phenomenon of word-of-mouth and electronic word-of-mouth communication, a crucial component of corporate interaction, is characterized as well. The main focus of this part of the book, however, is on Twitter. The chapter describes the functionality of the service and its main characteristics. The use of the medium in different areas of personal and professional communication is also presented. The chapter closes with a discussion of the use of Twitter in corporate communication.

Chapter 2 is devoted to the phenomenon of customer encounters. Customer encounters are defined as a genre of interaction and their basic structural and linguistic properties are described. The chapter then proceeds to the presentation of an overview of the existing research and analytical approaches devoted to customer encounters in face-to-face communication and call centre interactions, as well as in online communication. The discussion also embraces the phenomenon of crisis communication and review management in different channels of interaction.

Chapter 3 provides a description of the basic characteristic features of corporate profiles on Twitter, i.e. provides examples of the structure and types of posts published on the profiles. The interaction on the profiles is described as an instance of discursive blending, with different modes of interaction interweaving in the tweets and exchanges.

Chapters 4 and 5 constitute the main analytical components of the book.

Chapter 4 is devoted to an analysis of the strategies employed by companies in the management of positive evaluations and complaints posted on their Twitter profiles. The focus of the first subchapter in this part of the book is on positive evaluation management. Consumer tweets featuring positive evaluations are exemplified, followed by a review of company response strategies, such as, for instance, acts of appreciation, compliment acceptance and compliment return. The subsequent part is devoted to complaint management on the analyzed profiles. An overview of consumers' complaints, the main constituents of the complaints and means of expression are outlined. The primary focus of this part, however, is placed on the investigation of complaint management strategies employed by the companies in the interaction. Acts constituting responses, such as requests, apologies and thanks are discussed, amongst others.

Chapter 5 focuses on conventional politeness acts in the messages and selected lexicogrammatical properties of the tweets. Opening and closing units are characterized, as well as forms of address and self-identification used in the interaction. The chapter also comprises a description of properties, such as the presence of informal and non-standard language in the tweets, language mistakes, the use of emoticons, hashtags and links.

The final part of the book presents conclusions concerning the analyzed interaction.

The analysis was designed to provide an insight into interactional practices on the profiles in the context of positive and negative evaluation and complaint management, and, in this way, contribute to the understanding of the use of Twitter in corporate interaction.

Chapter 1. Social media and corporate communication

1.1. Social media as a channel of communication

Social media have been defined as "online tools and platforms that allow Internet users to collaborate on content, share insights and experiences, and connect for business or pleasure" (Strauss and Frost 2009: 329) or "a group of Internet-based applications that build on the ideological technological foundations of web 2.0 and that allow the creation and exchange of user generated content" (Kaplan and Haenlein 2010: 61). In other studies, the term "social media" refers to "activities, practices, and behaviours among communities of people who gather online to share information, knowledge, and opinions using conversational media" (Safko and Brake 2009: 6) or to "the sharing of information, experiences, and perspectives throughout community-oriented websites" (Weinberg 2009: 1). The aspects underlined in the above-mentioned definitions, determining the nature of social media, comprise engagement in connecting, sharing and creating user-generated content.[1]

Social media encompass different channels of online communication, such as blogs, social networking sites (e.g. Facebook, Twitter, Instagram), professional networking (e.g. LinkedIn), video sharing (e.g. YouTube), picture sharing (e.g. flickr), review sites and social bookmarking (e.g. delicious, digg), social sharing of knowledge (e.g. Wikipedia), discussion forums and virtual worlds (Palmer and Koenig-Lewis 2009, Zarella 2010).[2]

Basic functionalities of these services comprise allowing individuals to construct a profile (public or semi-public), compose a list of users with whom the

---

[1] As Page (2012) observes, social media "refer to Internet-based applications that promote social interaction between participants. (…) Social media is often distinguished from forms of mass media, where mass media is presented as a one-to-many broadcasting mechanism. In contrast, social media delivers content via a network of participants where the content can be published by anyone but is still distributed across potentially large-scale audience" (ibid.: 6).

[2] A significant amount of research has been devoted to different aspects of social media use. Analyses of social media from a linguistic perspective comprise, among others, Crystal (2006), Danet and Herring (eds.) (2007), Myers (2010), Thurlow and Mroczek (eds.) (2011), Page (2012), Zappavigna (2012), Barton and Lee (2013), Dąbrowska (2013), Herring et al. (2013b), Tannen and Trester (eds.) (2013), Lomborg (2014), Seargeant and Tagg (eds.) (2014), Vásquez (2014), Trottier and Fuchs (eds.) (2015), Pihlaja (2016), Farina (2018), Georgalou (2018), Zappavigna (2018).

individuals connect within the system,[3] navigate through the list of connections (boyd and Ellison 2008: 211), interact with connected users, disseminate, like or comment on the content distributed within the network.

Twitter represents an example of a social networking service. Social networks are a category of social media[4] defined as "virtual communities created for people to connect with others by means of popular web-based tools" (Wallace et al. 2011: 102). The tools comprise Web 2.0 applications[5] allowing users to create and share user-generated content within their network of connections.

Research has shown that Internet users exploit different services simultaneously because each medium offers unique affordances (Phua et al. 2017a, 2017b). The choice of the medium is motivated by prior attitudes, self-regulation, media self-efficacy or habitual behaviour (Dimmick et al. 2004, LaRose and Eastin 2004, Ko et al. 2005). The wide variety of social media allows users to satisfy different needs, such as the need for information, entertainment, socializing or escapism. Various studies into social media have applied the uses and gratifications approach to analyze the motifs behind the use of the media. Whiting and Williams (2013), for instance, outlined ten major uses and gratifications of social media: social interaction, information seeking, passing time, entertainment, relaxation, communicatory utility, convenience utility, expression of opinion, information sharing, surveillance/knowledge about others. Orchard et al. (2014), studying motivations for using social networking sites, found that the purposes include information exchange, conformity, freedom of expression, social maintenance, recreation and, most importantly, making new connections.[6]

---

[3] As boyd and Ellison (2008) underline, "[w]hat makes social network sites unique is not that they allow individuals to meet strangers, but rather that they enable users to articulate and make visible their social networks" (ibid.: 211).

[4] The term "social networking service" is nowadays often used interchangeably with the term "social medium."

[5] Newman et al. (2016) define Web 2.0 as "sites and services that rely upon the generation of content by their users, as opposed to editors or dedicated content creators" (ibid.: 591, cf. O'Reilly 2005). The defining features of Web 2.0 comprise interconnectivity, interactivity, social networking, focus on user-generated content and using the potential of collective intelligence (O'Reilly 2005, Newman et al. 2016). Web 2.0 is contrasted with an earlier stage of the Internet, i.e. Web 1.0, based on a networked hyperlinked set of non-interactive websites ("Web 1.0"). The next stage of the development of Internet services is referred to as Web 3.0. This stage integrates new technologies such as Cloud Computing and Big Data, and the idea of the Internet of Things (Newman et al. 2016).

[6] Other studies focus on the uses and gratifications of specific social media. Quan-Haase and Young (2010) outlined six gratifications from Facebook use, i.e. passing time, showing affection, following fashion, sharing problems, demonstrating sociability, improving social knowledge. Participation in Facebook groups, in turn, has been found to allow users to fulfil the need for socializing, entertainment, self-status seeking and information (Park et al. 2009). The study by Gülnar et al. (2010) proved that uses and gratifications of both Facebook and YouTube comprise mainly self-expression, media drenching, passing time, information seeking, personal status updating, relationship maintenance, and entertainment. It is also worth mentioning the study by Phua et al. (2017b), who investigated the influence of social media on online bridging and bonding social capital, and found that Twitter had the highest bridging, while Snapchat the highest bonding social capital.

An interesting observation, made in many studies, is that social media no longer serve as tools used primarily for communication and networking, but have become important means of obtaining information, in this way allowing individuals to satisfy informational, emotional and social needs at the same time (Quan-Haase and Young 2010).

1.2. Social media and marketing communication

The use of social media has grown from being a tool of interaction for and among ordinary users to enjoying a role in other areas of communication. They also make an important contribution to marketing communication.

Studies into the use of social media in business and marketing communication have investigated the use of those media by both companies and consumers. Research has proved that social media have significantly impacted (Gallaugher and Ransbotham 2010: 197-198) or even disrupted (Nitins and Burgess 2014: 293) traditional customer relations, intensifying existing relations and bringing about new opportunities (Gallaugher and Ransbotham 2010: 197-198). Before, the relations between consumers and companies were largely limited to mass communication, with companies diffusing content and influencing consumers through advertising and marketing activities. In this process, interaction was largely unidirectional and customers were passive recipients of content produced and controlled by companies (Van Norel et al. 2014). Moreover, direct contact was restricted to face-to-face interaction in individual retail purchases or customer services, as well as mediated telephone or e-mail communication (Gallaugher and Ransbotham 2010: 197-198). The new media, by contrast, allow a multidi-rectional and interconnected relationship between consumers and producers (Hennig-Thurau et al. 2010, Van Norel et al. 2014), with the emphasis placed on dialogue and engagement (Nitins and Burgess 2014: 302).

The potential of social media as a marketing tool can be utilized in various areas of corporate communication by consumers and companies, allowing both parties to fulfil their communicative aims and interests. As Larson and Watson (2011) show, social media can be successfully applied in business-to-consumer (B2C) communication, allowing companies to fulfil their aims to inform con-sumers of new products or campaigns, as well as in consumer-to-business (C2B) communication, enabling consumers to communicate with companies. Finally, social media can be applied in consumer-to-consumer (C2C) interaction, lending consumers an opportunity to share experiences, opinions and make other consumers aware of brands.

A number of studies have been devoted to the use of social media by companies, examining why and how companies exploit the potential of these channels of communication. The studies have assumed different approaches, comprising a qualitative or quantitative analysis of social media messages, as well as interviews with marketing managers. Social media have been analyzed as a marketing, engagement and reputation management tool.

Several factors are believed to have contributed to the shift of companies towards social media and their engagement in social media interactions with stakeholders. These comprise the development of social media technology and new tools which the media offer, the growth and popularity of social media, declining response rates among consumers towards conventional online marketing in the form of banners and e-mail advertising, the shift of young consumers to online media, the decline in the use of traditional channels of marketing, changes in customers' preferences,[7] greater trust towards other consumers' opinions rather than companies' communications, low cost of social media campaigns, their viral nature, widespread reach, visible, ubiquitous and relatively permanent character, as well as the presence of competitors in the media (Gillin 2007, Hennig-Thurau et al. 2010, Tsimonis and Dimitriadis 2014).

Owing to the affordances and functionalities of the new media and changes in consumers' practices, traditional methods of marketing management, advertising and campaigning proved inadequate or inappropriate and thus created a need for companies to adjust to the new conventions of new media interactions, expand their activities, to develop new ways of interacting with consumers, new marketing and interaction strategies, with a new approach to the consumer considered as an active partner (Hennig-Thurau et al. 2010).

Among the strategies aimed at increasing a company's efficiency in social media, a proactive approach has been advised, involving building relationships, establishing and strengthening a community, offering consumers a place for interaction with the brand, with other consumers, encouraging consumers to participate and contribute user-generated content, triggering conversations, engaging with consumers, providing relevant and valuable content, offering incentives and providing consumers with feedback, thus validating their partic-

---

[7] Consumers of the new generation, the so-called Customers 3.0, tend to be characterized by the following features and behavioural tendencies: are highly informed (are highly skilled in information gathering and comparison of offers), price sensitive (focus on value for money), socially connected (actively use social media), trust the crowd (are more willing to trust other consumers' views rather than the communications of the brand), self-promoting (publish and promote information about themselves, their decisions and opinions), expect instant gratification (expect quick and timely delivery of information and services), expect immediate satisfaction, are security unconscious (are not concerned about security online) ("Say Hello to Customer 3.0" 2013).

ipation (McWilliam 2000, Zemke and Connellan 2001, Smith et al. 2012, Shin et al. 2015, Phua et al. 2017a).

Effective discourse strategies which can help companies to fulfil those aims comprise a dialogic approach, which is said to enhance brand attitudes, evaluations and purchase decisions. Implementing a dialogic approach is said to be a sign of a company's greater care and credibility (Colliander et al. 2015: 191). Other strategies comprise the inclusion of emotional sentiment, i.e. emotionally charged messages, inclusion of corporate brand names, but avoidance of explicitly commercial statements (Swani et al. 2013a, 2013b). Culnan et al. (2010) suggest a list of principles underlying effective social media use in three categories of mindful adoption, community building and absorptive capacity, advising companies on actions which should be undertaken to successfully exploit the potential offered by the media.[8]

Moreover, the type of the social media channel is a crucial factor in determining the company's approach and strategy. The selection of social media is broad and each channel may be used to serve different purposes. Each medium, e.g. Twitter, Facebook, Instagram or YouTube, offers different functionalities and may help the company to reach different consumers. In order to be effective, marketers should adjust campaigning strategies to the medium and create appropriate content according to the gratifications which the medium offers and which the users expect (Phua et al. 2017a).

---

[8] The principles are as follows: Mindful Adoption: match your adoption of social media platforms to your organization's culture, your customers, and your business objectives; make applications easy to find (maintain an inventory of all social media applications, provide links from the firm's homepage or an accessible "community" or gateway page, provide easy cross-navigation between your social media applications, make sure the links between your social media sites or links back to other websites work); develop quantitative and qualitative metrics for measuring the value of your social media applications (design metrics to measure community outcomes, e.g. size of community, frequency of participation, sharing of content with other social media sites; design metrics to measure traditional outcomes, e.g. revenues, cost savings, increased customer satisfaction); address risk management issues, including security and privacy issues (create a formal policy for employee use of social media, post a privacy notice and "house rules" for participants, train employees, monitor social media applications for potential problems); Community Building: continually populate the site with engaging content (assign formal responsibility for creating content, have executives or other company "celebrities" post and interact with community members); provide incentives for participation (e.g. recognition); don't mention the company in every conversation; balance freedom with control and accountability; be selective in deleting content; be sensitive to the norms and policies of any public platforms you use; Absorptive Capacity: assign responsibility to designated employees or departments for monitoring social media based on the objective(s) of the social media application; build on your organization's existing processes and expertise in public relations, customer service, product development, or elsewhere for processing customer communications received via other media; to structure messages, where feasible, integrate your social media applications with your existing web services (e.g. link to existing web customer support application); develop new procedures for message processing as needed for (identifying and responding to both routine and urgent messages, exception-handling, answering messages on a timely basis, integrating social media with your existing related applications); share knowledge across the firm, develop procedures and metrics for reporting (Culnan et al. 2010: 251).

The use of social media, the implementation of the correct social media strategy and active engagement with consumers has critical importance for any company's image and operations. The benefits which companies may obtain from using social media are manifold. Studies devoted to social media use by companies have proved that the media can significantly impact the company's image and its relations with consumers and stakeholders. An increase in brand visibility and a presence in social media can significantly enhance a company's financial performance by increasing sales and profitability (Swani et al. 2014). Further advantages derived from social media use comprise improved stake-holder management, integration, open innovation and crowdsourcing activities (Stieglitz and Krüger 2014: 281-283). Social media afford companies access to new audiences, their opinions and needs, providing companies with an additional channel for promotion and easy interaction with customers, as well as enabling brands to communicate with consumers and measure their communication, browsing or purchase-related behaviours, and to measure brand attitudes and engagement (Hennig-Thurau et al. 2010). Companies may enhance brand equity, increase brand awareness, establish brand identity and significance, encourage brand responses, create and foster relationships and brand loyalty (Van Mulken and der Meer 2005, Taylor et al. 2011, Kumar and Michandani 2012, Rapp et al. 2013, Wiersema 2013, Swani et al. 2014).

The most important benefit comprises engagement between individuals and the brand, creating or enhancing the relationship with consumers, creating new communication opportunities owing to the availability of direct, personalized and customized communication. Companies may interact with consumers, provide advice and information, handle customer service issues (Tsimonis and Dimitriadis 2014). Social media have an important effect also in times of crises and are an important crisis management tool (Stieglitz and Krüger 2014: 283). In this case, the media may help the company to handle crisis situations, mediate reactions and work on image improvement (Gallaugher and Ransbotham 2010: 207).

As far as consumers' perspective is concerned, social media, as pointed out above, allow customers to communicate with the company and with other consumers. Social media may enhance collaboration, enable interaction and participation, encourage content sharing (Jansen et al. 2009). In the new media, users may not only consume content produced by companies, but also generate and distribute brand-related information.

Research devoted to consumers' use of social media has shown that it largely depends on the medium and each channel offers a different form of user-generated brand-related content (Smith et al. 2012: 111). Brand-related content broadcast on YouTube, for instance, has a largely self-promotional character, with brands here playing a supporting role rather than a central one. On Twitter, by contrast, self-promotional content plays a minor role, dominated by news publication, discussions and interaction with the brand, with a more central role of the brand. Facebook, in turn, is located somewhere in between, combining self-promotion with interaction.

The study conducted by Phua et al. (2017a) examined the use of four social networking sites (SNSs): Facebook, Twitter, Instagram or Snapchat, for following brands. The results of the study indicate that Snapchat is mainly used for passing time, sharing problems and improving social knowledge, while Instagram is utilized to show affection, follow fashion and demonstrate sociability. The strongest brand community identification and membership intention was observed among Twitter users, whereas Instagram users exhibited the highest brand community engagement and commitment.

In general, consumer activities on brands' social media pages comprise participating in competitions, communication with other users, asking questions, providing feedback, sharing complaints or expressing thanks (Tsimonis and Dimitriadis 2014).

At this point it is worth mentioning some of the critical views of the corporate use of social media. Social media are here perceived as tools of manipulation, exploited by companies for purely instrumental purposes. It has also been observed that the practices employed by social media blur the distinction between the public, institutional or corporate, and the private, personal and social spheres, and thus exemplify the processes of conversationalization, pseudo-social performance and technological interactivity (Thurlow 2013, Page 2014, Lillqvist et al. 2016).

Thurlow (2013), for instance, claims that the use of social media by companies represents an instance of the commodification and technologization of communication. This process is noticeable in the case of "'discourse technologies' (Fairclough 1989: 216), where otherwise informal and/or interpersonal communicative genres are strategically recontextualized for instrumental (usually economic) purposes" (Thurlow 2013: 228). Thurlow further observes that social media practices exemplify conversationalization, understood as apparent friendliness used for instrumental purposes, and synthetic personalization, in which equality is simulated in order to disguise an "instrumental and manipulative relationship to the mass of people beneath a façade of personal and equal relationship" (Fairclough 1989: 216). As Thurlow (2013: 235) claims, companies create an illusion of intimate and sincere engagement with consumers, try to persuade consumers that sociality and engaging practices are possible not only with friends but also with products and brands. In this way, corporate strategies create an instance of pseudo-sociality, with companies stylizing themselves as participatory, interactive and accessible.

The view that social media exemplify the process of conversationalization and create an illusion of personalization and familiarity is shared by Lillqvist et al. (2016). The scholars show how corporate rhetoric can make companies seem friendly and familiar as a result of manipulation. The authors investigated those practices in a study in which they contrasted monologizing and dialogizing practices used by companies on the example of Facebook. Dialogizing practices comprise being responsive, carnivalistic and polyphonic, allowing users to introduce topics and engage in a conversation. These practices diminish distance between the participants and lend all participants access to public discourse. The scholars, however, also highlight a tendency towards using monologizing practices, in which companies are engaged, i.e. practices by means of which companies control participation in discourse, which comprise coercive and manipulative strategies. The former involve, for instance, preventing users from posting, while the latter encompass avoiding ethics-related topics and focusing on subjects with pleasant connotations. Monologizing practices can also be seen in blocking consumers' voices, deleting posts or censoring consumer participation. The scholars further claim that social media enable exploitation of consumer labour in that companies appropriate consumers' posts and consumer-created content for strategic and economic purposes.

In an earlier study, investigating impression management strategies on corporate profiles on Facebook, Lillqvist and Louhiala-Salminen (2014) outline two major categories of such strategies, i.e. social acceptability and credibility, both of which may be perceived as more or less sincere and manipulative. More specifically, as regards acceptability strategies, three types of strategies serve to uphold social acceptability by following cultural norms and values, i.e. the use of conventional politeness, appealing to moral discourse, mainly in cases of disagreement with consumers, and the strategy of diversion, by means of which companies try to divert attention from issues which threaten the company's social acceptability. Among the strategies enhancing the company's credibility, the scholars single out the category of entitlement and stake, in which representatives are presented as experts, the category of footing, when representatives distance themselves or align with the users' comments, and the category of ridicule, in which the representatives undermine the credibility of others.

In a different study, Floreddu and Cabiddu (2016) examined communication strategies used by companies on social media and found different degrees of openness and transparency among the companies. Communication strategies which can be perceived as more genuine, transparent and customer-oriented comprise the so-called conversational strategy, where companies respond to users' comments, aiming to create or deepen relations with consumers. These strategies include the openness strategy as well, in which companies respond to all remarks in public, with the aim of improving the transparency of conversations, and the supportive strategy, in which companies provide information about products and offers to inform and facilitate purchases. Strategies which can be considered as more controlling and manipulative include the egocentric strategy, where companies focus on sharing information, with the sole aim of increasing visibility in social media, but do not engage in direct conversations with consumers, or the selective strategy, in which companies filter positive comments and ignore negative opinions. This group also comprises the so-called secretive strategy, in which case companies direct conversations to other channels in order to avoid public management of conflicts. The study also compares the communication strategies used by low, medium and high reputation companies, and proves that high reputation brands in particular exploit social media effectively as a reputation management tool, aiming to improve customer perceptions of the company.

1.3. Social media and electronic word-of-mouth communication

As mentioned above, social media lend consumers an opportunity to connect, produce and share brand-related content. The properties of the media make it an ideal channel for the consumers to engage in brand related word-of-mouth communication (Riegner 2007, Zhang and Daugherty 2009, Chu and Kim 2011).

Word-of-mouth (WOM) communication involves exchanging marketing information among consumers (Chu and Kim 2011), comprising both positive or negative evaluative communication (Buttle 1998, Carl 2008). Since opinions expressed by consumers engaging in WOM are considered more reliable, more authentic and less biased than the messages generated by companies (Dellarocas 2003, Phelps et al. 2004, Ha 2006, Keller 2007, Daugherty and Hoffman 2014), WOM is claimed to play a significant role in influencing consumers' attitudes and brand perception (Katz and Lazarsfeld 1955). WOM is perceived as a critical marketing factor and is claimed to have a significant influence on the consumer's decision making process (Daugherty and Hoffman 2014). It may affect the company's operations in a positive way, attracting new customers to the brand and increasing sales (Chevalier and Mayzlin 2006, Daugherty and Hoffman 2014).

Electronic word-of-mouth (eWOM) communication is defined as "any positive or negative statement made by potential, actual, or former customers about a product or company, which is made available to a multitude of people and institutions via the Internet" (Hennig-Thurau et al. 2004: 39).[9]

By means of eWOM, consumers express and exchange opinions about services and products. The motives which underlie engagement in eWOM involve

---

[9] The channels which allow consumers to engage in eWOM comprise not only social media but also a range of platforms and websites, such as Amazon, eBay, TripAdvisor or Booking.com.

social-psychological, identity and utilitarian motives (Hennig-Thurau et al. 2004: 47-48), such as concern for other customers, social and economic benefits, advice seeking, as well as positive self-enhancement, knowledge sharing and expression of emotions (Hennig-Thurau et al. 2004, Lovett et al. 2013, Swani et al. 2014). Positive eWOM is said to help consumers to enhance social and self-approval, while negative eWOM is more directed at expressing hostility and vengeance (Jansen et al. 2009).

Both WOM and eWOM practices have a significant impact on consumers' purchase decisions and opinions about a specific company, which may influence a company's reputation (Lee and Youn 2009, Chu and Kim 2011). eWOM, however, is said to exert a more powerful impact (Zhang et al. 2011) in shaping opinions, generating interest in products and services than traditional marketing communication. The advantages of eWOM over traditional channels result from its anonymous, wide-reaching and relatively permanent character. eWOM is immediate, more accessible, spreads faster and may reach a wide audience (Jansen et al. 2009). Research clearly shows that consumers perceive the information published online by other consumers as more trustworthy than the information published by companies (Coyle et al. 2012).[10] It is important for marketers to understand the impact and consequences of eWOM due to the influence it may have on attitudes, judgements and, consequently, on the company's sales results (Lee and Youn 2009, Chang et al. 2013). This is especially significant in the case of negative eWOM. Negative opinions spread quickly and have a greater influence than opinions spread via traditional media. Moreover, negative eWOM is said to have more impact than positive opinions (Park and Lee 2009). As a result, negative opinions may significantly influence consumers' brand perception and purchase decisions (Stieglitz and Krüger 2014: 283).

The widespread popularity of eWOM interaction posed questions for companies as to how to employ the data concerning brand attitudes published online, which marketing strategies are the most effective in this environment and, more importantly, how to react to public criticism and negative content. The choice of strategy is claimed to depend on the type of brand and marketed product or service (Daugherty and Hoffman 2014: 96). Studies underline the importance for businesses to engage in eWOM communication as both initiators and participants (Zhang et al. 2011), that is engaging consumers and actively interacting with them.

Social media and social networking sites in particular are considered an ideal tool to practice eWOM owing to the ease of creating and disseminating information within the social network of friends and acquaintances, but also

---

[10] According to Bickart and Schindler (2001), consumers value online sources of information about products owing to three major reasons: greater perceived credibility of user-generated information in contrast to company-generated content, greater relevance of the information presented online, increased empathy felt as a response to the information presented online.

on a more widespread range (Vollmer and Precourt 2008, Chu and Kim 2011). It has also been observed that social media make companies particularly vulnerable to negative eWOM. Companies tend to be more exposed to negative feedback than in other media, the range of the reach and the consequences of negative opinions published are also greater (Sparks and Browning 2011). The management of negative eWOM in social media may constitute a serious challenge for the company (Pfeffer et al. 2014) and requires implementing an appropriate strategy. The means which may help the companies to manage eWOM comprise, among others, the tools of Internet monitoring and sentiment analysis.[11] Companies may use software to extract mentions of the brand and opinions published online. The tools analyze positive and negative customer feedback, and can help a company to adjust management strategies to customers' expectations and current moods.

1.4. Twitter as a microblogging service

Twitter, introduced in 2006, is a microblogging service. Microblogs are a category of blogs,[12] which allow users to publish short textual or multimodal posts online. In contrast to blogging, communication is faster on microblogs and the publishing frequency tends to be higher owing to a lower effort which users need to invest in generating content (Java et al. 2007). Microblogs are considered an easy form of communication, by means of which users may broadcast information, opinions and share their status (ibid.). As norms specifying the content and form of interaction have gradually emerged, Twitter has been termed a new

---

[11] Sentiment analysis is defined as "a type of data mining that measures the inclination of people's opinions through natural language processing (NLP), computational linguistics and text analysis, which are used to extract and analyze subjective information from the Web – mostly social media and similar sources. The analyzed data quantifies the general public's sentiments or reactions toward certain products, people or ideas and reveal the contextual polarity of the information" ("Sentiment Analysis"). Sentiment analysis used in the context of marketing may allow companies to gain information concerning the attitudes to their products expressed in different online media (cf. Pozzi et al. 2016). There are many online tools and applications which may be applied to conduct sentiment analysis e.g. Hootsuite, TweetReach, HowSociable.

[12] Blogs, a shortened form of the term web log, were traditionally defined as instances of online diaries. Further classifications of blog categories comprise, for instance, the division of blogs into filters, i.e. blogs with lists of links, memoirs and diaries, knowledge-logs, devoted to specific knowledge domains, mixed types, combining the previous blog formats, and the category "other", which serve other functions (Herring et al. 2004). Currently, the format is used in an even greater variety of ways, which has led scholars to consider blogs as an online medium (Lutzky and Gee 2018: 174). More on the use of blogs can be found in Herring et al. (2004), boyd (2006), Myers (2010), Lutzky and Gee (2018).

communication genre (Fischer and Reuber 2011), "a new form of communicative engagement" (Hodgkin 2017: 2). As Hodgkin (2017) further observes, Twitter represents an innovative system of communication, "a significantly new way of using our language and expressing our intentions and interests" and constitutes "a prime example of our digital use of language" (ibid.: 1).[13]

As a microblogging service, Twitter allows users to publish brief updates and share them with others. Posts appear in reverse chronological order, with updates refreshed and the display of the posts having the form of a stream (Naaman et al. 2010). In contrast to traditional blogging practices, readers do not have a possibility to leave comments to posts and can only respond to them (boyd et al. 2010).[14]

Twitter comprises the basic components and functionalities of social media, i.e. the construction of a user's profile, composition of a network or list of connections and sharing textual and multimedia content. The profile structure on Twitter encompasses a thumbnail and background image, as well as a short bio.

The connections between profiles, as is the case with all social media, are based on an articulated network of connected users. The basic concept underlying the connections and the functioning of Twitter involves the idea of following – following is analogical to subscribing to updates by a specific user. If a user decides to follow another user, s/he automatically receives updates published by the selected tweeter (Schmidt 2014: 5). By default, tweets are public and accessible to all users. A user may also choose to manage a private account, in which case only followers are given access to the published content. Following does not require reciprocity and the relationships can be unilateral, which contrasts Twitter with other social media, such as Facebook (boyd et al. 2010).

The restriction on the length of the message is a further defining feature of Twitter as a microblog, as posts are limited to 140 characters. As of 2017, the addressee's address is not counted as part of the tweet, which gives authors a slightly higher number of characters for the message proper.

Interaction on Twitter may be conducted in the following patterns:
– one-to-one – a conversation between individual users;

---

[13] The innovative use of language which may be observed on Twitter, as Hodgkin (2017) claims, makes it a perfect space for the exploration of philosophical theories of language. Hodgkin (2017) then proceeds to apply the speech act theory to the interpretation of communication on Twitter. According to the scholar, the speech act theory may be helpful in explaining a range of aspects associated with the interaction on the microblog, such as the formation of Twitter membership – users perform linguistic acts upon joining Twitter, the relation between the members – Twitter users are related through the act of following, the substance of Twitter messages – the messages represent instances of individual speech acts, and tweets constitute Status Function Declarations, a foundation of what Hodgkin (2017: 2) terms "the institution of Twitter."

[14] As of January 2019, there are 262 million registered Twitter users; the total number of tweets sent per day amounts to 500 million; 37 percent of the users are 18-29 years old, while 25 percent are between the ages of 30-49; 79 percent of the accounts are based outside the United States; in the United Kingdom, there are 13 million Twitter users; 80 percent of the users use the medium on a mobile device ("Twitter by the Numbers: Stats, Demographics & Fun Facts," "Twitter – Statistics & Facts").

- one-to-many – interaction between the profile owner and other users;
- many-to-many – interaction of a group of users taking place on a specific profile.

In each case, communication may have a public or private character, being available to all Twitter users or to a restricted group of individuals/followers. As indicated before, interaction may take place in real-time or may be delayed, i.e. may be conducted in a synchronous or in an asynchronous manner.

Twitter allows users to interact via the following types of messages:
- updates – posts published by the profile owner;
- retweets – tweets of other users forwarded by the profile owner;
- @mentions or replies – tweets mentioning or addressed to a specific user in public;
- direct messages – messages addressed to an individual user in a private form, not accessible to the public.

Moreover, despite the 140-character limit on messages, selected features enhance the effectiveness and variety in the interaction on the microblog. The features comprise the following components and affordances:
- expanded tweets – messages in an expanded form, which allows users to preview content, view images and play videos;
- linking – sharing links is considered a central practice on Twitter (boyd et al. 2010); URLs are condensed to 19 characters, which allows users to save space within the tweet;
- hashtags – tagging messages allows users to organize conversations around specific topics and facilitate search.

Retweeting, hashtagging and @mentions are significant and defining components of Twitter interaction and as such deserve further explanation.

Mentions and replies are created by means of the @ symbol. With these messages, tweeters refer to other users and create a link to the referenced user's account. In addition to its function as a marker of "addressivity" (Honeycutt and Herring 2009), where it indicates the recipient of the message, or reference to another user, the @ sign may also be used as part of an emoticon, e-mail address, may be used to express locational or non-locational meanings of the preposition *at*, or as a sign used in representations of swear words (Honeycutt and Herring 2009).

Retweets, as indicated above, comprise messages forwarded to all of the followers of a specific user. The practice of retweeting is sometimes considered as an equivalent to forwarding mails (boyd et al. 2010) and has been regarded as a form of quoting (Puschmann 2015) or reported speech specific to Twitter (Draucker and Collister 2015).[15] The structure of retweets varies and may com-

---

[15] More on the practice of retweeting analyzed from different perspectives can be found in Suh et al. (2010), Kenney and Akita (2012), Wang et al. (2012), Manzanaro et al. (2018).

prise a mere retweeting of the post without modification or attaching a comment to the retweeted message, expressing the tweeter's stance towards the retweeted content and evaluation of the message.

In terms of retweeted content, boyd et al. (2010) single out the practice of retweeting for others, when tweeters forward messages with content of general interest or with interest to their followers only, retweeting for social action, which encompasses calls to protest or donate, show collective identity, enhance the popularity of a particular topic, messages aimed at enhancing knowledge or skills, as well as the so-called ego retweeting, i.e. retweeting messages referring to the self. boyd et al. (2010), however, do not perceive the latter as a narcissistic act and see it as a means of appreciating another user's attention and comments.

The major reasons for retweeting comprise amplifying or spreading tweets to new audiences, entertaining and informing a specific audience, commenting on another user's tweet by supplementing content, triggering a conversation or debate, marking one's presence, publicly agreeing with others, validating others' posts, gaining followers and saving tweets for future access (boyd et al. 2010). The reasons for retweeting thus go beyond distributing a particular tweet, but also encompass reacting to others' opinions and engaging other users.

As boyd et al. (2010) observe, retweeting is a means of participating in a diffuse conversation. Retweeting "contributes to a conversational ecology in which conversations are composed of a public interplay of voices that give rise to an emotional sense of shared conversational context" (boyd et al. 2010: 1). The sense of participation is also underlined by Page (2012), who investigated tweeting from the perspective of narrative theory. Page (2012) interprets retweets as "co-constructed narratives" and retweeting as one of "co-tellership practices" allowed by social media, in which two or more parties are involved in the process of discourse creation. Unlike other forms of collaboration in social media, however, the contributions of both parties are compressed in the same unit in the case of retweeting (Page 2012: 113). Retweeting has also been found to play a significant community-building function. Zappavigna (2014b: 191), namely, interprets retweeting as a means of social bonding and enacting interpersonal relations.

The use of hashtags, i.e. keywords preceded by the # symbol, and the process of tagging messages needs to be mentioned as an important aspect characterizing Twitter interaction. Though the practice of using the # symbol is specifically associated with Twitter, tagging has become a popular phenomenon in social media in general.[16] The origin of the practice comes from the tradition of naming Internet relay chat (IRC) channels.

---

[16] Hashtags have also become a popular means of expression in other social networking sites apart from Twitter, as well as in other contexts. Increasing research has been devoted to the phenomenon of tagging (see, for instance, the volume edited by Rambukkana (2015), Giannoulakis and Tsapatsoulis (2016), analyses by Heyd and Puschmann (2017), Erz et al. (2018), Lee and Chau (2018), Matley (2018a, 2018b), or Zappavigna (2018)).

A number of studies have been devoted to the practice of tagging and the function of hashtags on Twitter. The phenomenon has been analyzed from different perspectives. It has been termed "a form of conversational tagging" (Huang et al. 2010), of "social tagging or folksonomy" (Vander Wal 2007). Using tags has even been considered as "linguistic innovation" (Cunha et al. 2011). It has been claimed that hashtags may serve various roles ranging from organizing information to establishing relationships (Zappavigna 2015). As Zappavigna (2015: 276) observes, hashtags function as "social metadata" or "descriptive annotation," added by the users and not by the channel. One of the most frequently identified functions of hashtags is that of contextualizing the message. The # symbol is a label assigned to the message by the user. By assigning a hashtag to the tweet, the user classifies the message, placing it in a specific thematic category. In this way, hashtags connect messages focusing on the same topic. By using the Twitter search engine, users are able to extract all the tweets marked by a particular tag and trace all messages concerning a specific issue. Tagging thus helps to "coordinate the exchange of information relevant to such topics" (Bruns and Moe 2014: 17). This, as Zappavigna (2014a: 151) states, "increases the interactivity of the microposts by rendering them a form of 'searchable talk.'" Moreover, subscribing to a hashtag allows users to collect all tweets marked by a specific tag and keep track of the discourse associated with a specific topic. Hashtags are also used to mark tweets associated with specific events. The use of hashtags to establish backchannels to live-events is especially frequent in live-commentaries to events published on Twitter. Hashtags allow users to establish an additional network of relations to the relatively stable follower-followee set of connections, namely short-term relations based on the interaction concerning trending topics among a dispersed unconnected audience "coordinated by a common hashtag" (Bruns and Burgess 2012: 803).

Drawing on the framework of systemic functional linguistics, Zappavigna (2015) identified three main communicative functions of hashtags: marking experiential topics, enacting interpersonal relationships and organizing text. More specifically, the experiential function is associated with the topic marking and subject classification by means of hashtags. The interpersonal role of hashtags refers to their function of enacting relationships and expressing evaluative meta-comments. The textual function refers to the role hashtags play in organizing the posts typographically, where they serve as a form of punctuation. Hashtags may also function as emotional metacomments, when they mark topics which are not likely to be searched, but "invoke a possibility of an imagined audience of users who feel the same way" (Zappavigna 2015: 275). As Zappavigna (2015: 279-280) observes, the above-mentioned functions are not mutually exclusive and it is often the case that a single hashtag adds to the meaning of the tweet in complex ways. Hashtags are also syntactically flexible and may be used in different positions, both at the beginning, in the middle and at the end of the post (positions termed as prefix, infix and suffix by Tsur and Rappoport (2012)).

Tagging, @mentioning and retweeting can be seen to enhance the richness and the interactive potential of communication on Twitter and to influence interpersonal dynamics and communication patterns in the medium in significant ways.

Based on the above-mentioned functionalities, Bruns and Moe (2014: 16-20) singled out three layers of communication on Twitter: the micro level of interpersonal communication, the meso level of follower-followee networks and the macro level of hashtag-based exchanges. The meso level, the default level of Twitter communication, involves the dissemination of updates by the profile owner to all followers. The micro level of interaction encompasses individual exchanges between users by means of @mentions and replies. Interaction on this level may have a private or public character. Finally, interaction on the macro level comprises hashtagged tweets and exchanges. As mentioned above, a tagged message may reach the audience beyond the group of followers. Tagging suggests that the tweeter wishes to participate in a wide communicative process, in interaction with others interested in the topic. As the scholars underline, the layers are inherently interconnected, interweave and do not exist separately and in isolation from one another.

What distinguishes Twitter communication from other channels of online interaction is lack of "shared location" (Schmidt 2014: 6). Interaction on Twitter, as boyd et al. (2010) suggest, is not constrained within bounded spaces, but dispersed throughout a network of Twitter users. Communication takes place in "networked, distributed conversations" (Schmidt 2014: 6). Tweets "are bundled in the constant stream of information within personal timeline, filtered via social connections made explicit, as well as in the spontaneous and ad hoc 'hashtag publics' (Bruns and Burgess 2011) filtered via shared keywords and phrases" (Schmidt 2014: 6).

As boyd et al. (2010: 1) observe, "the stream of messages provided by Twitter allows individuals to be peripherally aware without directly participating." Twitter, in this way, creates a space of ambient conversation, information stream and ambient affiliation with other users (boyd et al. 2010, Bruns and Burgess 2012, Zappavigna 2012, 2014b). The term "ambient," used in the above-mentioned studies, clearly emphasizes this potential which Twitter offers for users to directly or indirectly participate in a public conversation, associate themselves with others, bond around common values, topics and interest areas (Zappavigna 2012, 2014b).

Tagging, @mentioning and retweeting help users to enact their social identity, practice affiliation and bonding. They allow users to be engaged in the practice of "searchable talk," defined as "online conversation where people render their talk more findable and hence bondable" (Zappavigna 2014b: 210). In the community of tweeters, it is bonding around searchable topics rather than direct interaction that is the basis of affiliation and social interaction (Zappavigna 2014a: 156).

It has also been observed that Twitter offers different interpersonal dynamics and, unlike other social media, is characterized by low reciprocity in following (Kwak et al. 2010), which is reflected in the prevalence of one-to-many over one-to-one communication (Page 2012: 94). Twitter has therefore been termed as an example of "news media, where users broadcast or narrowcast to followers" (Rogers 2014: iv). Clearly, Twitter is a perfectly suitable medium for one-way communication but a large part of the interaction concerns phatic communication and social bonding. As Zappavigna (2014a) concluded, microblogging is a "highly social activity involving communicative practices in which conversational reciprocity is central" (Zappavigna 2014a: 141).

Motivations behind microblogging are many and depend on the type of profile and its purpose. The study by Java et al. (2007), which represents one of the first investigations of the practices on Twitter, identifies three categories of Twitter users: information sources, friends and information seekers. Users of the first category, which comprises individuals or automated services, focus on posting news and usually have a numerous group of followers. The category of friends comprises most of the ordinary users, while the category of information seekers encompasses users who post rarely but regularly follow others. According to Java et al. (2007), the main intentions behind tweeting across the three categories of users comprise daily chatter (posts concerning daily activities), conversations (interaction with other user/s), sharing information and links, as well as reporting and commenting on latest news.

Subsequent studies investigating user practices on Twitter have focused on specific groups of users and underlined the utility of Twitter in individual, institutional and public communication. In addition to its use by ordinary users, Twitter has been successfully adopted by mass media, institutions or politicians, and has become an important channel of news providing, information and opinion sharing, a place for political and social debate, business and marketing, as well as a platform for entertainment and celebrity world (Marwick and boyd 2011a, 2011b, Weller et al. 2014).[17]

Zappavigna (2014b) observes that ordinary tweeters use the microblog to communicate their experience of reality, to share values and affiliate with others. For such users, Twitter provides a platform to disclose and exchange routine experiences, to bond around daily life matters. As a result, Twitter discourse offers insight into users' experiences which have so far been private and not accessible to the public audience (cf. Thornborrow 2015). Users' engagement in

---

[17] As of January 2019, the most popular profiles on Twitter measured by the number of followers comprise celebrities' accounts (e.g. Katy Perry, Justin Bieber, Rihanna), politicians' profiles (e.g. Barack Obama, Donald Trump), profiles of entrepreneurs (e.g. Bill Gates) and the media (CNN, BBC, The New York Times) ("Top 100 Twitter Users by Followers").

such public disclosures and the performance of public identities is explained by the need for affiliation and connectedness (Zappavigna 2014a, 2014b).[18]

Twitter's role in journalism has been underlined in many studies. The design of the medium, its public and one-to-many capacity makes Twitter a suitable medium for journalistic practices. Bruns and Burgess (2012) underline the usefulness of Twitter for both live-reporting, encompassing live-coverage of events from the scene, for second-hand discussion and sharing of news and comments. What contributes to the utility of Twitter in journalistic practice are the many affordances it offers, i.e. the possibility to use additional materials, multimedia and links. This enables users to disseminate both user-created materials of events as they unfold as well as additional secondary content in the form of links and screen captures. The combination of different practices on Twitter, comprising uploading, sharing and disseminating materials, highlighting important content, commenting and evaluating news in public allow the production of a comprehensive depiction of a news event (Bruns and Burgess 2012).

Twitter's use for news dissemination and commentary is additionally enhanced by the platform's ability to establish discursive communities around breaking news coordinated by means of hashtags, which are often created instantaneously as the events unfold, and which increase the visibility of news and allow communication with the whole community of users (Bruns and Burgess 2012: 803). As Bruns and Burgess (2012) claim, Twitter offers a merger of a social networking site and a broadcasting channel, allowing users to engage in both networking practices, establishing connections and interpersonal communication, in broadcasting original content and disseminating news and information.[19] This may be successfully exploited in journalistic practice, broadening the range and impact of the news broadcast and of the journalistic commentary.[20] Twitter has mainly become a reporting tool in the coverage of breaking news, accidents, terrorist attacks, as well as the coverage of political events.[21]

---

[18] Naaman et al. (2010) also focus on personal accounts on Twitter and identify a set of categories of intentions behind microblogging among the so-called ordinary users. The intentions comprise information sharing, self-promotion, opinions/complaints, statements and random thoughts, the "me now" category, questions to followers, presence maintenance, anecdote (me), anecdote (others).

[19] Owing to the functionalities offered by the medium, Twitter is extensively used as a tool of citizen journalism. An interesting discussion on the use of Twitter as a citizen journalism channel can be found in Murthy (2011).

[20] Extensive research has been devoted to the use of Twitter in journalism. See, among others, Hermida (2010), Bruns and Burgess (2012), Verweij (2012), Artwick (2013), Broersma and Graham (2013), Horan (2013), Murthy (2013), Parmelee (2013), Vis (2013), Canter (2015), Malik and Pfeffer (2016), Al-Rawi (2017), Einwiller et al. (2017), Simon (2018), Bouvier (2019).

[21] A particularly significant role of Twitter as a news providing and information sharing medium came to the fore during the so-called Arab Spring. Twitter has been considered as one of the primary tools of disseminating news concerning the war in Syria, as well as Tunisian or Egyptian revolutions, a major news source on the events from the site, at times even replacing traditional media (Lotan et al. 2011, Murthy 2013, Rogers 2014, Kharroub and Bas 2016). The potential of the medium to converge

Twitter has also exerted an impact on sports journalism, where it brought about changes in news gathering and publishing techniques, as well as new real-time interaction possibilities. It has been observed that Twitter is used to break and monitor news, promote stories, to retweet posts by athletes, sports organizations and fans, and to interact with the audience (English 2016, cf. Shermak 2018).

Mass media utilize Twitter not only for news dissemination, but also as a promotion and branding tool. Twitter is used by media channels to share news stories and attract followers to specific programmes (Clark et al. 2011).[22] Twitter is extensively used as a backchannel to access programmes broadcast by mass media, offering a platform for a live commentary on the programmes, and thus offering access to the audience's reactions and opinions (Thornborrow 2015).

A number of studies have also been devoted to the use of Twitter in the sphere of political communication.[23] Many studies have underlined Twitter's importance in political campaigns in particular. Research into the use of Twitter in presidential elections has revealed that the medium can be successfully exploited as an information dissemination channel and a tool to influence voters (Adams and McCorkindale 2013, Jungherr 2015, Mourão 2015, Kreiss 2016, Galdieri et al. (eds.) 2018).[24] The potential of Twitter as a dialogic platform, however, has proved not to have been adequately utilized (Adam and McCorkindale 2013, Jungherr 2015). It has been suggested that focusing on a meaningful dialogue with supporters and voters would increase the authenticity of political figures and the feeling of connectedness (Adam and McCorkindale 2013).[25] Further important factors influencing the effectiveness of tweets in political campaigns comprise good timing, resonance and rhetorical effectiveness (Kreiss 2016). Research has proved an opinion-making potential of Twitter and the influence it may exert on political debate. It has been observed that news and comments published online tend to be diffused offline, i.e. political discussions are transferred from Twitter to face-to-face interaction, which increases the reach of their

---

different news sources and different perspectives, i.e. that of journalists, activists, bloggers, witnesses of events could be clearly observed. Twitter proved a useful medium uniting the dispersed voices and conversations among participants of events, directly and indirectly involved in the events, the media and general interest readers (Lotan et al. 2011).

[22] Studies on the use of Twitter by mass media comprise, for instance, research by Lin and Peña (2013), Harrington et al. (2013), Moon and Hadley (2014), Larsson et al. (2017), Atifi and Marcoccia (2017).

[23] Further studies devoted to the use of Twitter in politics involve, among others, Grant et al. (2010), Jackson and Lilleker (2011), Lee and Oh (2012), Bastos et al. (2013), Jungherr (2015), Coesemans and De Cock (2017), Schneiker (2018).

[24] For more research on the use of Twitter in political elections see Larsson and Moe (2012), Dang-Xuan et al. (2013), Graham et al. (2013), Freelon and Karpf (2015), Jungherr (2016), Pancer and Poole (2016), Buccoliero et al. (2018), Shmargad (2018).

[25] The need to utilize Twitter as a tool of direct communication with citizens was also pointed out in a study by Golbeck et al. (2010), evaluating the use of the medium by congressmen in the US. It was observed that Twitter is mainly used to disseminate information, to report on activities and as a vehicle of self-promotion, but its interactive potential remains largely underexploited.

influence (Ceron and d'Adda 2016). Owing to its prominent role in political communication, Twitter has started to be recognized as a channel which enables the prediction of voting intentions and election results (Tumasjan et al. 2010).[26]

It is worth noting the use of Twitter in 2016 US elections. Research has pointed to a prominent role of the medium and demonstrated how Twitter affected political communication and citizen politics during the elections. The studies have pointed out different uses of Twitter by candidates, i.e. to attack opponents, but also to promote organizational efforts, provide information and make policy statements (Granberg-Rademacker and Parsneau 2018). Quite interestingly, it has also been shown that tweets posted by a candidate may reveal information on his/her image and character (Hixson 2018).[27] The analyses have also concerned the use of humorous political images in the campaign (Belt 2018). It has been shown that images shared via the platform constitute a means of communicating a candidate's stance on a particular issue. Research has pointed to an important difference in the use of images on Twitter and other media, and showed that images on Twitter tend to be more partisan, less emotionally charged and less stereotypical, and as such are more likely to appeal to a more politically educated audience (Belt 2018).

Twitter has also been found useful as a medium used in organizational communication. The research into the use of Twitter in this area has underlined its potential to function as a tool of information dissemination, dialogic communication and promotion (Jansen et al. 2009, Lovejoy and Saxton 2012). Lovejoy and Saxton (2012) show how Twitter is effectively exploited by non-profit organizations. Three major areas of use were identified, i.e. disseminating information concerning the organization, community building, encompassing fostering relationships and creating networks, as well as mobilization and calling users to action, such as donation, attendance of events and joining specific movements.

The use of the microblog has been particularly extensive in the arena of health communication, being employed by health organizations as well as health professionals. In this regard, the medium serves as a channel of information dissemination and exchange, health advice, support-seeking, promotion of a healthy lifestyle, as well as a channel of knowledge dissemination and self-promotion for health professionals (Lee and Sundar 2013, Murthy 2013, Park et al. 2013, Myers 2015, Park et al. 2016).

Finally, Twitter has also been successfully applied in scientific and academic communication. The service is used to spread scientific messages, updates on research and publications (Letierce et al. 2010). Its use as a conference backchannel

---

[26] The analysis by Jungherr (2015), however, revealed that, contrary to a popular belief, Twitter data do not constitute a fully reliable source of information on political sentiment and voting intentions of the users.

[27] Similar observations are made by Shane (2018), who applied semiotic analysis to Donald Trump's tweets and uncovered authenticity cues, defined as indexes of the candidate's self in the tweets, comprising such cues as the typographic texture, the tweets' timestamps and the operating system tags.

has proved particularly useful, where it has introduced new interaction options for the participants and observers, is used to promote and provide account of conference events, presentations, paper summaries and to trigger further discussions (Chaudhry 2011, Ross et al. 2011, Chaudhry et al. 2012, Desai et al. 2012). Studies investigating the use of Twitter by colleges and universities have proved that Twitter is mainly used as an institutional news feed addressed to a general audience, only rarely being used in dialogical communication (Linvill et al. 2015, cf. Palmer 2013).

Focusing on celebrity practices on Twitter, Page (2012) shows that celebrities exploit the medium as a tool to promote the self and emphasize their professional identity. As the study proves (Page 2012: 116), Twitter is not really utilized as a channel of direct interaction with fans, but rather as a medium by means of which celebrities broadcast their identity to followers, thus offering only pseudo- rather than real interaction between fans and celebrities.[28]

Owing to its functionalities, Twitter has become a useful tool facilitating public social debate. Discussions on Twitter, trending hashtags may serve as means reflecting public sentiment and opinions on current affairs and social matters. So far, based on data obtained from Twitter, researchers have investigated public reactions and attitude to such issues as the economic crisis (Maragh 2016), racial relations (Chaudhry 2016), gender (Cummings 2018, Scarborough 2018), as well as the refugee crisis and immigration problems (Kreis 2017, Siapera et al. 2018).

Based on the wide-ranging application of Twitter, it can clearly be seen that owing to a unique structure and many affordances, Twitter represents a medium with a wide range of potential applications in various areas of communication. As Weller et al. (2014) emphasize, "the highly personal use by each user as a tool for outreach, spreading information, connecting to friends is at the very heart of Twitter's utility for individuals and organizations alike and underpins its success as a global news media and public communication platform" (Weller et al. 2014: xxx).

1.5. Twitter in corporate communication

In addition to its use in the areas of communication mentioned above, Twitter has been successfully exploited in the domain of marketing and corporate communication, affording important possibilities for both brands and consumers.

---

[28] More on the use of Twitter by celebrities can be found in Marwick and boyd (2011b), Kehrberg (2015), Kim and Song (2016), Yan and Zhang (2018).

Jansen et al. (2009) consider microblogs as key applications and "a competitive intelligence source" (Jansen et al. 2009: 2186) due to the ease of monitoring brand perception among users. Zhang et al. (2011) named Twitter "one of the best social tools empowering the brand to connect with customers" (Zhang et al. 2011: 162). Among the most important advantages and assets of Twitter, which make it particularly useful for corporate interaction, are its dialogic character, which allows the company to cultivate relationships (Rybalko and Seltzer 2010, Kwon and Sung 2011), as well as the ease of use, simplicity, openness and flexibility (Zhang et al. 2011). As Zhang et al. (2011) emphasize, short, micro-messages are easy both to produce and then to process by the consumer. Further advantages comprise their many interaction options, i.e. one-to-one and one-to-many interaction, in the private and public mode, involving textual and multimedia content. These affordances offer companies invaluable opportunities to shape brand image, foster relations and enhance brand engagement.

The importance of Twitter as a branding and promotional tool cannot be denied. It offers a wide range of application areas, encompassing target and real-time marketing, as well as broadly defined customer services (Wood and Burkhalter 2014). Twitter facilitates direct access for brands to consumers' opinions and preferences, which, in turn, aids marketing and the management of customer relations. By monitoring consumers' Twitter profiles, companies may obtain market information, review consumers' decision-making processes, disseminate information to consumers' profiles, engage in dialogue and exert influence on consumers' perceptions (Jansen et al. 2009, Van Norel et al. 2014). Microblogging communication offers companies an opportunity to obtain immediate feedback, to advertise products, increase brand awareness, attract consumers' attention and, in this way, increase sales and revenue (Jansen et al. 2009, Kumar and Mirchandani 2012, Smith et al. 2012, Rapp et al. 2013, Wood and Burkhalter 2014). Twitter is also a useful medium in crisis situations, offering companies a channel to manage its consequences and rebuild damaged reputation (Van Norel et al. 2014).

The success of Twitter in both ordinary and commercial use depends "on the willingness of users to follow others and allow others to follow them" (Wood and Burkhalter 2014: 130). The potential and appeal of Twitter is attributed to the opportunity that users have to follow and engage with any other user, be it politician, celebrity[29] or brand, someone who they admire, like, who inspires and

---

[29] Wood and Burkhalter (2014) investigated how brands employ celebrities to promote their products on Twitter. The research indicates that celebrities may indeed help to disseminate brand information and draw attention especially to unfamiliar brands. On the other hand, celebrity endorsement appears to have little influence on changing brand attitudes among consumers. The study advises cautious use of celebrity endorsement, because, if wrongly managed, it can lower consumers' opinions of the brand. What the researchers see as the best strategy of influencing engagement is direct interaction with consumers, which corroborates the results of other studies mentioned before.

attracts them. This makes consumers more receptive to the communications and content which they receive from the users they follow (ibid.).

According to Wood and Burkhalter (2014), a consumer's decision to follow a brand is motivated by their engagement with the brand and an emotional connection to the brand. Brand engagement is said to develop through a set of stages, comprising the stage of connection, interaction, satisfaction, retention, commitment, advocacy and the final stage of engagement (Sashi 2012). Wood and Burkhalter (2014) illustrate the development of the process of brand engagement on Twitter with the stage of connection enacted by the consumer's decision to follow the brand, the stage of interaction by replying to tweets, exploring multimedia and links, the stage of satisfaction by providing positive feedback, the stages of retention and commitment by continuing to follow the brand and by accepting tweets, the stage of advocacy by retweeting branded content, all of which lead to the stage of engagement, in which consumers maintain the relationship.

The potential of Twitter may be utilized not only by companies, but also by consumers, whom it offers innumerable possibilities and solutions. Consumers may follow brands, subscribe to company tweets, disseminate brand-related information, follow brand communities, engage in eWOM, exchange opinions, concerns and recommendations with other consumers, compare products and offers and interact with companies (Burton and Soboleva 2011, Swani et al. 2014). Research has shown that consumers consider Twitter a reliable and trusted source of information and opinions (Jansen et al. 2009). Consumer practices and the uses to which they put Twitter offer important insights and information about their needs, impressions and concerns.

In order to fully and effectively exploit the potential of the medium, companies need to design an appropriate strategy concerning branding activities and customer encounters on Twitter. Researchers underline that in order to be effective, companies need to know and follow the norms and expectations of their audience (Li and Li 2014). Companies should also be aware of the factors which influence the consumer's interpretation of the message, which comprise habits, expectations, as well as familiarity with social media (ibid.).

The studies into commercial uses of Twitter underline the importance of implementing the following strategies:
- regular and frequent updates – tweets should be published every 1.5-4 hours; a higher number and intensity of tweets published gives a company a greater chance to reach more consumers and thus have a bigger impact;
- lending messages an emotional value – emotionally charged messages, namely, tend to be forwarded and posts with positive or negative sentiment receive more attention than neutral posts;
- development of a unique style of communication;
- active engagement in the interaction, listening and providing feedback;

– a presence not only on Twitter – company's presence on different social media is important, as it increases potential influence and reach (Zhang et al. 2011: 172, Smith et al. 2012: 111, Stieglitz and Krüger 2014: 283).

Moreover, other studies indicate that companies using a "multi-dimensional communicative stream" (Fischer and Reuber 2014: 566), entailing a high volume of high-quality posts with relational orientation and positive affect, considerably increase the impression of quality and distinctiveness of a company (ibid.). Since, as mentioned above, the success on Twitter is measured in the rate of tweeting, retweeting, sharing and transmission of content, companies should also understand factors which enhance these practices. Research (Lovett et al. 2013, Rapp et al. 2013, Swani et al. 2014) has proved that messages which enhance engagement with content comprise tweets containing brand names as well as messages with emotional and functional content. The study by Liu et al. (2012) indicated further factors which have a positive impact on retweeting and these comprise source trustworthiness, expertise, attractiveness and the amount of multimedia content in the message.

In the majority of studies, the need to engage consumers through dialogue and to offer consumers an opportunity to inquire, express feelings and to obtain answers has been underlined (Jansen et al. 2009, Rybalko and Seltzer 2010, Lovejoy and Saxton 2012).

It is worth mentioning specific examples of the use of Twitter in business interaction and marketing in general. Numerous studies have already been devoted to different aspects of marketing communication on Twitter and have revealed diversified applications of the service.

The study by Jansen et al. (2009), devoted to a content analysis of tweets concerning brands, shows that consumers use Twitter to obtain, share and exchange news and information, share activities concerning brands and express attitudes and opinions. Another important finding of this research is that nearly 20 percent of the messages expressed positive or negative sentiment concerning the brand, which, as the authors observe, proves that microblogging can affect brand image and companies should therefore be actively involved in managing brand perception online. The scholars underline the potential microblogs offer to monitor brand-related discussions and the opportunity they lend to influence consumers. Tweets, both positive and negative, constitute important feedback concerning products and can be effectively exploited by the companies. They may help the company to investigate consumers' preferences, product and service flaws, and, consequently, to improve the offer.

Rybalko and Selzer (2010) focused on the use of Twitter as a tool of dialogic communication. The study shows how companies try to utilize the affordances of Twitter by entering into a dialogue with consumers, reacting to consumers' comments, simulating discussions and trying to engage consumers into a conversation. Their analysis, which contrasts the use of Twitter with the use of websites, indicates that using those two channels of communication, companies target different audiences. While companies' websites publish content designed for specific groups of addressees, such as the media, investors, customers or employees, Twitter posts are addressed to an unspecified general audience or to specific individual Twitter users.

The analysis by Swani et al. (2013b) presents the following message strategies employed in service and product marketing: company brand name, product brand name, functional appeal, emotional appeal, direct calls to purchase, information search, hashtags, image and video. The information tweeted across services and products comprises newsletters and news, information on job openings, information and promotion of products and services, information on events, testimonials, goodwill and community information.[30]

Krüger et al. (2012) show how Twitter can be utilized in three areas of corporate communication, i.e. business-to-consumer (B2C), consumer-to-business (C2B) and consumer-to-consumer (C2C) interaction. The scholars propose a classification of the most frequently posted tweets in each of the types of communication. In the case of C2C communication, tweets mainly comprise messages with product and sales promotion information, tweets in which users make others aware of products, messages presenting experiences about a specific brand, comments concerning other people's use of products, as well as positive and negative statements about the brand. B2C communication tweets comprise the category of brand related news, service and customer care messages, tweets concerning products (information about product lines, product features) promotions and discounts, as well as the question and answer categories, which involve conversational and customer service tweets. C2B communication, in turn, encompasses messages with product and sales promotion-oriented content, tweets including statements about the brand and consumer's self-expression, as well as tweets with questions and wishes.

In a similar vein, focusing on different areas of marketing communication, the study by Swani et al. (2014) revealed differences in the use of Twitter in B2B and B2C interaction. The investigation shows that B2B in contrast to B2C messages comprise more links for additional information, hashtags and functional appeals, while B2C messages include more emotional appeals and direct calls to purchase. The use of brand names in tweets is similar in both cases. The scholars underline the use of emotional appeals not only in B2C but also in B2B tweets as an effective tool which can strengthen brand relationships and add valuable dimensions to the company's operations. The use of links in B2C

---

[30] The analysis identified differences between strategies applied in service and product marketing. The study revealed that service tweets in contrast to product tweets use more messages related to services and products information and promotion, events and testimonials. Emotional appeal turned out to be more frequent in service tweets as well. The analysis shows that the use of direct calls to purchase and hard sell strategies is infrequent in both product and service tweets (Swani et al. 2013b: 54).

tweets, though less frequent than in B2B messages, is also substantial, which, as the scholars claim, demonstrates the important function of Twitter as an information sharing platform. The study indicates that since the medium is often used as an informational platform, companies could enhance their relationship with consumers by providing useful brand news. The research also proved that Twitter and other social media are not fit for direct sales, but are more applicable for community building and establishing relations with consumers (Rapp et al. 2013, Swani et al. 2014).[31]

Twitter has also been observed to play a powerful role in consumers' eWOM communications. Twitter, referred to as a socialization agent, facilitates the exchange of eWOM and influences brand engagement practices (Chu and Sung 2015). Owing to its characteristics, tweets being "immediate, ubiquitous, and scalable" (Jansen et al. 2009: 2170), the microblog represents an efficient tool allowing consumers to share and exchange brand-related content and information, express opinions, interact with other consumers and companies (Chu and Sung 2015). The use of Twitter in eWOM communications may constitute both an advantage and a threat to the company. Positive news and opinions shared across the medium may enhance the company's image, but negative eWOM may pose a threat to its reputation. A report on the use of social media in customer services referring to Twitter stated that "one too many negative tweets can seriously tarnish a brand's image" (Andrews 2014). Moreover, the viral nature of negative eWOM hinders the easy management of such posts and their consequences.[32]

A potential threat to the image may only be diminished by an immediate and suitable reaction. Companies may exploit access to Twitter to monitor negative opinions and undertake appropriate measures to prevent the spread of negative communications. A number of studies have investigated how companies handle negative communications on Twitter and how they utilize Twitter as an image management or repair tool. These studies will be described in the next chapter.

---

[31] Among the analyses devoted to corporate Twitter use, the study by Gallaugher and Ransbotham (2010) also deserves mention. On the basis of Starbucks Twitter account, the scholars show how Twitter can be applied in the three above-mentioned areas of corporate communication. The functions of Twitter comprise its use as megaphone, as monitor and as magnet, respectively. Twitter used as megaphone (to share communications with customers) broadcasts store and partner promotions, sponsored tweets, offers specialized additional accounts (e.g. Starbucks jobs, My Starbucks ideas), sends commentary from nutrition and corporate social responsibility staff. Twitter as magnet (to engage consumers in dialogue) provides a platform for followers, a place to share opinions, send suggestions and vent complaints. Twitter as monitor is used to investigate customer-to-customer interaction and intervene appropriately. It provides metrics such as keyword mentions and retweets, offers insights on campaign click-throughs and customer sentiments, suggests hashtags to followers, thus encouraging further customer dialogue, allows staff to reply to consumers, to apologize, correct, offer help and also provides insight on competitor activities.

[32] There have been numerous cases of the so-called online fire-storms in which consumers expressed their strong dissatisfaction, irritation or even anger directed at a company (Pfeffer et al. 2014).

Chapter 2. Customer encounters as a genre of social interaction

2.1. Customer encounters as a genre of social interaction – basic characteristics

Customer encounters, i.e. encounters between customers/users and company representatives, represent an instance of institutional discourse, defined as "verbal exchanges between two or more people where at least one speaker is a representative of a work-related institution and where the interaction and the speakers' goals are partially determined by the institution at play" (Freed 2015: 809, cf. Drew and Heritage 1992).

One of the earliest definitions of customer encounters was provided by Merritt (1976), who defines a service encounter as "an instance of face-to-face interaction between a server who is 'officially posted' in some service area and a customer who is present in that service area, that interaction being oriented to the satisfaction of the customer's presumed desire for some service and the server's obligation to provide that service" (Merritt 1976: 321).

The above-mentioned definition concerned face-to-face encounters carried out in a store, but service encounters may also take place in institutional and professional contexts (Gutek 1999: 605), and may be carried out in a mediated form through a phone call or, increasingly, through online channels of communication.

A broader definition encompassing the different contexts and purposes of a service encounter was suggested by Ventola (2005), who refers to encounters as "everyday interactions between the customer and the server whereby some commodity (information or goods) will be exchanged" (Ventola 2005: 19).

Customer encounters represent a ritualized communicative situation (Bayyurt and Bayraktaroglu 2001, Economidou-Kogetsidis 2005) and are viewed as a standardized genre with characteristic actions and moves, as social activities characterized by socially shared, regular patternings (Ventola 1987, Biber and Conrad 2009). The most important distinctive features of such an interaction in offline communication, i.e. face-to-face, telephone or written communication, comprise its incidental and short-term character. The participants are usually strangers and motivated by transactional or instrumental goals (Coupland 2000). With regard to language and politeness conventions, encounters tend to be characterized by the use of conventional politeness acts and the use of the standard variety of language (Economidou-Kogetsidis 2005: 257). The discourse of service encounters is referred to as "quasi-conversational" (Hutchby and Woofitt 2008: 151).

More specifically, customer encounters have the following properties:
- differ in style and functionality from everyday talk;
- exemplify a "specialized kind of spoken interaction" (Biber and Conrad 2009: 102), "standard situations," i.e. situations with clearly defined, pre-scribed roles of the speakers (buyer/seller), with "a pre-fixed constellation of rights and obligations" (Blum-Kulka and House 1989: 142), where the listener has a high obligation to comply and the speaker has a strong right and low degree of difficulty to pose the request, as indicated in Merritt's (1976) definition provided above. The roles assumed by the customer and provider are unchangeable;
- the interaction is conversational – involves two participants in a face-to-face communicative situation;
- display a routine structure; compositional structure comprises three stages: opening, offering and closing;
- the interaction is task-based, single-topic and goal-oriented; the emphasis is on making and supplying a demand;
- the result benefits the addressee;
- official character of the communicative situation – the service often involves first-time speakers, the level of familiarity is low or non-existent, determined by an institutional relation between the participants, their social roles and lack of emotional ties between them;
- asymmetric relations – the salesperson is the primary sender in the talk; s/he assumes a superior position towards the client owing to his/her expert knowledge, familiarity with sales methods and control of the talk, selection of topics and persuasion methods;
- participants typically preserve their anonymity and do not reveal their status;
- the degree of imposition the speaker makes on the hearer is low;
- the interaction is characterized by politeness and low level of emotion-ality, brevity and explicitness, conventional and ready-made linguistic calques and a limited set of expected speech acts tend to be used, as well as a restricted repertoire of forms of address, with an occasional and sponta-neous use of uncommon attention getters or address terms (Goffman 1967, Merritt 1976, Jefferson and Lee 1981, Ventola 1987, Drew and Heritage 1992, Lubecka 1993, Bayyurt and Bayraktaroglu 2001, Economidou-Kogetsidis 2005, Biber and Conrad 2009, Pałka 2009).

The above-mentioned features define a conventional customer encounter situation. Encounters, however, tend to be locally managed in a particular communicative situation, which may make the pattern of the overall organization of an encounter less standard. The setting, the sociocultural context, participants' roles, the sociopragmatic knowledge of the interlocutors, the gender of the participants, the degree of familiarity between them, as well as the nature of the product or services purchased may impact an encounter in significant ways, influencing the organization of an encounter and its discourse (Kerbrat-Orecchioni 2005, Félix-Brasdefer 2012). Similarly, the speakers' roles and identities are said to be continually negotiated in an ongoing inter-action (Gavioli 1997: 137).[33] A more detailed description of differences in the encounters arising due to the influence of various contextual factors will be presented in the following subchapters.

2.2. Previous research into customer encounters

2.2.1. Face-to-face customer encounters

Service encounters have been analyzed using different theoretical and meth-odological approaches. Studies have been devoted to structural, pragmatic and sociolinguistic issues, and have examined the sequential organization of encounters, discourse structure and politeness conventions, patterns of selected speech acts used in the encounters, interactional styles of the speakers, as well as relational components in the encounters.

Customer encounters have been analyzed from an intracultural, as well as from a contrastive inter- and cross-cultural perspective, in which encounters in different languages and cultural contexts have been compared. Studies comprise research on face-to-face as well as mediated telephone encounters, i.e. phone calls to shops and stores or call centre interaction.

A review of literature concerning customer encounters will be provided below, focusing on research devoted to organizational patterns of encounters, analyses discussing customer-encounters in different cultural and social contexts, as well as in different communication channels.

As mentioned above, customer services are structured and typically com-prise a beginning, middle and an end stage. Typical communicative activities

---

[33] Research has shown that small shop encounters, for instance, tend to be characterized by lower levels of formality and more intimate and familiar relationships between the participants (Placencia 2005, Kerbrat-Orecchioni 2005).

and components of a retail service encounter, when the customer must request a product from the provider, comprise the basic stages of opening, request and closing, or, more specifically, the stage of greetings, opening, request for a product/service, negotiation of the exchange, provision of the product/service, payment and closing (Bailey 2000: 95, Shively 2011: 1819). The encounters, however, may vary in complexity, involving additional stages, requests and/or offers. The organization of the sequences of the interaction may also be influenced by the context of the encounter. In a study devoted to open-air market interactions, Mitchell (1957/1975), for instance, identified the following sequences: salutation, inquiry about the object of sale, investigation of the object, bargaining and a conclusion.

An extensive discussion of the organizational and structural properties of direct sales encounters is included in Pałka's study (2009). Focusing on Polish, the author investigated the strategies applied by representatives and communicative aims typical of each stage of the talk, i.e. opening, offering and closing. The author outlines the following communicative aims: opening stage – to establish contact and initiate the talk; offering – to maintain contact, to continue conversation and share knowledge about a product; closing – to close the talk and terminate contact. The study proved, however, that the realization of additional communicative aims and extending each of the stages is typical of the encounters. In the opening sequence, the salespersons may aim at becoming familiar with the client, creating a positive relationship, establishing credibility and trust, raising a need to possess the product, threatening the consumer with consequences resulting from lack of activity and possessing the product; in the sequence of offering and maintaining contact, they may aim at establishing a positive relationship with the client, raising his/her willingness to purchase the product by informing the client about its value, present the product as a solution to problems; while in the sequence of closing, the representatives may try to prolong the act of closing, express a wish for a second meeting, enhance credibility, try to terminate contact in a pleasant atmosphere, try to strengthen the consumer's willingness to purchase the product (Pałka 2009: 272).[34] The study showed that exchanges have the form of an illusive or one-sided rather than a proper dialogue and are based on a planned scenario of linguistic actions and the use of strategic activities associated with extending the sequences of opening, offering and closing.

Research concerning sequential organization of service encounters has been to a large extent associated with the analysis of request patterns. Owing to the purpose of service encounters, requests are considered as the principal or one of

---

[34] The study presents conventional and less conventional activities and strategies employed by salespersons. Among the less conventional strategies associated with initiating a relationship, the author mentions acts aiming at establishing credibility and a positive relation with the client, such as performing the role of an expert or the role of a friend. The least conventional strategies and the most creative ones, in turn, comprise acts aiming at raising the consumer's anxiety and raising the need to purchase the product, presenting the product as a solution to the consumer's problems (Pałka 2009).

the most significant components of the interaction. Requests tend to be divided into two main categories, i.e. requests for information and requests for action (Merritt 1976). The studies have investigated requests from a single language or a cross-cultural perspective, showing pragmatic norms underlying the formulation of requests. The studies have demonstrated that a range of factors, such as the context, the degree of familiarity between the interlocutors or the gender of the participants may influence the shape of requests in the encounters (Gavioli 1997, Bailey 2000, Antonopoulou 2001, Marquez Reiter and Placencia 2004, Kerbrat-Orecchioni 2005, Félix-Brasdefer 2012, Fink and Félix-Brasdefer 2015). The type of request acts used may also be influenced by the time factor.[35]

In a seminal paper on requests, Merritt (1976) investigated request response sequences in service encounters in a convenience store. The study lends important insight into the role of inference in structuring a request sequence. In particular, the study concentrated on the pragmatic interpretation of elliptical structures in sequences where questions followed questions, as exemplified by the response to a question "Do you have coffee?" with another question "Cream and sugar?" instead of an assertion or denial (Merritt 1976: 325). According to the scholar, the direct request in the above-mentioned act tends to be interpreted as a request for service and not as a request for information. Merritt argues that the specific and conventionalized nature of an encounter leaves room for a greater degree of inference, as a result of which participants may eliminate the inferred sequences of the interaction.

Downey Bartlett's (2005) study also focused on coffee shop encounters and investigated sequences used in placing an order. The study points to a significant degree of complexity of an encounter and technical language used in coffee shops. The study shows that encounters contain a high degree of ellipsis, phatic communication, implicitness, colloquial and idiomatic language. The analysis proved that the most frequent request types comprise conventionally indirect requests, assertions and want statements.[36]

Structural aspects of request sequences in service encounters are the main focus of a study conducted by Bowles (2006). Applying conversation analysis methods, the study investigates how participants negotiate requests. More specifically, based on a corpus of telephone calls to bookshops in Great Britain, the analysis compares strategies used in pre-sequences introducing the reason for the call by native and non-native speakers of English. The results demonstrate differences in the sequential organization of pre-sequences between the two groups. It was found that non-native speakers tend to use more combined pre-sequences, while native

---

[35] As Kerbrat-Orecchioni (2005) shows, for instance, requests tend to take an elliptical form when consumers have to queue up to obtain the product.

[36] Analyzing the encounters from the perspective of foreign language learning, the scholar concludes that L2 textbooks are inadequate since they misrepresent the language which naturally occurs in coffee shops (Downey Bartlett 2005).

speakers use individual pre-sequences more often. Native speakers also use more turn constructional unit pre-sequences in combination with other pre-sequences. The concluding observations of the study emphasize a crucial role of a correct management of pre-sequences in the process of negotiating the request.

Pragmalinguistic variation in the production and perception of requests in café encounters in the US is the main concern of a study by Fink and Félix-Brasdefer (2015). The analysis proved that conventionally indirect requests are the most frequent type of requests used, followed by elliptical requests, while the least common requests comprise want and need statements and implicit requests. A high frequency of this request pattern led the authors to interpret it as a socioculturally expected unmarked request type. As far as the further structural properties of requests are concerned, the study showed that internal modification is more frequent than external modification. The most common internal modifiers comprise the politeness marker *please*, the downgrader *just* and the conditional form. External modification encompasses greetings and relational talk, with greetings being more frequent. The analysis also showed that relational talk occurs in the encounters involving regular customers or when the interlocutors are acquainted with each other.

Studies have investigated pragmatic variation in requests according to the gender of the speakers. Though the studies have been carried out in different cultural contexts, they have reached similar results, showing that female customers prefer conventionally indirect requests, while male customers tend to employ elliptical requests (Antonopoulou 2001, Félix-Brasdefer 2012, Fink and Félix-Brasdefer 2015, Taylor 2015). Differences in the pragmatic norms underlying the realization of requests in the encounters have also been found across cultures. Studies have shown that depending on the cultural context, requests may differ in the degree of directness, formality and deference (Gavioli 1997, Bailey 2000, Marquez Reiter and Placencia 2004, Kerbrat-Orecchioni 2006, Callahan 2009, Fink and Félix-Brasdefer 2015). More detailed results of these studies will be presented below.

Research has also been devoted to the opening and closing sequences of customer encounters. Openings and closings constitute politeness routines, the function of which is to manage interpersonal relationships and reinforce the relational sphere of the encounter. Though openings and closings in the form of greetings and leave-taking formulas are not necessary to perform the transaction and tend to have a highly ritualized character, they are used in most of the encounters, regardless of the context or channel of the interaction. The presence of the formulas shows that the speakers consider them as relevant and important or even procedurally essential (Kerbrat-Orecchioni 2005, Reiter 2008, 2009). Openings in particular have been the object of analyses due to their significant function in an encounter. As sequences initiating the interaction, they constitute stages at which participants establish their relationship.

Openings and closings have been analyzed as part of broader research focusing on strategies serving relational work and the management of social relationships in customer-provider interaction. As part of this investigation, the research has also focused on address terms and politeness formulas, as well as phatic communication and small talk, and other activities employed for rapport-building purposes, such as jokes and compliments used in customer encounters conducted face-to-face or in a mediated telephone interaction (Aston (ed.) 1988, Cheepen 2000, Coupland 2000, Kuiper and Flindall 2000, McCarthy 2000, Marquez Reiter and Placencia 2004, Placencia 2004). The studies have emphasized the important and meaningful role which relational aspects may play in the interaction. Politeness formulas, greetings, the choice of address terms constitute tools which allow speakers to express social distance and thus may construct the encounter as deferential, egalitarian, overfriendly or even abusive (Placencia 2015: 38). Drawing on conversation analysis, Aston (1988a) identified the different linguistic resources used to negotiate friendly relations in the context of a customer encounter. These comprise phatic communication, small talk, but also language play activities, teasing and joking. Coupland's (2000) collection of studies highlights the centrality of phatic communication in task-oriented interactions in English. The studies by McCarthy (2000) as well as by Kuiper and Flindall (2000), included in the volume, focus on instances of small talk in different encounters and show how small talk serves as a strategic tool used by companies to achieve interactional goals and establish an in-group relationship with the consumer. McCarthy's (2000) study examined small talk in two types of encounters, i.e. in a hairdresser's salon and during a driving lesson. The study distinguishes four types of talk in an encounter: phatic exchanges (greetings), transactional talk (requests, enquiries, instructions), transactional and relational talk (evaluations and comments), and relational talk (small talk, jokes, topics of mutual interest). Though the study makes a distinction between relationship-oriented talk and task-oriented talk, a constant intertwinement of these two types of talk is underlined. Kuiper and Flindall (2000), in turn, show how small talk, idiosyncratic and creative acts intersperse counter closings and openings enacted by speakers who deflect routine and formulaicity.

Studies have shown differences in the use of relational strategies in service encounters depending on the cultural background of the interaction. As far as openings and closings are concerned, for instance, openings and closings tend to be used frequently in Ecuador (Placencia 2008), as is the case in Greece (Antonopoulou 2001) and France (Kerbrat-Orecchioni 2006), where they perform a politeness function. In Mexican encounters, by contrast, openings and closings tend to be omitted (Félix-Brasdefer 2012). Examining shop encounters in Ecuador, Placencia (2004, 2008) showed that rapport-building activities in which the participants are engaged comprise phatic communication, individualized exchanges concerning different topics from the private and public domain (health, politics, school), as well as instances of creative language play activities. Kerbrat-Orecchioni (2005, 2006), who investigated encounters in small shops in France, observed that the degree of relational talk and the choice of address terms are influenced by the relationship between the interlocutors. When the customer and the seller know each other, warmer address terms tend to be used and a more frequent recourse to jokes, humour and small talk tends to occur. The study also showed that polite formulae are a distinguishing feature of small shop interactions, functioning as "lubricants" aiming to "polish" and soften the transaction (Kerbrat-Orecchioni 2005). Placencia and Mancera Rueda (2011), in turn, analyzed rapport management strategies between customers and bartenders in breakfast bars in Seville. The following rapport building strategies were identified in the interaction: greetings, goodbye wishes, bypassing the request sequence, as well as individualized rapport building strategies, such as complimenting, teasing, gossiping, sharing personal stories, offering advice, discussing future plans or disagreeing with the consumer. The scholars claim that the strategies serve to "reduce interpersonal distance and reaffirm friendly relations" (Placencia and Mancera Rueda 2011: 192) and the customer's refusal to engage in such rapport building behaviour would be perceived as unfriendly.

Interactional talk is seen as a tool allowing the interlocutors to maintain positive rapport and friendly relations. As Aston (1988a) claims, thanks to interactional talk, a transaction may become a pleasant and an entertaining encounter. However, beyond its function to establish and maintain positive rapport, relational talk may serve further strategic goals. Coupland (2000) points to the phenomenon of commercialization of small talk and argues that small talk constitutes a part of the commercial context of the transaction and serves as a tool of attaining commercial goals.

As mentioned above, research into customer encounters comprises studies carried out in an intracultural context, examining encounters in a single language, as well as cross-cultural comparisons of the encounters in various cultural contexts.

Many studies have assumed a contrastive approach, comparing service encounters in different cultural backgrounds. The studies have focused on the organization of the encounters as well as interactional styles of the speakers involved in the encounter, similarities and differences in the norms underlying the encounters. Research has also highlighted the socio-pragmatic variation in the practices found in customer encounters. Cultural differences identified in the studies concern the sequential organization, interactional patterns, the degree of formality, directness, deference, as well as the degree of relational and transactional orientation (Aston 1995, Gavioli 1997, Bailey 2000, Marquez Reiter and Placencia 2004, Kerbrat-Orechioni 2005, Callahan 2009).

Among the most important cross-cultural studies of service encounters, the research conducted by scholars of the PIXI (Pragmatics of Italian/English

Cross-Cultural Interaction) project needs to be mentioned. The project involved a contrastive English-Italian analysis of bookshop service encounters conducted within the conversation analysis approach. Studies carried out as part of the project, based on an investigation of the structural organization of the interactions, outlined differences in the interactional style in the two languages (Aston 1995, Gavioli 1997).

As part of the project, Aston (1995) investigated openings and closings in customer encounters on the English and Italian corpus. The analysis showed that Italian openings were characterized by greater variability than the English ones. A higher frequency of reciprocal prefaces, both customer and assistant-initiated, also occurred in the Italian corpus. Moreover, Italian exchanges included a more personalized approach to the exchange, both on the part of the customer and the assistant, which was absent from the English interactions. As far as closings are concerned, the study showed that English and Italian speakers expressed similar concerns of referential and role alignment. However, these concerns tended to be approached in different ways. In the cases where it was necessary to ratify role alignment, Italians adopted a two-part closing sequence, involving the customer's acceptance, thanks and the assistant's ratification. This difference, as the scholar claims, results from the organization of remedial work in the case of dispreferred assistant responses in the two languages. In Italian, remedial work was initiated by the customer, with the role of the assistant reduced to the ratification of the remedy and closure of the interaction, while in English, it is the assistant who typically suggested the remedy, leaving acceptance and closing of the encounter to the customer.

The study by Gavioli (1997) argues against the maintenance of cultural stereotypes of Italians as personalized and involved, and of the English as impersonal and neutral in the context of service encounters. The study proved that both attitudes can be found among the speakers of both cultural contexts, though achieved in different ways. The differences between the cultures pointed out in the study concern the structure of dispreferred responses, which in English tend to be prefaced by mitigators or delayers. The study also proved that English customers are less likely to discuss personal experiences during an encounter.

An investigation of openings in telephone encounters in English, French, German, Italian and Spanish was conducted by Pallotti and Varcasia (2008). The authors examined both inter- and intra-linguistic variability in these acts, as well as the presence and structure of such moves as summons-answer, identification, greetings, how-are-you's and getting-down-to-business. The study pointed to the presence of different pragmatic routines unique to each of the languages, but also a degree of intra-linguistic variability in the openings. The analysis showed that self-identification is frequent in German but absent from English and French calls. The results also show that responding to calls with *hello* tends to be used in Italian, French and Spanish, but that it is infrequent in

German and English. Differences also concern the sequencing of moves within turns, with openers or greetings occurring either at the beginning or at the end of the turn, depending on the language. Low variation in answers to phone calls in an institutional setting was observed in French, while a greater variation in German and English.

Traverso (2006), in turn, contrasted Syrian and French encounters, focusing on the use of conversational routines and ritual acts. The analysis showed that selected acts in the encounters tend to be routinized in both languages, e.g. accepting the product or requests, while eliciting the request is not routinized in either of the languages. The main difference is that in Syrian, in contrast to French, the acts of acknowledging the acceptance and the request tend to be routinized. The analysis proved that in both ethnic groups, politeness tends to be constructed in different ways. In French encounters, politeness emerges from the use of linguistic devices, such as minimization, additional devices and substitutive devices. In Syrian, where fewer such devices can be found, polite behaviour is expressed through the systematic use of ritual acts.

A more recent contrastive study of service encounters comprises Varcasia's (2013) research into telephone encounters in English, German and Italian, conducted within the contrastive analysis tradition. The study compared the organization of interactional turns of providers. The analysis focused on the responses provided by receivers to callers' pre-requests for service. The aim of the analysis was to investigate the conversational patterns occurring in the responses in these languages. More specifically, the study aimed at investigating the conversational architecture in response sequences, as well as the strategies applied in the responses in the three languages.

The study showed that a shared set of strategies can be found in the responses used across the three languages. The analysis revealed that speakers follow specific response patterns, using simple and extended structures, which comprise responding to callers' queries by providing the relevant information, asserting or denying the availability of the service, extending the response with an explanation or solution, asking relevant questions to clarify the request and responding accordingly, and adding more information. The study showed that the speakers try to avoid abruptness and leave the customer with more information than initially desired. Differences concern the preference for a specific response format in the analyzed languages. The most significant difference was observed in the occurrence of the extended response format, which proved the most frequent in English in contrast to other languages.

Drawing on material from English and Greek, Sifianou (2013) focused on the impact of globalization on the expression of politeness and impoliteness in various areas of social life, in the area of service encounters, among others. The study examined whether and, if yes, how the process of globalization influences the practices in service encounters. The scholar concludes that changes in politeness conventions should not be attributed only to the homogenizing force of globalization, arguing that they may result from internal processes of variation and change occurring in a particular language.

A cross-cultural investigation of customer encounters was also undertaken by Félix-Brasdefer (2015). The study, devoted to service encounters in commercial and non-commercial settings in Mexico and in the United States, examined a variety of issues, such as relational and transactional talk, and, more specifically, address forms, request patterns and the use of small talk in the two cultural contexts. Focusing on request patterns, the research supported previous observations that the gender of the participants, topics of the interaction and the setting influence requesting strategies in service encounters. As for the differences between the analyzed contexts, the US data indicated a preference for indirectness, whereas the Mexican data revealed greater variation in the use of imperatives, elliptical requests and assertions. The research also concerned intra-lingual differences between two regions of Mexico and revealed that customers in Mexico City, in contrast to Guanajuato, more often tend to delay requests, use assertions, implicit requests and imperatives. As far as the non-commercial setting of a visitor information center analyzed in the study is concerned, the analysis showed that initial requests are expressed by means of clarification requests, repairs or reformulated questions.

Analyses have also contrasted customer encounters conducted in regional or dialectal varieties of a single language. A rich line of research has been devoted to customer encounters in the Spanish speaking world, offering further interesting insight into the nature of customer interaction. The studies have demonstrated differences in the interactional styles of the participants of customer encounters in sub-varieties of Spanish.

The study by Marquez Reiter and Placencia (2004), conducted from the perspective of pragmatics and conversation analysis, investigated similarities and differences in the organization of service encounters and the relationship between the customer and assistant in Montevideo (Uruguay) and Quito (Ecuador). The analysis revealed numerous differences between the speakers of both cultures, with Uruguayan encounters characterized by a greater variety and number of selling strategies, higher verbosity of the encounters indicated by a larger number of turns per an encounter, a greater occurrence of personalization strategies and a preference for a closer and friendly relationship. Ecuadorian speakers, by contrast, showed a preference for formality, formulaicity and maintenance of interpersonal distance.

The studies by Placencia (2005, 2008) focused on shop transactions in different varieties of Spanish spoken in Quito, Manta and Madrid, respectively. The analyses concerned pragmatic variation in expressing interpersonal concerns in the encounters and indicated that the interaction proceeds according to different norms in the studied contexts. Focusing on the patterns in request realizations, the analyses showed that although direct requests predominate in both groups, a more frequent use and a more complex form of internal modification of the act could be seen among the Quitenos. It is this group that expressed a preference for a more personalized service and displayed more interpersonal concerns as well. It was shown that Quiteno customers tend to use more deferential address forms, as well as a range of terms of endearment and rapport-enhancing strategies with the aim of expressing interpersonal concerns to the interlocutor. Less formality and politeness in the choice of greetings and address terms was observed among Manteno and Madrileno customers. The studies showed a more task-oriented character of the encounters, less formality, especially in the choice of greetings and politeness formulae, as well as little relational talk and little engagement in interpersonal work among Manteno and Madrileno customers.

Studies into service encounters conducted from a cross-cultural perspective have also concerned different practices of interlocutors in intercultural and interethnic encounters. For instance, Bailey (2000) compared interactional practices in service encounters between Koreans and African Americans, and found a difference in the perception of customer-assistant relationship in the two groups. In a study devoted to language choices in service encounters in Barcelona, Torras and Gafaranga (2002) showed that the choice of either Catalan, Spanish or English serves the speakers as a tool to construct social membership and display different linguistic identities.

Research by Callahan (2006, 2009) focused on interethnic Spanish-American encounters. The aim of the studies was to examine the choice of language used in the workplace by Spanish vendors in response to American customers' turns initiated in Spanish. The analyses found a generally high percentage of accommodation in the encounters, with the exception of young Latino workers who tended to choose English in responses to younger female non-Latino customers. The lack of accommodation in this case is explained by two main factors, i.e. a greater psychosocial need to establish boundaries in this group and by a higher use of English or even English dominance among young members of bilingual populations.

In a more recent study, Ramírez-Cruz (2017) investigated customer encounters in an intercultural setting comprising Hispanic service providers and Anglo-American and Hispanic customers. The analysis examined the occurrence of two types of stancetaking, i.e. transactional and friendly, and showed that transactional stances constitute the majority in both groups of speakers. The comparison of the ratio of both stances in the two examined groups showed, however, that Hispanic customers use the friendly stance more often. The employment of a friendly stance also occurred more frequently among female than male American customers.

The analysis by Shively (2011), devoted to pragmatic development in the second language among American students studying in Spain on the basis of customer service interactions, found that students' choices changed over time, as they started to employ more direct strategies, thus reflecting the process of linguistic socialization and accommodation to the practices common in a foreign language.

Studies in different cultural contexts have also investigated pragmatic variation in service encounters according to the gender of the participants, with a particular consideration of sequential organization of the encounter, politeness strategies used and the shape of requests.

Antonopoulou (2001) examined the influence of gender on service encounters in small shops in Greece, with the focus on the shape of customer-initiated requests and politeness strategies. The study showed both similarities and differences in the linguistic behaviour and in the approach to the encounter among male and female customers. The similarities comprise the use of questions to secure cooperation with the seller and the use of apologies and excuses to reduce the imposition on the seller. The study showed that both male and female consumers use positive politeness strategies to express friendliness and concern. The strategies, however, tend to be different, with males more often resorting to the use of jokes and teasing, and females using more self-deprecating funny comments. Further differences concern the form of requests, with males more often using elliptical and non-verbalized requests, and female consumers more often resorting to fully verbalized request acts. The most significant difference between the two gender groups of consumers, which impacted the linguistic behaviour of the consumers, comprises the perception of the encounter, i.e. males perceive the encounter as purely transactional, which excludes the need for an interactional focus and an exchange of civilities. Female consumers, by contrast, put more focus on interactional exchanges, which is reflected in a more frequent use of greetings, partings and thanks. However, the study also showed that both gender groups tend to accommodate to the addressees and choose strategies which are considered more preferable for the opposite sex. This means that women addressing men tend to select elliptical constructions, while men addressing women sellers opt for fully verbalized requests. Moreover, both groups use more civilities when addressing the opposite sex, which, as the author concludes, shows that both male and female customers consider greetings as essential formalities in the context of a distant relation with the interlocutor.[37]

---

[37] The issue of gender was the object of a study conducted by Hall (1993), who examined how restaurants of differing prestige gendered service encounters. Based on an interview analysis, Hall singled out three scripts of good service, i.e. friendliness, deference and flirting. The author showed that a server job can be gendered as female or male, depending on the degree of subservience and deference. In the case of the former, a server is expected to show deference, act in a subordinate way, take care of customers and even flirt. The study also showed that the gender of the server influences customers' linguistic behaviour, e.g. the form of requests.

Pragmatic variation in service encounters according to the gender of the participants was also investigated by Félix-Brasdefer (2012), who examined encounters in Mexican open air markets. Three levels of pragmatic variation were analyzed in the study, i.e. actional, interactional and stylistic levels, with the focus on the type of requesting behaviour, sequential structure of the transaction and forms of address used in the encounter, respectively. The study exhibited selected intra- and cross-gender similarities and differences in speech patterns among male and female participants of the encounters. The study showed that imperatives, followed by elliptical statements and implicit requests were the most frequent request types. The analysis also showed that internal modification was rather infrequent.

With respect to differences between the two gender groups, the analysis found that imperatives were more common among male than among female consumers. It was also shown that female customers used more openings, elliptical statements, modification by *please* and leave-taking formulas. The author claims that request sequences are not produced in isolation but tend to be co-constructed by the interlocutors, the customer and the vendor, with both parties focusing on conducting the transaction and achieving meaning in social interaction. The research showed only individual instances of greetings in the data, as well as an infrequent use of openings and closings. It was female consumers who tended to use the above-mentioned politeness formulas more frequently. As the author argues, the direct form of requests as well as an infrequent use of politeness routines should not be interpreted as impolite, as it represents an appropriate and expected strategy in the context investigated.

Similarly to the above-mentioned study by Antonopoulou (2001), the analysis showed that speakers tend to accommodate their linguistic behaviour to the addressee. It was observed, for instance, that female consumers tend to follow the male speech behaviour and choose direct requests in the form of imperatives while addressing male sellers. An accommodation of the interlocutor was also observed in the choice of address terms. It was shown, namely, that the gender of the seller determined the address term and its function used by the consumers. Informal forms of address predominated in male-male transactions, while formal address terms were more frequent in female-male encounters. The study also showed that sellers used a wider range of address forms, comprising names, titles or terms of endearment, which the author interprets as a sign of greater involvement and solidarity politeness on their part.

In a similar vein, focusing on three layers of pragmatic variation, Yates (2015) investigated service encounters in corner stores in Buenos Aires, Argentina. The study proved that direct questions and elliptical requests are used the most frequently, with an uncommon use of lexical downgraders. It was observed that on an interactional level, the participants tend to use short and informal openings and closings, as well as informal terms of address. As far as the influence of gender is concerned, selected differences between males and females were observed only on the stylistic level.

Gender variation in the production and perception of requests in café encounters in the US was investigated in the above-mentioned study by Fink and Félix-Brasdefer (2015). The analysis showed similarities and differences between female and male customers in their requesting behaviour. It was found that although both gender groups use conventional indirect requests the most frequently, they differ in their preference for other request patterns, with male customers employing elliptical requests and assertions more often than female clients, which confirms the results obtained by Antonopoulou (2001) or Félix-Brasfeder (2012) in other cultural contexts. The two gender groups also differ in their use of internal modification. It was found that female customers tend to use more politeness markers such as *please* and the conditional form. External modification proved similar in both groups, with male and female customers utilizing relational talk and greetings, the latter being more frequent. In general, the study showed that female customers are more concerned about being polite to the barista and show more concern for the barista's autonomy and negative face, while male customers express more focus on attaining the transactional goal of the encounter. In line with other studies (Antonopoulou 2001, Félix-Brasdefer 2012), the analysis demonstrated that speakers tend to accommodate and change their speech to match the interlocutor's preferences. Male customers are more likely to use greetings and decrease the use of elliptical requests when addressing female than male baristas.[38]

The study by Taylor (2015) also focused on requests in café service encounters in the US and produced analogical results showing that conventional indirect forms tend to be the most frequent, followed by assertions, imperatives, want and need statements, and elliptical forms. The study demonstrated gender

---

[38] The study referred to also examined baristas' perceptions of the encounters and showed that the request form and the completeness of the order influenced the perception of the politeness of the request. It showed similarities and differences in the perception of politeness between female and male baristas. Both baristas pointed out that modification increased the degree of politeness of the requests. It was only conventional indirect requests that were perceived as polite by both female and male baristas regardless of modification used by the consumer. This, as the authors claim, points to the inherent politeness of this request form. Moreover, both baristas did not consider relational talk as expected in the encounter. The baristas, however, differed in a few respects. The female barista pointed to the query preparatory conventional indirect request as the most polite, while the male barista considered the conditional form as the most polite. Baristas disagreed as to the degree of politeness of the possibility subtype of the conventional indirect request, which the female barista considered as polite, while the male as impolite or neutral. The baristas also differed in their perception of want and need statements, considered as demanding or rude and impolite by the female barista and polite or neutral by the male barista, respectively. Both baristas perceived assertions and implicit requests without modification as neutral, while verbless requests and suggestory formulae without any internal modification as impolite. As the authors claim, the differences clearly indicate that gender may impact one's perception of politeness (Fink and Félix-Brasdefer 2015).

differences in the request forms used as well, with females using more conventionally indirect fully verbalized requests and males employing elliptical verbless requests more frequently. The scholar, drawing on Antonopoulou's (2001) claims, stated that the differences result from the perception of a service encounter by the two groups, i.e. males in contrast to females perceive service encounters as a transaction which does not require interpersonal exchanges between the two parties involved.[39]

As the review of the studies provided above shows, customer encounters, though considered routine forms of interaction, exhibit considerable organizational and discursive diversity, with different contextual factors, such as the degree of familiarity, gender and cultural background having an important impact on the shape of the interaction.[40]

2.2.2. Call centre interactions

A rich line of research into customer care discourse has focused on call centre interaction. Call centres, despite the growth of other channels for customer interactions, are still considered important, since they allow a company to establish and manage customer relationships, conduct transactions, provide information, handle problems and complaints at a relatively low cost (Feinberg et al. 2002). The popularity of call centres and their use for different purposes has been attributed not only to the low cost of their management, but also to their accessibility and, from the perspective of the caller, the intimate anonymity which they offer, the availability of an anonymous expert with whom one may discuss problems and the conversational engagement of the call taker (Firth et al. 2005: 16-20).

Call centre interaction constitutes an important area of linguistic research. As Cameron (2000b: 328) observes, in call centres, language and communication are of primary significance since the quality of the talk determines the standards of the service and is key to offering successful customer care (cf. Jagodziński and Archer 2018).

Call centres comprise inbound centres, which focus on providing information and answering customers' queries and problems, and outbound centres, which deal with telesales and customer surveys (Forey and Lockwood 2007: 309). The research into call centre communication has focused primarily on the interaction carried out in the inbound centres. Such calls, usually initiated by customers,

---

[39] Taylor's (2015) analysis additionally examined the influence of modality on request forms, contrasting face-to-face with drive-through encounters. In drive-through encounters, the above-mentioned gender differences were not observed and conventionally indirect forms were used the most frequently by both gender groups. This is explained by the lack of direct visual contact with the barista.

[40] Selected studies have also focused on nonverbal communication in service encounters (see, for instance, Dorai and Webster (2015), Loth et al. (2015), Svinhufvud (2018)).

are considered more demanding than outbound calls, as the nature of the call cannot be predicted and agents need to manage more complex issues. Outbound calls, by contrast, have a more predictable and routine character.

The research into call centre interaction in English has focused on the language of centres located in the UK or the US, where the agents comprise predominantly native speakers of English, and offshore call centres located for instance in India or the Philippines, where the agents are mostly non-native speakers of English. Both lines of research have examined different aspects of call centre interaction and uncovered different practices associated with call centre talk. The studies have concerned discourse features of the interaction as well as the structural organization of the talk.

In a series of studies, Cameron (2000a, 2000b, 2008) focused on the scripted and codified character of call centre interaction. Based on an analysis of agent training materials, assessment forms, scripts, prompts, as well as interviews with workers and the management staff of call centres in the UK, Cameron discusses the practices of "styling" the agents, i.e. imposing specific interactional behaviours. Regulations encompass the sequencing and the content of the talk, the use of politeness formulae, lexical choices, as well as voice quality, prosodic, paralinguistic and nonverbal behaviour. As Cameron (2008) demonstrates, call centre talk constitutes an example of "top-down talk," characterized by a significant degree of codification, with the shape of the interaction determined beforehand, designed and imposed by managers and consultants, rather than managed naturally or spontaneously by the participants. The primary aim of styling agents' talk is to reduce variability and maximize productivity of the interaction. The scholar interprets the process as a consequence of globalization and a high degree of competitiveness in the corporate world (Cameron 2000a, 2000b). Cameron (2000b) draws an analogy between the preferred style of speech required from the agents and women's language. The agents, namely, are advised to use expressive intonation, be cooperative, show support, concern, empathy and interest through minimal responses, questions, favour indirectness through hedging and mitigation. Since these characteristics are symbolically associated with women's language, as the author claims, the process of styling has contributed to the valorization of the feminine linguistic style (Cameron 2000b: 323).

Adolphs et al. (2004) investigated telephone conversations between callers and advisers in NHS Direct health advisory service in the UK. Applying discourse and conversation analysis perspectives and corpus analysis, the study uncovered selected linguistic and discourse features of the interaction. More specifically, the analysis presents strategies which advisors use to involve the caller, establish a relationship with the caller, to lend authority to the advice given and to end the interaction. The interaction is shown as a strongly caller-oriented discourse, which is reflected in a frequent use of the personal pronouns *you* and *your* by the agents, indicating focus on the caller, as well as a frequent use of backchannel responses, used to invite involvement from the caller and elaboration of the caller's health concerns, and further to affirm the patient's concerns. The study showed that agents' language is also characterized by a preference for politeness strategies, strategies minimizing the imposition of the advice given, marking optionality and hypotheticality, which is reflected in a high frequency of modal verbs *can* or *may*, as well as of *if* and *or*. In order to enhance the credibility and authoritative nature of the advice given, the agents often depersonalize the advice by referring to secondary sources or third parties. The analysis also pointed out that advisors tend to end the interaction with a "convergence coda," i.e. a turn summarizing the talk and advising the adoption of the advice given.

A range of aspects associated with call centre interaction are discussed in the volume edited by Baker et al. (2005). The studies included in the volume concern calls of a different nature, i.e. calls focusing on technical assistance, healthcare provision and customer assistance, examining aspects of call management as well.

Baker et al. (2005) focused on technical support calls and examined sequences of turns in the openings of customer calls. The study found certain regularities in the sequential ordering of the talk and a series of interrelated though separate components. The components identified in the study comprise a sequence in which the identity of the caller is established and the preferred address forms are selected, the assistant's offer of help, which is followed by the customer's narrative describing the problem and reason for the call. Examining the above-mentioned components in detail, the study demonstrated "how intricately and delicately talk is designed and interactionally managed" (Baker et al. 2005: 56). Further studies presented in the volume concern the procedures in the sequence of problem description, underlining the advantages of collaboration between the caller and the call taker (Houtkoop et al. 2005), the use of spatial metaphors by callers and call takers in their narratives describing computer problems (Kraan 2005), the strategies of advising used by call takers employed in support lines (Pudlinski 2005), the use of a non-standard opening in children's counseling service calls (Danby et al. 2005), as well as identity construction among callers and call takers in an emotional counselling helpline (Molder 2005). The studies included in the volume also discuss research devoted to help-seeking behaviour among the callers, strategies of problem-description (Leppänen 2005), advice-giving practices (Landqvist 2005), strategies of problem-solving and negotiation (Chappell 2005), language games in complaint calls (Torode 2005), the structure of adjacency pairs comprising instruction giving and receiving (Murtagh 2005), and, finally, the important role of monitoring each other's interaction performed by the personnel of call centres (Whalen and Zimmerman 2005).

Studies into call centre interaction have also focused on different im/politeness phenomena. For instance, Jagodziński (2013) and Jagodziński and Archer (2015) investigated instances of impoliteness and verbal aggression in British call centre interaction. Examining impoliteness strategies, Jagodziński and Archer (2015) provide examples of "sanctioned face-attack," instances of impoliteness which are tacitly accepted by call centre agents.

Additional studies into call centre communication worthy of mention comprise research conducted in different cultural contexts.

Economidou-Kogetsidis (2005) undertook a contrastive analysis and compared requesting behaviour among British and Greek consumers in call centre interaction of an airline company, focusing on the assessment of social variables, social power, familiarity and imposition of the act, as well as the degree of directness employed by the speakers. The analysis proved that Greek requests are more direct. According to the author, directness in the requests is motivated by clarity, goal orientedness and minimizing imposition, thus expressing negative politeness. Comparing the function of politeness markers *please* and *parakalo*, the scholar observes that the two markers are employed differently, with the Greek marker being less conventionalized, with its use supporting negative politeness of Greek requests.

The research into call centre interaction in Polish has encompassed analyses of selected features of the encounters and strategies used in the exchanges by consumers and an insurance company (Ptaszek 2008, Kaszewski and Ptaszek (eds.) 2009). On the part of the company's representatives, studies have indicated a customer-oriented form of discourse, reliance on conventional politeness, with a general tendency towards "excessive politeness" (Ptaszek 2008: 111). Analyses have shown that customers are treated in a highly civil and polite manner. The above-mentioned choices constitute evidence of a preference for an institutional, rather formal tone in the representatives' statements (Ptaszek 2008, 2009b, Kaszewski 2009, Wierzchowska 2009). As far as consumers' interactional practices are concerned, the study by Ptaszek (2009a), devoted to the ways of communicating criticism and negative emotions among consumers, proved that consumers use swear words, try to discredit the consultants, negate their competence or show superiority. The study shows how consumers direct criticism at the company, exposing its dishonest or corrupt practices.

As far as other cultural contexts are concerned, it is worth noting research into Spanish and Slovenian encounters.

The study by Marquez Reiter (2006) analyzed the practices found in service calls to a Montevidean company and showed that greetings and self-identification play a major role in achieving interactional closeness among the participants of the interaction. In a further study, Marquez Reiter (2009) examined the opening sequence of a service call between an Uruguayan agent and an Argentinean client, with a particular focus on the manifestation of face in the interaction and shows that face concerns underlie ritualistic politeness acts in the openings, such as "how are you" exchanges. The analysis provided an example of how face work is carried out in the interaction both on the part of the customer, who tries to diminish the agent's professional face, and of the agent, trying to re-establish her professional identity.

Orthaber and Marquez Reiter (2011) investigated complaining practices typical of Slovenian. The scholars analyzed the form of complaints to a transport company and showed that complaints expressed by consumers tend to be explicit and intensified by expressions of criticism, insults and threats. In their 2014 study (Orthaber and Marquez Reiter 2014), in turn, the authors focused on the company representative's responses in the calls and investigated instances of impoliteness in service calls, forms of disaffiliation, disengagement and non-recipiency, comprising the agent's passivity, delayed responses, pauses, withdrawal from his/her role as a source of information, assigning responsibility to third parties or offering unreliable information.[41]

Analyses of offshore call centres have focused on a range of aspects. The studies have investigated, among others, the influence of globalization and managerial practices on national identity and language policies in professional or institutional settings.[42] The research has also comprised analyses carried out from a linguistic perspective. Since for agents working in such centres English is usually a second language, the studies have investigated, for example, communicative competence and cultural awareness of the agents, problematic stages and communication breakdowns in the calls (Forey and Lockwood 2007), expression and management of emotions in the interaction (Hood and Forey 2008), the problem of employee language assessment (Friginal 2007) or training in accent neutralization (Cowie 2007, Forey and Lockwood 2007, Friginal 2007, 2008, 2009).

More specifically, the study by Forey and Lockwood (2007) investigated the genre, discourse structure and selected language features of the interaction, with the primary aim of establishing the causes of language and communication problems occurring during the call. The research showed that the generic structure of the talk comprises obligatory stages of opening, gathering information, establishing the purpose, servicing the customer and closing. Optional stages involve the statement of purpose of the call by the customer, summarizing the

---

[41] The authors attribute impoliteness to both internal and external factors, comprising the type of company and its services, job characteristics of agents, the agent's interactional style and broader socioeconomic factors underlying the functioning of the company under investigation (Orthaber and Marquez Reiter 2014).

[42] For instance, research by Poster (2007) examined the managerial practice of national identity management in Indian call centres requiring agents to assume different national identities, i.e. either American or British, depending on the location of the company they serve. Taylor and Bain (2005) investigated Indian call centre labour process and pointed out problematic issues and practices associated with it.

call and restating its key points. It was found that most communication problems occur at the stages of establishing the purpose of the talk and servicing
the customer. It is at these stages that agents' comprehension skills and their
ability to formulate a clear response with servicing solutions are tested. Calls
which most frequently result in communication breakdowns comprise those
with complaining, frustrated and aggressive customers, customers who were
vague, demanding or had complex problems. It was observed that in dealing
with such customers, agents tend to "lose control of the call" and respond with
silence or formulaic, unhelpful, rude or contradictory answers (Forey and
Lockwood 2007: 315). The study found that the choices made by the agents
at three levels, i.e. phonological and lexical, interpersonal and discourse level,
influence the degree of success in the interaction. The choices made on the
phonological and lexical, as well as on the discourse level, reflect the agent's
ability to form an expression understandable for the customer. Interpersonal
choices reflect their ability to establish relationship with consumers, manage
and direct the interaction, understand the context and the agent's cultural
competence.

Hood and Forey (2008) investigated interpersonal dynamics in offshore calls
between Filipino representatives and American customers. Drawing on appraisal
theory, the study examined how the caller and the representative manage the
emotive intensity of the interaction in the case of problematic calls. The study
proved that the speakers resort to implicit rather than explicit expression of
attitude. The analysis showed how agents utilize such concessive contractors as
already, *actually*, *just*, *yet* or *only* as a means serving to reduce the emotional
intensity of the interaction.

Cross-cultural interaction in a US outsourced call centre in the Philippines
was also analyzed by Friginal (2009). The study offers a linguistic perspective,
investigating discourse patterns practiced in the interaction by both callers and
agents. The work contains a detailed corpus-based analysis of a range of lexicogrammatical features, as well as pauses and dysfluencies in the interaction.
The corpus of interactions is further contrasted with the corpora of spoken
face-to-face conversation and spontaneous telephone exchanges. The research
proved the occurrence of systematic patterns of speech typical of the language
of outsourced call centres. The main distinguishing features comprise a high
frequency of politeness and respect markers, procedural language, addressee
focused turns and a high degree of nominalization. These features reflect the
specific roles of the agents – attending to consumers in a respectful manner,
delivering instructions and specialized information, and managing the conversation. A higher frequency of dysfluencies and filled pauses, repeats, respect
markers and apologies by the agents, as the scholar observes, results from the
cross-cultural nature of the interaction, inadequate language competence of
the agents and the pressure of a direct contact. These properties distinguish call

centre interaction from both face-to-face and spontaneous telephone conversations. The procedural and highly polite language of the agents is contrasted with more involved, personal and less managed discourse of the callers. The study also indicates differences in the discourse resulting from speakers' gender and agents' experience. Agents' experience proved to have a considerable influence on all aspects of their language. With regard to gender and differences between male and female callers, the analysis shows that female speakers tend to use more involved, personalized and polite language than male callers. Interestingly, however, similar differences were not stated for the language used by the agents, as the language of male agents resembled the language of female rather than male callers, which may corroborate Cameron's (2000a, 2000b) observations concerning the female communication style among call centre agents.

2.2.3. Online customer encounters

Research has also been carried out into different aspects of online customer encounters, i.e. into online interaction practices and image management, online crisis communication, as well as into the discourse and management of customer complaints and reviews.

Studies of customer encounters comprise analyses of different channels of communication, asynchronous and synchronous interaction, i.e. communication via e-mail, platforms, websites, review websites or social networking sites. The studies underline the impact of the medium on traditional service encounters, on interactional practices, politeness conventions, show how traditional genres are transformed when transferred online and how new genres develop. A short review of the research devoted to different aspects of the encounters concerning different languages and cultural contexts will be presented below.

E-mail communication, which was one of the first channels of online interaction between a company and its customer, was perceived as a channel which could improve the relationship between consumers and web-based companies, allowing for a degree of personalization, which, in turn, constitutes one of the primary factors enhancing a consumer's experience as a customer (Zemke and Connellan 2001). Selected aspects of e-mail customer communication were investigated in a study by Van Mulken and der Meer (2005). The study examined e-mail replies to consumers' questions posted by e-mail, focusing on rhetorical and interpersonal strategies used in the replies. The investigation was conducted with a contrastive approach comparing Dutch and American replies. The moves identified in the responses comprise salutations and closings, presentation of the company, thanks, response to the customer's enquiry, explanation and invitation for further contact. The study did not find many differences in each of the compared aspects. The identified differences concern the use of thanks, which were more frequent in American responses, and apologies, which proved more frequent in Dutch e-mails.[43] The scholars conclude that traditional, established generic structure of customer paper-based communication was transferred to electronic communication. As the scholars claim, though medium characteristics impact the structure of moves, with selected moves being more often omitted (e.g. opening and closings) or added (e.g. literal citations) in e-mails, there is no need to define e-mails as a sub-genre of customer communication.

Potential differences between traditional and electronic customer encounters were examined by Blitvich (2015). The author argues that there is a clear need for new hybrid methods of researching e-encounters. Methodologies which would be useful in the new context, according to the author, should merge natively digital approaches with digitized models of analysis.

Placencia (2015) investigated online service encounters interaction on an e-commerce platform in Ecuadorian. The analysis showed that online encounters are characterized by more informal, egalitarian and less personalized relationships between the participants than in traditional face-to-face interaction. The change in the conventions of address terms was attributed to the anonymity of the speakers online.

Ivorra-Perez (2015), in turn, conducted a cross-cultural investigation of engagement markers on toy selling websites. The analysis was devoted to Spanish, British and North American websites. The study showed cross-cultural differences in the strategies used by the companies, with Spanish websites using more indirect strategies in their interactions with consumers, a preference for direct strategies on American websites and a tendency to combine direct and indirect strategies on the British pages. The analysis revealed visible differences in consumers' preferences of specific strategies in different cultural backgrounds. The results are interpreted in the context of globalization in the corporate world, advising a careful adjustment of interaction strategies to a specific cultural context.

---

[43] The study additionally compared practices by Dutch companies with a long and short tradition. The results showed that there was not much difference in the practices of old and new companies, apart from a more frequent use of the moves of invitation to further contact and presentation of the company among the new companies (Van Mulken and der Meer 2005).

2.3. Crisis communication, complaint and review management

Extensive research devoted to customer encounters focused on crisis management and, more specifically, complaint and negative review management strategies in different communicative contexts. Research on crisis management in the context of traditional offline and online communication will be described below.

2.3.1. Crisis communication, complaint and review management in traditional channels of interaction

Crisis management comprises communication expressed by a company as a response to an organizational crisis defined as "the perception of an unpredictable event that threatens important expectancies of stakeholders and can seriously impact an organization's performance and generate negative outcomes" (Coombs 2007a: 2-3). It includes messages and strategies used by the company and distributed to stakeholders and the public in general. Crisis situations may involve a range of events, such as natural disasters, rumours, workplace violence, challenges, technological-error and human-error accidents, organizational misdeeds, boycotts or strikes (Coombs 2007b: 168, Ki and Nekmat 2014: 143). Post-crisis communication, depending on its form, may either diminish or aggravate the results of a crisis (Roshan et al. 2016: 351). A timely reaction suitable to the state of affairs can help the company to diminish negative sentiment and eliminate confusion, whereas the lack of any reaction or an inappropriate response can have significant negative consequences for the image of the company (Nitins and Burgess 2014). Complaint and negative review handling, in turn, encompasses "the strategies firms use to resolve and learn from service failures in order to (re)establish the organization's reliability" (Tax et al. 1998: 61) and manage customers' dissatisfaction.

The research on crisis and complaint management comprises analyses of the responses conducted from different perspectives.

Extensive research has been devoted to complaint management from the perspective of marketing research. Consumer complaining behaviour is here defined as "an action taken by an individual that involves communicating something negative regarding a product or service" (Jacoby and Jaccard 1981: 6).[44] As part of

---

[44] Other definitions view complaining behaviour as "a set of all behavioral and non-behavioral responses which involve communicating something negative regarding a purchase episode and is triggered by perceived dissatisfaction with that episode" (Sing and Howell 1984: 42) or "a subset of all possible responses to perceived dissatisfaction around a purchase episode, during consumption or during possession of the goods or services" (Crié 2003: 62).

research devoted to complaining, types of consumer complaint behaviours and complaint-related personalities have been investigated (Singh 1988, Davidow and Dacin 1996, Berry et al. 2018), managerial reactions to complaints (see, for instance, Resnik and Harmon 1983, Fornell and Westbrook 1984, Baer and Hill 1994, Bolkan and Daly 2009, Bradley and Sparks 2012, Mauri and Minazzi 2013, Wei et al. 2013, Levy et al. 2013, Knox and Oest 2014), as well as consumer reactions to complaint management processes (Conlon and Murray 1996, Cranage and Mattila 2005, Wirtz and Mattila 2005, Homburg and Fürst 2007, Singh et al. 2016). Within this line of study, a number of classifications of complaint management strategies have been suggested. For instance, Coombs (1998) discusses a range of crisis management strategies placed on a continuum from accommodative strategies, which comprise full apology, corrective action or ingratiation, to defensive strategies, which include attacking the accuser, denial, with excuses and justifications placed in the middle of the continuum. Coombs and Holladay (2008), in turn, compared apology, perceived as the best strategy in crisis management, to other crisis response strategies. The results indicate that apology and equivalent strategies, such as sympathy and compensation, are perceived in a similar way and can be equally effective as crisis responses. As far as other classifications are concerned, Sparks (2001) proposes a class of "nonrecovery" strategies of denial and avoidance, and "recovery strategies" of an apology, rectification, explanation, invitation of input and compensation. Liao (2007) enumerates the strategy of apology, problem solving, courtesy, explanation and promptness.

Within crisis management research performed from a rhetorical perspective, Benoit's (1995, 1997) approach has been considered particularly influential. The scholar outlines five categories of image restoration strategies and sub-strategies, i.e. denial: simple denial and shifting the blame; evasion of responsibility: provocation (response to act of another), defeasibility (lack of information or ability), accident, good intentions; reducing offensiveness of event: bolstering (stressing good traits), minimization, differentiation, transcendence (underlining more important considerations), attack accuser (reducing credibility of accuser), compensation (reimbursing victim); corrective action (planning to solve or prevent problem); mortification (apology).[45]

---

[45] In the context of studies carried out within the area of marketing and management, it is also worth mentioning studies by Davidow (2000, 2003), who investigated organizational responses to customer complaints and reviewed how those responses influenced post-complaint behaviour among customers. Six dimensions of organizational responses to complaints are presented, i.e. timeliness (speed of providing a response), facilitation (procedures supporting customer engagement in complaints), redress (outcome of a response that a customer receives), apology (acknowledgement of the consumer's complaint), credibility (company's readiness to offer an explanation of the problem), attentiveness (interpersonal communication between organization and customer) (Davidow 2003: 232).

From a pragmatic perspective, Trosborg and Shaw (1998) discuss strategies used in responding to complaints in business interaction.[46] According to their account, the management of customer complaints should involve the use of ritual acts of thanking, apologizing for the infraction, requests for information and promising correction, offers of repair, checking customer satisfaction and preventing future mistakes.

Complaint handling was also studied from a discourse-oriented perspective by Marquez Reiter (2008). The analysis, devoted to service calls to two Montevidean telephone service centres, found a common use of explanations in the interaction. The frequent use of such acts was associated with a non-severe nature of the offence on the part of the company. The study further compared strategies used by the two companies and showed similarities and differences in the interaction. Both companies resorted to explanations, but differed in their approach towards the infraction, expressing justifications and explicit apology acts or excuses and acts evading responsibility, respectively.

Finally, working from the perspective of genre theory, Giannoni (2014) compared British and Italian customer complaint forms. The study uncovered similarities and differences in the structure and wording of complaint forms in both languages. Structurally, complaint forms in both languages exhibited a similar degree of complexity. Differences were observed in the wording of directive acts used in the forms, with more such acts used in British forms, which shows a greater degree of interaction with the consumers. Further differences were found in the reference to the complaint and the consumer. It was observed that in British forms, the event tends to be personalized and the customer is addressed directly, while in Italian forms, the event is objectified, while the consumer is not explicitly referred to or is addressed as a third party. The study interprets the differences as a reflection of national perceptions of the complaint management process, of duties and obligations of the company and the customer. As the author claims, differences reflect the cultural context in which the texts are produced, i.e. British, being a low-context culture, in which the relationship between the company and the customer is explicit and foregrounded, and Italian, representing a high-context culture, in which customers need to refer to their cultural competence and background knowledge to uncover implicit meanings.

---

[46] The scholars distinguish between complaint handling strategies used in business interaction and in everyday communication. As far as everyday communication is concerned, Trosborg and Shaw (1998) name the following categories of responses: apology, acknowledgement of blame, explanation and offering repair, as well as a group of strategies in which the speakers opt out and deny their responsibility for the offence, evade responsibility or attack the complainer.

2.3.2. Online crisis communication, complaint
and review management

A significant proportion of research into online corporate interaction and customer encounters has concerned the problem of crisis communication, review and complaint management.

As stated before, the introduction of social media, as well as portals and services designed specifically for the purpose of sharing and distributing information and opinions about goods and services, has contributed to a considerable increase in customers' engagement in eWOM practices. Consequently, managing reviews and comments published online has become a significant component of any company's reputation and image management strategy.

Research into consumer eWOM has focused in particular on negative customer reviews and complaints, the response strategies employed by companies to such reviews, as well as customer perception of the strategies used. Studies have been dedicated to reviews, complaints and responses published in social media, as well as review and e-commerce websites offering user-generated content.[47] Research has been carried out mainly in the area of marketing and organizational communication.

Studies devoted to complaints and reviews have focused on investigating the characteristics of online reviews, their communication and informational properties, with the aim of uncovering how they shape consumers' choices and opinions (see Chatterjee 2001, Lee and Hu 2005, Brown et al. 2007, Sen and Lerman 2007, Chen 2008, Gretzel and Yoo 2008, Lee et al. 2008). Sparks and Browning (2011), for instance, examined the factors associated with reviews which have the most salient impact on consumers' decisions, i.e. the content or target of reviews, the overall tone or valence of the reviews, the framing of the review and peripheral information (e.g. rating). The research confirmed that positive reviews tend to increase consumer trust, but it is negative information that has a greater influence on consumers' evaluations and that the negative valence and frame of reviews tend to intensify consumers' distrust. The study also proved that consumers' judgement is influenced by peripheral information included in reviews, such as rating, due to the ease of processing such data.

The studies have also investigated the motives governing consumers' engagement in online reviews. The research has focused on negative reviews and complaining behaviour in particular, and showed that the motives comprise the need to vent anger and dissatisfaction, to express concern for others, to warn other consumers or to express dissatisfaction with previous complaint

---

[47] Websites which allow and/or encourage users to publish reviews of services and products include, among others, Oyster, Yelp, Amazon, TripAdvisor, Hotels, Booking.com.

management (Harrison-Walker 2001, Zheng et al. 2009, Sparks and Browning 2010, Vásquez 2011, Levy et al. 2013, Einwiller and Steilen 2015).

Extensive research conducted to date has focused on the management of negative reviews and complaints, i.e. review and complaint handling strategies used by companies in online encounters. Crisis management strategies have received considerable attention, since proper management of reviews, in particular negative reviews and complaints, constitutes a significant tool of enhancing customer relations.

The management of consumer complaints by companies on Twitter and consumer reactions to the messages was investigated by Coyle et al. (2012). Two major kinds of responses were singled out, i.e. empathetic posts, including a suggestion or expression of concern, and problem-solving posts, comprising a solution to consumers' problems. As far as consumers' perception of the strategies is concerned, it was observed that problem-solving posts contribute to a positive attitude towards the brand and the feeling of a company's trustworthiness and benevolence.

Romenti et al. (2014), in turn, investigated dialogue strategies applied by organizations in a crisis situation on Facebook, Twitter and YouTube. The analysis proved that of the companies engaged in crisis communication, all applied a dialogic approach but adopted different dialogue strategies. The study reviews the use of such dialogue strategies as concertative strategies, i.e. informative responses aiming at reaching consensus, framing strategies, in which companies attempt to guide conversations to a different topic or issue, transformative strategies, which aim at finding solutions to crisis collectively with stakeholders, as well as generative strategies, in which companies encourage conversations between stakeholders but remain external observers themselves. Each set of strategies allows the company to achieve different aims, i.e. framing strategies constitute a means of reinforcing a company's image, concertative strategies are a means of offering solutions, while transforming strategies represent a way of engaging consumers to collect solution ideas. The study showed that concertative, framing and transformative strategies were the most frequent.[48] The scholars proved that companies are aware of the potential benefits of a dialogic approach to crises. In times of crisis, by approaching affected consumers and engaging them in dialogue, companies may protect their image. Using a dialogic approach, as the scholars underline, allows companies to share their position on the crisis, their ideas and communicate with stakeholders to reach consensus. A dialogic approach contributes

---

[48] The analysis also proved that companies apply different strategies depending on the phase of crisis. It was shown that concertative strategies are more frequent in the first stage of crisis, followed by transformative strategies used to collect ideas and solutions to crisis (Romenti et al. 2014).

to a positive perception of the company among consumers, who perceive it as interested in and appreciative of their suggestions.[49]

An analysis of complaint handling on both Twitter and Facebook was undertaken by Einwiller and Steilen (2015). The study showed a moderate degree of responsiveness towards consumers' complaints and indicated that companies do not fully utilize the potential of the medium to interact and assist consumers. Strategies which enhance consumers' satisfaction were identified and these comprise offering corrective action, which is in line with the results obtained by Coyle et al. (2012) mentioned above, as well as connecting consumers to representatives who can solve the complaint and expressing thanks for the complaint. The most frequent strategy used in handling complaints encompassed requests for further information, which, however, as it was observed, do not impact consumers' satisfaction in a positive way.

A typology of responses to reviews was also suggested by Sparks and Bradley (2017), who investigated responses to hotel reviews. The so-called "Triple A" typology comprises 19 forms of managerial responses in broad categories of acknowledgements, accounts and actions. Each category includes more specific moves, i.e. the category of acknowledging the review encompasses the acts of thanks, appreciation, apology, admitting or dismissing the review. The category of account comprises excuses, justifications, penitential and denial acts, while the category action may involve investigating, referral, rectification, training, direct contact and compensation.

Research has also concerned consumers' evaluation and perception of review management strategies. The studies have shown that the so-called accommodative responses, in which the companies try to assist stakeholders affected by crisis, the use of such moves as apology, explanation and appreciation of feedback are rated highly and thus can help a company to achieve service recovery (Sparks and Fredline 2007, Levy et al. 2013, Ye and Ki 2017). It has also been found that the use of referential explanations resulted in higher levels of satisfaction and loyalty than justification (Sparks and Fredline 2007).[50] The factors which are appreciated by the consumers also comprise the responses' immediacy, authenticity and an individual treatment of each review (Zheng et al. 2009, Chan and Guillet 2011, Levy et al. 2013). By contrast, explicit marketing messages or third-party endorsement and bolstering strategies, in which companies seek to

---

[49] With respect to users' approaches to the strategies applied by companies, the study also pointed out that framing strategies, in which companies try to regain control and shift conversation towards different topics, were not appreciated but interpreted as a means of escaping from responsibility (Romenti et al. 2014).

[50] Similar results were obtained by Wei et al. (2013), who contrasted general and specific responses, and observed that the use of specific responses is positively evaluated by consumers, increases consumers' trust and positive perception of the company's communication quality.

publish positive information about the company were not welcome by respondents (Dekay 2012, Ye and Ki 2017).

The above-mentioned studies into the management of complaints and crisis situations in social media from the marketing-oriented perspective offer insight into successful and unsuccessful management strategies applied by companies. It is in the context of crisis management that the difference between traditional and new media is particularly visible. It has become clear that traditional, top-down approaches to campaigns do not find application online and it is no longer possible to maintain control over consumers' experiences (Nitins and Burgess 2014). Approaches to crisis which proved unsuccessful in the new media and which originate from a more traditional approach comprise silence or lack of responsiveness as a solution to crisis or attempts to control users' feedback. A successful crisis management approach, by contrast, comprises an introduction of immediate damage control activities, establishment of a social media group dedicated to crisis management, offering immediate explanations and updates on corrective processes, which may help the company to diminish negative feedback and confusion.

According to Levy et al. (2013), it is important that companies implement a reputation management plan, with clear objectives, encompassing encouraging more consumers to write positive reviews, improving review ratings of review channels and clear strategies, such as active monitoring and responding to feedback, soliciting reviews from satisfied consumers, responding to reviews in a positive and personalized manner in a short period of time, all of which may help the company to achieve service recovery. The authors also emphasize the importance of social networking sites as places where consumers share reviews and underline a necessity to adapt review management practices to social networking and to monitor feedback published there. As mentioned before, responding to reviews and handling consumer complaints effectively is believed to help companies to gain new customers, improve relationship with existing clients, increase customer satisfaction, loyalty and repurchase or return intentions (Sparks and Fredline 2007).

An increasing amount of research into complaints, reviews and review responses has also been undertaken from a discourse and genre perspective, analyzing structural and discursive properties of these texts. Reviews and review responses have been recognized as new genres of computer-mediated communication. The two text-types belong to the same genre chain due to intertextual connections between them (Zhang and Vásquez 2014). The most significant properties of online reviews, which determine their structure and content, comprise their participatory, collaborative and user-generated nature (ibid.: 54). The purpose of a customer review is to present an opinion and evaluation of the goods or services offered. The purpose of a review response, in turn, comprises public acknowledgement of the customer's review, apology and, consequently, repair and maintenance of the relationship with the consumer, or denial and rejection of the review.

As far as consumer reviews and complaints are concerned, research has focused on strategies exploited by consumers in presenting their evaluations, as well as on the structural and lexical shape of the posts. The study by Meinl (2010) investigated complaints expressed on eBay by English and German customers. Based on this analysis, Meinl draws conclusions concerning differences between complaints in spoken interaction and in computer-mediated communication. The study shows that, in contrast to oral communication, complaints in computer-mediated communication are characterized by greater directness and more prominent upgrading modification. The direct and strong form of complaints is said to result from the public and anonymous context, in which consumers are not constrained by face considerations. Drawing on the original classification by Olshtain and Weinbach (1987), the author identifies eight complaint strategies, i.e. expression of disappointment, expression of anger or annoyance, explicit complaint, negative judgement, drawing one's own conclusion, warning others, threat and insult. The strategies can be used in isolation or in combination, forming a complaint speech act set. The study shows that while in face-to-face complaint communication British and German speakers rely on different norms, their communicative behaviour is more uniform in online complaints. The study found that both British English and German consumers use the same range of complaint strategies. The use of an explicit complaint strategy proved the most frequent in both analyzed corpora. It was shown that both groups employ a similar amount of upgrading and downgrading modification in the complaints. The occurrence of elliptical comments was also similar among both groups of consumers. As regards differences, the study pointed out that German consumers demonstrate a tendency to use more direct strategies and more frequent intensification in selected types of complaints.[51]

Working with data obtained from Polish, Smól (2010) analyzed strategies used by customers in expressing negative emotions in reviews posted on Allegro.pl, an e-commerce service. The means of expressing emotions comprise the use of negatively evaluating vocabulary, as well as punctuation, i.e. the use of capital letters or multiple punctuation marks. Analyzing negative reviews on the same e-commerce website, Kaszewski (2014) focused on forms of addressing sellers and demonstrated that most negative comments contained some address terms, such as neutral (e.g. *seller*) and impersonal forms, the pronominal form *they*, indicating distance and depreciation, but also negatively evaluating forms (e.g. *liar, fraud, thief*). An infrequent use of

---

[51] Certain differences in intensification patterns were also observed, with German consumers using exclamation marks more frequently to express their anger. British English consumers, by contrast, more often used first person pronouns to emphasize personal involvement and second person pronouns to underline the complainee's guilt and aggravate their complaints (Meinl 2010).

mitigation in the comments was observed, contrasted with a common use of strategies enhancing the illocutionary force of the messages.

Customer reviews were extensively researched by Vásquez (2011, 2012, 2014, 2015), who investigated online reviews published on different websites, such as Yelp, Amazon, Epicurious, Netflix and TripAdvisor. The studies present discourse and genre features of the reviews, both positive and negative, showing how customers express their evaluation and stance, how they construct their identity as a reviewer, establish their trustworthiness and reliability. The analyses also discuss involvement strategies, strategies used to engage other readers and forms of intertextuality in the reviews.

The genre properties of online complaints were studied by Tereszkiewicz (2015a), who analyzed complaints expressed by Polish customers on the Twitter profile of a telecommunications company. The study shows the components of an online complaint as well as complaint strategies. The strategies used in the complaints comprise questions with a pejorative undertone, exclamatives, imperatives, the use of negation and irony. The analysis shows that complaints may also be expressed by means of hashtags accompanying the messages. The study demonstrated how the context influences the genre of a complaint, its structure and content.

A cross-linguistic comparison of complaints in e-mail encounters was presented by Decock and Spiessens (2017). The study focused on complaint negotiation practices by German and French language customers. The aim of the analysis was to examine and compare complaint and disagreement strategies used by the two groups of consumers, as well as the presence of internal and external modification. The study showed an evolution from a more professional, neutral, problem-oriented and routinized tone in the first complaints, to confrontational and person-oriented discourse in subsequent disagreements. Disagreement e-mails were characterized by an increased use of upgraders, less routinized language and a decreased use of formulaic politeness. In disagreements, in contrast to complaints, in which customers typically resorted to an expression of dissatisfaction and a request for repair, consumers also tended to use a wider and more diversified range of strategies. With respect to cross-cultural differences, the major differentiating feature was that German customers tended to use a more explicit, while French consumers a more confrontational style.

Drawing on the material from social media and e-mail communication, Decock and Depraetere (2018) discuss the problem of indirectness in complaining. The scholars propose several complaint strategies based on the number of constitutive elements in the message (from one to four) and on their implicit or explicit nature.

Studies into companies' responses to consumers' complaints and reviews have focused on the analysis of moves and strategies constituting the structure of the responses.

Rhetorical moves present in responses to complaints and negative reviews were investigated by Zhang and Vásquez (2014). The moves outlined in the study comprise opening pleasantries, expression of gratitude, apology, a move which may comprise a proof of action, acknowledgement of feedback, reference to customer's review, avoidance of reoccurring problems, as well as an invitation for a second visit, soliciting response and closing, with thanking and apologizing being the most frequent among the strategies. The study points to different approaches to problems reported by consumers and the use of generic and specific responses, differing in the reference to the original review, with generic responses being vague, underspecified and not elaborating on the problems mentioned by consumers. In such responses, the authors stick to a template with recurring syntactic and lexical patterns. In specific responses, by contrast, a clear reference to the review is made and either a brief or a detailed explanation of the problems is provided. The study indicates a predominance of a generic approach in the reviews. The use of such responses is explained by a number of factors, comprising the speed and efficiency in publishing, facilitating the task of responding for the representatives or by a wish to standardize the responses.

Companies' responses on Twitter were investigated by Page (2014), who examined components of companies' apology acts. Results showed a frequent use of offers of repair and compensation, and an infrequent use of explanations. Questions and imperatives tended to be used as follow-up acts directed at offering repair and maintaining interaction with the consumer. The study also points to the use of greetings, discourse markers and emoticons accompanying apologies as rapport building and image repair tools.

Marquez Reiter et al. (2015) examined strategies of disaffiliation practiced by the company on Facebook. The study analyzes moderators' responses and customers' reactions. The analysis showed that companies use Facebook to associate with consumers and increase the company's visibility, while customers utilize the platform to associate with other customers and voice their dissatisfaction with the company. The study showed that companies tend to ignore customers' criticism.[52]

The investigated issues have also comprised responses to complaints on Polish corporate Twitter profiles. The analysis by Tereszkiewicz (2017b) outlined the most frequent strategies used in responding to complaints, i.e. attending to the complaint by means of requests for information and further contact, apologies, explanations, offers of assistance and evasive acts in which companies denied responsibility, diminished blame or criticized the complainer. A contrastive English and Polish analysis of strategies used in responding to complaints

---

[52] The important role of moderators managing interactions on the profile was emphsized, as individuals bearing the ultimate responsibility for the shape of interaction, with the company's role being only indirect (Marquez Reiter et al. 2015).

(Tereszkiewicz, forthcoming-b) showed a lower number of apologies and a higher number of evasive strategies in the Polish corpus. In both corpora, a similar use of requests for further contact and of offers of help and repair was observed, which proves a customer-oriented approach of the companies willing to show readiness to attend to the customer and thus protect their image.

An analysis of moves in review responses was also included in the studies by Ho (2017a, 2017b). According to the author, obligatory moves in responses to negative reviews comprise acknowledging the problem, expressing feelings and thanking the reviewer. Ho (2017b) focused on the strategy of denial and distinguished different strategies used by hotel managers, such as challenging the reviewer's decision, framing the problem as an isolated incident, suggesting other services or highlighting practice and facility, and further showed how the managers try to manage rapport and diminish the threat to the customer's face by acknowledging the problem, explaining, apologizing, rectifying the problem, showing appreciation and minimizing imposition. The author showed how these strategies work to achieve service recovery.

Chapter 3. Corporate profiles on Twitter – general characteristics

3.1. Company profiles – structure and types of posts

As indicated above, Twitter allows users to create individual profiles by means of a number of affordances, comprising visual and text-based means of communication.

The component parts of the profiles comprise profile data, a background image, a thumbnail image, a bio and a list of posts. All of these serve as important image management tools which allow the company to create and project a desired identity.

a) Profile data

Profile information comprises the data concerning the number of posts, followers, followees, likes, lists and moments. The data may have a significant persuasive potential, as they reflect the company's activity, degree of responsiveness and popularity.

b) Background images

Background images represent different degrees of complexity, comprising only text-based forms or highly multimodal, image- and text-based shapes. Background images may present company products, services, the company's logo and brand name, as well as advertising slogans and messages. The images may refer to recent advertising campaigns and as such may serve additional promotional purposes.

c) Thumbnail images

Thumbnail images in corporate profiles, in contrast to background images, tend to have a simpler form. The images most frequently involve the company's logo or the company's name.

d) Bios

Bios assume different forms and include short basic information concerning the profile, its purpose and content. The notes may also provide information on the company's location, company's website address, the date when the company joined Twitter, as well as links to multimedia content posted on the profile.

In their bios, most companies clearly state the function of the profile, i.e. presentation of news concerning the company and/or customer service. Bios are structured differently, with a more information-oriented form, as exemplified in (1), where the note includes plain statements of the two purposes of the profile, or a more information- and promotion-oriented form, as exemplified in (2). In such bios, companies promote the company and the profile, introduce and advertise new products, and encourage consumers to check the company's offer. For instance:[53]

> (1) The official channel of Company9 UK mobile and home. Providing support from 9am – 9pm. (@Company9)

> (2) Official Twitter account for Company3 UK. For customer service support, please tweet @Company3EUhelp. Create the answer. Discover more: http://xxx/6000DiXXX (@Company3)

The use of strategies typical of corporate discourse and advertising with a clearly persuasive function can be seen in the messages. The following properties and the use of the following strategies characterizes the notes:

- self-identification – the companies self-identify by means of the company's name, as exemplified in (7) and (11), or, more frequently, by the use of second person plural forms of pronouns (e.g. (3), (4)). The use of identification in the pronoun form enhances the degree of personalization of the statements;
- dialogicality – bios make frequent use of dialogical strategies, most frequently involving external dialogicality, in which companies address consumers. Dialogicality is expressed in the form of questions addressed to users, most often questions in the function of offers of help and support (e.g. (3), (6)). Dialogical structures also comprise imperatives, encouraging customers to follow the profile and use the company's services, or directing consumers to further channels of communication (e.g. (4), (6), (7)). Imperatives are also used in more promotion-oriented notes, in which the companies persuade consumers to try the company's products. In this case, the notes may assume the form of a company's slogan, as exemplified in (8). A dialogical orientation of the messages is also reflected in addressing users by means of the second person singular form of the pronouns as well. The use of these forms may enhance the company's consumer-orientation and a wish to cater for consumers' needs (e.g. *to provide you, your queries*);
- evaluation – the strategies commonly found in the notes comprise the use of evaluation by means of positively loaded lexical items, enumeration, boosting, comparative and superlative statements, used with a persuasive function to advertise the company's services. Promotion of the profiles

---

[53] Examples have been anonymized. Company and product names have been removed from the messages. Otherwise, tweets are quoted in their original form.

is often expressed by means of an evaluative and playful reference to the company's products (e.g. *tastiest food updates, delicious updates*).

For example:

(3) Need to ask us something? We're here to help you 24 hours a day, 7 days a week. We'd never ask you for personal data on Twitter, please never post any. (@Company5)

(4) Track your parcel at http://www.xxx.co.uk. If you need to get in touch, DM your parcel number, name & delivery address. We are here Mon to Sat 8am-10pm & Sun 9am-5pm (@Company6)

(5) We're here 24/7 to provide you with the latest updates, news and assist with your queries. It's all part of our Customer Promise http://xxx.do/LrXXX (@Company12)

(6) Follow us for the tastiest food updates and news to snack on. Got a question? Our customer service team is here to help. (@Company10)

(7) Delicious updates from the UK Company11 team – head over to http://bit.ly/xxxtact for customer service support. (@Company11)

(8) Enjoy everything the world has to offer, through the power of technology. Breathe it all in. (@Company1)

(9) We're here for the box set bingers, telly ninjas, all-night gamers and biggest streamers. Need help? We're online 8am-10pm Mon-Fri & 8am-4pm on weekends. (@Company7)

(10) We're Company2, the UK network with 4G in more places than any other. Welcome to our official Twitter page! We're here to help from 7am-11pm (weekends 8am-8pm) (@Company2)

(11) Keep up to date with Company12 Coaches – offering great value travel to thousands of destinations across the UK & Europe. (@Company12)

As far as the posts are concerned, as indicated in Chapter 1, Twitter offers a range of communication options, i.e. by means of:
- updates,
- retweets,
- addressed messages: one-to-one interaction and one-to-many interaction (public); direct messages (private).

Updates, retweets and addressed messages may be purely textual, pictorial or comprise a combination of textual and multimedia content. Twitter allows users to include links to other sources in the tweets as well in the form of shortened website addresses or multimodal attachments to the posts. The links refer consumers to further sources, primarily concerning the company's offer or services. As such, the links perform the function of sales funnels directing consumers to the company's e-shop.

a) Updates

Updates comprise information-oriented tweets, promotional messages, promotion- and action-oriented tweets, as well as response solicitation messages (Lovejoy and Saxton 2012: 344).

Messages with a primarily informative purpose comprise tweets informing consumers on the availability of the company's services, on service breaks, disruptions or technical problems. For example:

> (12) Company7 @Company7
> We will be carrying out upgrade work Nov 3rd 7pm – Nov 5th 7am. This means some of our customer and [product name] services may be disrupted. Please bear with us your services will be back up and running first thing Monday! (@Company7)

> (13) Company12 @Company12
> #Company12Update Some of our services between Lincoln – Grimsby have been cancelled this morning due to urgent work being carried out on the track. Network Rail are currently working hard to get the line reopen. You can see further details here: http://ow.ly/WHRg30mYXXX (@Company12)

Promotional messages, which constitute the majority of the updates, encompass tweets publishing information on the company's offer, products and services. The tweets also involve updates on the company's achievements, such as obtained prizes or distinctions:

> (14) Company1 @Company1
> Just announced. The #[product name] is now available on an Company1 custom plan. Flex your data every month and spread the cost over 3 to 36 months. Get yours here: http://xx.uk
> [multimedia component] (@Company1)

> (15) Company2 @Company2
> We're the UK best network for the fifth year on the bounce according to RootMetrics®. Find out more: http://po.st/2HeXXX (@Company2)

Promotion- and action-oriented posts comprise tweets informing about the company's campaigns and events, encouraging consumers to participate in the activities. Updates also include polls, surveys, contests, tweets with questions addressed to the users, i.e. messages which are aimed at response solicitation (ibid.). The purpose of the messages is to encourage a conversational response from the users and create a dialogue, which serves further promotional functions. For instance:

> (16) Company1 @Company1
> Fancy winning a weekend wine-tasting trip to France, with flights included? Plus two brand new Bordeaux Red #[product name]? Enter now on #xxPriority:xx.uk/Bordeaux How's that for a #FridayFeeling (@Company1)

> (17) Company9 @Company9
> Get more done, wherever you are with the [product name]. Perfect for heading #BackToSchool! What are you looking forward to most?
> Entertainment overload
> Intelligent connectivity
> Multitasking like a pro (@Company9)

b) Retweets

Retweets comprise forwarded messages published by other users on Twitter or in other media. The companies forward reviews, important facts concerning the company, cite news, analyses or reports. Retweeting information has a promotional purpose. The use of other sources may also help the company to achieve an impression of objectivity. Quoting others may enhance the reliability of the information provided and thus convince consumers of the quality of the company's offer. Examples of retweeted posts are provided below.

(18) Company9 Retweeted
     user @user
     Company9 brings picture-perfect beauty to the screen with the [product name] TV
     bit.ly/2G2CXXX (@Company9)

(19) Company11 Retweeted
     user @user
     Our friends @Company11 have partnered with us to say #ThankYou100 to the #WW1
     generation who changed our world. Watch the video to find out more about the wom-
     en who kept the factories running, and sent care packages to troops on the frontline:
     http://ow.ly/Z38F30mwXXX (@Company11)

c) Addressed messages

Units initiating individual interaction on Twitter may be posted by both a customer and a company.

– Customer-initiated interaction – comprises the interaction between the company and the consumers initiated by an addressed message sent to the company's profile by the user or by means of @mentions. The messages may involve, for example, inquiries, requests for help, positive evaluation or complaints and negative evaluation. The messages are publicly visible to others. Users may also choose to send a direct message, which is not posted on the profile. The examples provided below illustrate public messages addressed to the company on the profile:

(20) when's custom cases coming to bristol?
     Company9 @Company9
     @user Hi [name]. We're happy to hear you're interested in these. No word on this at
     the moment, but we recommend you keep an eye on our website, and social media
     channels. ^ [initials] (@Company9)

(21) I just got the watch and it's great so far!
     Company9 @Company9
     @user We're glad to hear that, [name]. We'd love to hear any additional feedback, once
     you've had a chance to get grips with all the different features. ^[initials] (@Company9)

(22) the [company name] payg website is not working properly please fix ittt I need to top up
     Company1 @Company1
     @user Hi there 🏠 We're unaware of any issues, what's happening when you try to top
     up? Let us know, we'd like to help. (@Company1)

— Company-initiated interaction – company-initiated addressed interaction comprises persuasive and promotional messages expressed in response to a user's tweet mentioning the company's name or product but not addressed specifically and purposefully to the company. The strategy results from the use of tools of Internet monitoring, which lend the companies an opportunity to extract messages mentioning the company's name or the name of the product, even though the message is not addressed to the company itself, and respond to it in a desired way. This practice may be exemplified in the exchanges quoted below, where the companies reply to messages containing a hashtag with the company's product or the company's Twitter address:

(23) user @user
     Let's do this... #[product name]
     Company3 @Company3
     @user Welcome to #[product name] [name]. You've got this! (@Company3)

(24) user @user
     please sponsor me already @user
     user @user
     I want these so bad. [+ added picture of a product]
     Company3 @Company3
     @user We'll just leave this here [name]👀....http://xxx/6015EHXXX
     user @user
     Ok wow I didn't realise there were so many options 😵
     Company3 @Company3
     @user 👜👜*Adds to bag* *Adds to bag* *Adds to bag* (@Company3)

As examples (23) and (24) above show, individual interaction with the consumers may have the form of a dialogue or a polylogue, respectively, as other consumers may join the interaction at any moment. The exchanges on Twitter may proceed in a synchronous as well as an asynchronous manner.

The above-quoted threads of interaction prove that Twitter creates a perfect environment for practicing "receiver-oriented persuasion" (Simons 1986: 121-139) or even what may be termed "individualized receiver-oriented persuasion." Twitter allows companies to "adjust the time and circumstances of the persuasive act to the needs" (ibid.: 121) of a specific user. The companies may learn about the consumers, their activities, practices and desires from observing their profiles and adjust the persuasive strategy to the consumer, may respond to the consumer's message with appropriate persuasive content.

Individualized receiver-oriented persuasion is more clearly visible in messages which are addressed to users in response to their comments not associated with the company's product. Using the previously mentioned tools of Internet monitoring, companies may search the Twitter feed for tweets not only with references to the company's offers, but also for messages touching upon a particular theme, e.g. mentioning a specific phenomenon or issue. Companies may then respond to such posts with promotional messages attuned to the content of the consumers' tweets. In these acts, the companies practice unsolicited promotion, interweave the product into the response and adjust it to any context mentioned by the consumer. Although the messages are addressed to individual customers, they remain public and visible to others, which widens the scope of their influence. Using tools of Internet monitoring, the companies practice what may be referred to as "search and connect" practices, in which they search for tweets mentioning a specific type of content and connect to interact with the specific consumer. Internet monitoring thus allows companies to engage with the consumer directly and introduce the brand into consumers' interactional activity. The companies may enter and mark their presence in the user's timeline and their interactional space. So far, for ordinary users, the Twitter sphere has been considered as a sphere of "searchable talk" and "ambient affiliation" (Zappavigna 2012), a sphere allowing users to share and exchange everyday life experiences or opinions with other users. For companies, it seems to have created a perfect environment for what can be termed "ambient product engagement," "searchable persuasion" or "searchable product placement." This appears to be a novel approach to product promotion, originating from the functionality of the microblog.

3.2. Modes of interaction on the profiles – discursive blending

With respect to discourse, the interaction practices on Twitter reflect a degree of discursive blending (Roberts and Sarangi 1999, Myers 2015), visible in an interweaving of corporate, institutional and personal modes of discourse in the tweets. The interaction on the profiles reflects a merger of conventions typical of institutional discourse, traditional written and face-to-face service encounters, as well as social media conventions of interaction between ordinary users.

More specifically, the three modes can be identified in the following strategies applied by the companies and the properties of the messages:
  – corporate mode – branding mode:
    • internal – between companies,
    • external – to consumers and stakeholders,
    • backstage tweets – e.g. updates from corporate events and campaigns,
    • information- and promotion-oriented tweets (updates, retweets, tweets to consumers),
    • advertising and persuasive strategies;

- institutional mode – customer-relations mode:
  - addressed messages, interaction with consumers,
  - ritual acts in customer care exchanges – e.g. requests, apologies, explanations, offers of help, thanks,
  - the use of acts of self-identification, greetings,
  - the use of *we* underlining collective identity,
  - language formality, formulaic and conventional politeness;
- personal mode:
  - addressed messages, interaction with consumers,
  - conversations of the private and public sphere – small talk and phatic communication,
  - relational strategies,
  - overt expression of opinions and emotions,
  - language informality, social media slang, emoticons, emojis, gifs.

The blending of the above-mentioned modes results from the multi-functional structure of the medium, the availability of a range of forms of interaction in the medium and forms of contact with the users. Each of the modes may be exemplified on the basis of the following tweets and exchanges:

Corporate mode:

(25) Company1 @Company1
The new #[product name] is now available on our new flexible custom plan. And you can upgrade again at any time xx.uk
[multimedia component] (@Company1)

Institutional mode:

(26) your find my phone feature has helped me retrieved my phone in a taxi I left in Naples. Thanks for making your technology so good and easy to use!
Company9 @Company9
@user We're happy to hear you've found your phone, [name]. Enjoy the rest of your weekend! ^[initials] (@Company9)

Personal mode:

(27) [name] future kid: "How did you & dad meet?""Someone stole my bank card & I called Company5 fraud department & well the rest was history..."
Company5 @Company5
@user Hi [name], it sounds like a true love story to me :) ^[initials] (@Company5)

The institutional mode is reflected in the maintenance of the conventions of customer encounters found in the interaction in other communicative contexts and channels, i.e. the conventions typical of the interaction in face-to-face and telephone customer encounters, while the personal mode is reflected in the use of the conventions underlying the interaction of ordinary users in the social media. The former can be seen in the use of formulaic acts and formal language, while the latter are detectable in the relational strategies, conversations of the private domain, the tendency towards establishing social bonds with the consumers and an emotional tone of the messages. The personal mode tends to be foregrounded in conversations with a primarily relational orientation. In these cases, the interaction concentrates on aspects related to topics not associated or only indirectly associated with the company's operations, to news and current events, as well as to the consumer's life. The exchanges may be interpreted as an instance of phatic communion (Malinowski 1972), which allows the speakers to establish and/or support their relationship (cf. Placencia and Lower 2013: 639). The function of the acts is to enhance rapport and engage with the consumer, creating interactional closeness and solidarity. Interactions in which the representatives share emotions with the consumers, be it a genuine or an artificial act of "synthetic personalization" (Fairclough 1989), indicate that the authors accept the conventions of the medium, where sharing emotions is an integral component of the interaction. The corporate mode is to be found mainly in the updates advertising new products and publishing corporate news, or retweets forwarding news and opinions concerning the company posted by other users, but it can also be identified in individual interactions focused on promoting products or sharing positive news concerning the company, and in acts of self-praise.

It is rare for the modes to form separate threads of exchanges within the profile. The modes typically interweave with one another, with corporate and/or professional and personal content intertwined in the interaction. Such a co-existence of modes can be exemplified in the following exchanges:

(28) Getting ready for America got a new phone today all ready for next week. #8days#[product name]
Company9 @Company9
@user We can't think of a better travel companion! Whereabouts in the States are you heading too?
user @user
@Company9 Great Barrington, MA :) going to work in a summer camp
Company9 @Company9
@user Ooo, lots of photo taking opportunities. You're going to love using the new dual pixel camera & we would love to see them. (@Company9)

(29) Company9 @Company9
[product name] stands the test of time, just like the works of Michelangelo and Rodin. Introducing our 'Modern Masterpieces' #BuiltToLast
user @user
@Company9 So true I've got a 12 year old [product name] tv, it's starting to get dark patches still works perfectly fine for now.
Company9 @Company9
@user Hey [name]. Thanks for reaching out! Could you drop us a DM with more information? Then we'll go through some troubleshooting steps with you. ^[initials]

user @user
@Company9 Bought a [product name]. Wi fi will not work. 4 emails sent no reply.
Product does not do was what is was sold to do and nobody seems bothere now they
have our money. Poor show Company9
Company9 @Company9
@user Hi [name]. Can you please DM us more information on this? What's the model
of your [product name]? ^[initials] (@Company9)

Example (28) shows an interweaving of the personal mode with the corporate
mode of promoting the product purchased by the consumer and anticipating the
consumer's positive experience associated with using it. The relational orientation of the message is intertwined with promotional content. Example (29), in
turn, is an instance of a complex exchange, with two customers' messages posted
in response to a company's update. The exchanges exemplify an intertwining
of the corporate mode in the form of a message advertising a product and the
institutional mode developing in response to the update, comprising interaction
concerning the consumers' use of the product, its positive and negative evaluation, respectively, and the review management process initiated by the company.

Chapter 4. Positive evaluation and complaint management on Twitter

4.1. Methods and materials

4.1.1. Methods

The analysis focuses on company responses and management strategies. An overview of consumers' messages is provided for additional background and the illustration of the practices of interaction in the medium. A detailed analysis of the acts of positive evaluation, complaining and complaint strategies posted by consumers on Twitter, however, was not the main object of the study.

The study comprises the analysis of structural and pragmatic components in companies' tweets. Due to a diversified nature of the interaction and the research topics, the analysis drew from a number of methodological approaches.

In investigating the organization of the encounters, the study relies on speech act theory (Searle 1969) and conversation analysis (Schegloff 2007).

More specifically, as regards the analysis of the strategies used in the management of the reviews, the investigation of positive evaluation was conducted with reference to the frameworks developed in the context of complimentary behaviour. The strategies were classified based on previous typologies of compliments and compliment responses developed by Manes and Wolfson (1981), Holmes (1986) and Herbert (1989).

The discussion of consumers' tweets also draws from the research devoted to the phenomenon of evaluation in language. Evaluation devices were identified inductively by a close reading of the tweets. The identification of the mechanisms was performed based on findings of the previous research devoted to evaluation in different contexts (e.g. Hunston and Thompson (eds.) 2003, Martin and White 2005, Bednarek 2006, 2008, Myers 2010, Zappavigna 2012, Vásquez 2014). The means of expression were identified with reference to three broad areas of appraisal, i.e. emotional affect, aesthetic appreciation and moral judgement (Martin and White 2005). The overviews of consumers' tweets show the most frequent lexicogrammatical and discourse-level means of expression the customers use to evaluate products and behaviour, and to indicate emotional reactions.

As far as complaint management is concerned, consumer complaints were identified based on previous research on complaint strategies, i.e. classifications developed by House and Kasper (1981), Olshtain and Weinbach (1987, 1993),

Trosborg (1995), Meinl (2010), Decock and Spiessens (2017), Decock and Depraetere (2018), as well as evaluation studies mentioned above.

The investigation of complaint management strategies employed by companies was conducted with reference to research devoted to the speech act of apology. Complaints and apologies, namely, are said to constitute an adjacency pair, where an apology represents the "preferred" act which follows the speech act of complaining (Trosborg and Shaw 1998: 72). The analysis of the responses was based on the frameworks developed by Blum-Kulka et al. (1989), owing to its widespread popularity and application in different contexts, expanded to include Page's (2014) framework for the structure of corporate apologies, as well as Benoit's (1995, 1997) and Coombs' (1998) typologies of crisis management strategies.

In the course of the analysis of companies' strategies, each of the company's responses was coded for the constituents, i.e. the type of speech act and the number of speech acts in the tweet. This approach allowed the extraction of the speech acts used in isolation and in the form of speech act sets. As Vásquez (2011) explains, "any speech act can be realized by using a single discourse strategy or by combining two or more discourse strategies, some of which may represent other types of speech acts" (ibid.: 1708). A speech act set is "a combination of speech acts that, taken together, make up a complete speech act. That is, it is often the case that one utterance alone does not perform a speech act. Some examples are apologies and invitations where several utterances are necessary for the intended act to be accomplished" (Murphy and Neu 1996: 214). Due to a lack of consistency and standardization in speech act segmentation observed in the tweets, the coding of the acts was conducted solely with reference to their pragmatic content.

The interpretation of consumers' and companies' practices was conducted with reference to the principles of Brown and Levinson's politeness theory (1987), the distinction between positive and negative politeness in particular. The notion of professional face was also applied in the interpretation of the data (cf. Charles 1996, Decock and Spiessens 2017, Jagodziński and Archer 2018). The concept of professional face was introduced by Charles (1996) to account for face considerations typical of corporate interactions. In customer encounters, namely, face considerations are different than in everyday private interactions owing to the distinct participant roles, goals, rights and obligations of the speakers. In such interaction, it is transactional goals that gain prominence. These goals and the speakers' roles shape the behavioural expectations of the participants, expectations of "professional conduct" (Decock and Spiessens 2017: 79). The professional face is thus distinguished from the speaker's personal and social face, and the needs which the speakers wish to satisfy in each of the cases. Personal face needs are associated with a wish to be viewed in a positive way and social face needs with a desire to be respected and valued in social roles. Professional face needs are associated with the tactical aspects of business interactions and the transactional goals which the speakers wish to attain (e.g. selling-buying). The distinction also results in a different perception of which acts are face-saving and which may pose a threat to the speaker's face. In this context, an act threatening the speaker's professional face occurs when the participant's behaviour violates and is contrary to status and role expectations (Charles 1996: 25). In a business encounter, for instance, acts showing interest or disinterest, which might be considered face-threatening in other situations, in this context are perceived as "tactical moves," strategies protecting the speaker's professional face.

The analysis of the acts combines a qualitative and quantitative examination. The number of the respective speech acts was calculated.

4.1.2. Materials

The material for the analysis comprises tweets exchanged by consumers and company representatives in the public and official Twitter profiles of selected English companies. The analysis concentrates on one-to-one interaction with consumers, on individual encounters, i.e. addressed messages only, with the exclusion of updates, retweets and direct messages, which are not available publicly. The material encompasses the customer's message and the company's response published on the profile and thus visible to all users of the medium. The analysis does not include private messages exchanged between the company and the consumers.

The examples were collected from the profiles of companies belonging to different branches of industry. More specifically, the tweets were collected from profiles of the companies representing the following areas: telecommunication, technology, sportswear, food, communication and travel, media providers, banking and postal services. Profiles of twelve companies were included in the analysis. The profiles were selected based on their popularity measured by the number of followers. Tweets were collected in the period between November 2015 and March 2016.

In the course of gathering the material for the analysis, 100 tweets were collected from each profile, comprising the same number of tweets from each of the profiles on a particular day. In the next step, consumers' tweets expressing positive evaluation and complaints or negative evaluation with ensuing company responses were extracted from the corpus.

The final corpus involves 1020 corporate tweets and 994 consumers' messages. More specifically, positive evaluation tweets comprise the total number of 258 tweets, with 129 user comments and 129 company responses, respectively. The corpus of complaint management messages involves 865 consumers' comments and 891 responses posted by the companies. A more detailed description of the corpus is provided in Table 1.

Table 1. Tweets analyzed in the study

Type of tweet	Number
Positive evaluation management	
Number of exchanges	87
Single adjacency pair exchanges	67
Multiple adjacency pair exchanges	20
Consumer comments	129
Company responses	129
Total number of tweets	258
Complaint management	
Number of exchanges	531
Single adjacency pair exchanges	364
Multiple adjacency pair exchanges	167
Consumer comments	865
Company responses	891
Total number of tweets	1756
Total number of exchanges	618
Consumer tweets	994
Company tweets	1020
Total number of tweets	2014

Source: own work.

The messages are quoted in their original form. For the sake of privacy concerns and to avoid personal identification, the messages have been anonymized (cf. Page 2014, Decock and Depraetere 2018). All personal names of individuals have been deleted and replaced with [name] or [initials]. Consumers' Twitter addresses have been removed from the examples. Corporate names and Twitter addresses have also been deleted and replaced with Company+number (e.g. Company1, Company2, etc.). Any reference to a different company has been replaced with [company name]. Names of specific products have been replaced with [product name].

4.1.3. The structure of customer encounters on Twitter

The interaction comprises exchanges of different levels of complexity. Both positive evaluation and complaint management sequences may have the form of a two-component exchange comprising an adjacency pair, i.e. compliment + compliment response or complaint + complaint response, as shown in (1) or (2):

> (1) The man who drove this train needs a pay rise-sharp, honest, funny and had carriages clapping him!
> Company12 @Company12

@user Hi [name]. That's great stuff! We've let [name] and his manager know. Thanks for getting in touch. (@Company12)

(2) just opened a [product name] to find a pathetic stick. Weighed it and it is underweight. Not happy #needstobulkup
Company11 @Company11
@user Oh dear, sorry about that [name]! Please call our team on 0800 818XXX & they'll be able to help. :) (@Company11)

The interaction may be continued, in which case the consumer exchanges further information with the company, until a final closure of the encounter:

(3) Well done @Company9 the #[product name] is amazing and puts all other devices to shame ! Absolutely in love! #[product name]
Company9 @Company9
@user Thanks for the love, [name]! What's your favourite feature so far? ^[initials]
user @user
@Company9 Have to say I am in love with camera! Was worried about it being only a 12mp compared to s5 16mp! Really impressed! #welldone
Company9 @Company9
@user We aim to please! ^[initials] (@Company9)

(4) For the second time this week. 17 minutes and counting… unbelievable. After 25 mins I am told I will need to wait in another 10 minute queue.
Company4 @Company4
@user Hi, I'm [initials]. Sorry to read your tweets. Have you managed to speak to this department since tweeting?
user @user
@Company4 yes finally. Another random fraud check and 45 mins I won't get back!
Company4 @Company4
@user I'm glad to hear you've been able to resolve your query. I'll certainly ensure your comments are recorded for feedback. ^[initials] (@Company4)

The exchange, however, may also be discontinued at any of the stages. An instance of a discontinued exchange is provided below in example (5). In this case, the company's request for further information is left without a response on the part of the consumer:

(5) Sort it out half my loaf is missing.,,
Company10 @Company10
@user Sorry about that [name]! Can you send us the barcode number? Which store did you buy it in? [name] (@Company10)

In the analyzed corpus, single adjacency-pair exchanges proved more frequent both in the case of positive and negative complaint management, with 70 percent of the encounters comprising a single adjacency pair exchange and 30 percent including multiple adjacency pair sequences (more specifically, in the case of positive evaluation management, 77 percent of the encounters comprise a single adjacency pair exchange and 23 percent include multiple adjacency pair sequences, whereas in the case of complaint management, 68 percent of the encounters involve a single adjacency pair and 32 percent encompass multiple adjacency pair sequences).

Tweets posted by consumers and companies assume different forms. The tweets may comprise a turn with the following constructional units (cf. Sacks et al. 1974): an opening unit with a greeting, self-identification, the main speech act or a speech act set constituting the message and a unit enclosing the message. The conventional politeness acts of openings and closings represent optional components of the tweets. The structure may take the following shape:

(opening unit: e.g. greeting, self-identification) the main act(s) (closing unit: e.g. thanks, self-identification).

Within the analyzed corpus, exchanges can be encountered in which turns are condensed in a single message as well as those in which the customer's and the company's turns are sequentially organized and distributed over a number of tweets. The following formats of the messages were identified, exemplified on the basis of companies' messages.

- Simple tweets: simple tweets, apart from opening and closing units, comprise a single speech act, a single move:

(6) @user What can we help you with today? ^[initials] (@Company9)

(7) @user There doesn't appear to be any known issues [name]. –[name] (@Company2)

(8) @user These are automated as you are abroad. – [name] (@Company2)

- Complex tweets: in the case of complex tweets, the messages assume the form of speech act sets and a number of moves are combined in a single tweet. It is worth underlining a frequent occurrence of non-standard segmentation of speech acts in the tweets. The tweets below exemplify various patterns of speech act combination in a single tweet: the use of coordination, the use of standard segmentation by means of dots, the use of commas and a lack of segmentation of the acts:

(9) @user You can call us on (0)800111XXX for free using Skype and we'll be happy to discuss your account. ^[initials] (@Company5)

(10) @user Hi [name]. That's great stuff! We've let [name] and his manager know. Thanks for getting in touch. (@Company12)

(11) @user Hi [name], we don't like the sound of this, what's happened? We'd like to help. (@Company1)

(12) @user Okay please let us know how you get on and have a lovely day – [name] (@Company2)

(13) @user It can be busy at this time on the weekend many apologies. [name] (@Company2)

- Multi-tweet messages: due to the restrictions on the length of a single tweet, a message may be expanded over several tweets, which leads to the production of a multi-tweet response:

(14) ?637 to sit on the floor @Company12 sort it out, this is insane
Company12 @Company12
@user Hi [name], We are sorry that you have been unable to locate a seat this evening. We do try to strengthen 1/2 our busier services but we do not have the availability within our fleet at the moment. 2/2 (@Company12)

(15) Blimey, another dodgy packet of [product name] @Company11 what's happening with quality control in Company11 World?
Company11 @Company11
@user Hi there, sorry about the shape of your [product name]! Please contact our customer care team here: http://bit.ly/YCpDXX...1/2 or call on 0800 818XXX and our team will take your feedback. :) 2/2 (@Company11)

As will be shown in the course of the analysis, complex tweets tend to be used the most frequently, with a less frequent occurrence of simple and multiple-tweet messages, both on the part of the consumers and the company.

4.2. Consumer positive evaluation on Twitter

The following subchapter focuses on positive evaluation management. The interaction in this case is triggered by customers' tweets in which they compliment the company, express praise, convey positive evaluation of the products and services they have purchased and used. Though, as mentioned before, positive evaluation may be a result of the company's strategy and manipulation, it is difficult to judge by the comment whether it expresses genuine or fake appraisal.

In the present analysis, the focus is placed on the form of the company's responses to positive evaluation and the strategies used by the company aiming at brand engagement. The company's responses to positive feedback, be it fake or real, constitute an important strategy of enhancing the company's image, marking cooperative involvement and interactional closeness with the consumer.

Strategies of positive evaluation used by consumers are briefly outlined first, followed by a description of companies' responses to the tweets.

4.2.1. Consumer positive evaluation on Twitter

Messages expressing positive evaluation comprise tweets in which consumers express positive attitude and positive feelings associated with products or services, and compliment the company.

In linguistic research, the means of expressing feelings and assessments have been subsumed under such terms as "stance" (Biber and Finegan 1989, Conrad and Biber 2003), "affect" (Ochs and Schieffelin 1989), "evaluation" (Hunston and Thompson (eds.) 2003) or "appraisal" (Martin and White 2005), among others.

Conrad and Biber (2003) define stance as "a cover term for the expression of personal feelings and assessments in three major domains: epistemic stance – commenting on the certainty (or doubt), reliability, or limitations of a proposition, including comments on the source of information; attitudinal stance – conveying the speaker's attitudes, feelings, or value judgement; stylistic stance – describing the manner in which the information is being presented" (Conrad and Biber 2003: 57). In earlier definitions, stance was also defined as "the lexical and grammatical expression of attitudes, feelings, judgments, or commitment concerning the propositional content of a message" (Biber and Finegan 1989: 9) or "personal feelings, attitudes, value judgments, or assessments" (Biber et al. 1999: 966).[54]

In a different approach, Hunston and Thompson (eds., 2003) use the term "evaluation" to refer to the linguistic mechanisms used in expressing feelings and attitudes. It is defined as "the broad cover term for the expression of the speaker's or writer's attitude or stance towards, viewpoint on, or feelings about the entities or propositions that he or she is talking about. That attitude may relate to certainty or obligation or desirability or any of a number of other sets of values" (Hunston and Thompson (eds.) 2003: 5). As the scholars underline, evaluation performs multiple functions. In addition to its role in expressing the speaker's opinion, it may construct relations and organize the text (ibid.).

To account for the above-mentioned mechanisms, Martin and White (2005), in turn, propose the system of appraisal, comprising three categories of affect, judgement and appreciation. In this approach, affect refers to "registering positive and negative feelings: do we feel happy or sad, confident or anxious, interested or bored?" (Martin and White 2005: 42). Appreciation expresses attitudes about objects, states and processes: "our reactions to things (do they catch our attention, do they please us?), their 'composition' (balance and complexity), and their 'value' (how innovative, authentic, timely, etc.)" (ibid.: 56). Judgement, in turn, critiques human behaviour: "judgements of esteem have to do with 'normality' (how unusual someone is), 'capacity' (how capable they are), and 'tenacity' (how resolute they are); judgements of sanction have to do with 'veracity' (how truthful someone is) and 'propriety' (how ethical someone is)" (ibid.: 52).

Research into evaluation has shown that it is an extremely complex phenomenon. Studies devoted to evaluation in different contexts and settings, applying different methodological frameworks, have identified a range of evaluative patterns typical of or occurring across various areas of discourse

---

[54] An important perspective on stance was put forward by Du Bois (2007), who suggested an interactional concept of stance, claiming that stance "can be approached as a linguistically articulated form of social action whose meaning is to be construed within the broader scope of language, interaction, and sociocultural value" (Du Bois 2007: 139).

(Hunston 1994, Bednarek 2006, 2008, Englebretson (ed.) 2007, Clark 2009, Lombardo 2009, Bednarek and Caple 2012). Studies have also identified different patterns of evaluation in online communication (Myers 2010, Langlotz and Locher 2012, Page 2012, Zappavigna 2012, Barton and Lee 2013, Vásquez 2014, Chiluwa and Ifukor 2015, Jakosz 2016).

Myers (2010) investigated stance-taking strategies applied by bloggers in his analysis of the discourse of blogs. The study focused on the presence of epistemic, attitudinal and stylistic stance, and indicated that bloggers the most frequently express an attitudinal stance to express aesthetic appreciation, moral judgement and emotional affect. Grammatical means used in the expression of stance comprise the use of verb plus clause complementation (with a common use of verbs *think, hope, suppose*), declarations, the use of adverbials (*fortunately, in my view, certainly*), modal and semi-modal verbs, adverbs (*so, totally, absolutely*), nouns, as well as reported speech, rhetorical questions, irony, concessions and conversational devices, such as interjections and discourse markers.

Applying the system of appraisal and corpus linguistics to the discourse of Twitter, Zappavigna (2012) showed how collocates with *love* and *good* are used to express tweeters' affect, how the use of linking and retweeting functions as an expression of appreciation. Further means of expressing appraisal identified in the study comprise emoticons. It was also shown that tweeters tend to upscale appraisal by means of punctuation marks.

Analyzing evaluation in online reviews, Vásquez (2014) identified such lexicogrammatical evaluative resources common in reviews as the use of adjectives (*good, great*), lexical chunks (*will definitely make this again*), stance adverbs (*definitely, unfortunately, literally*), the use of slang terms (*meh, whatever*), interjections, rhetorical questions, declarative statements, including the assessment of others in the reviews, as well as the justification of star rating.

Studies have shown that evaluation may be expressed by means of a variety of resources at different levels of language, i.e. on the lexical, syntactic and discourse levels. Moreover, evaluation may be expressed either explicitly, for instance by means of evaluative lexis, or implicitly (may be implied or invoked), when "the selection of ideational meanings is enough to invoke evaluation, even in the absence of attitudinal lexis that tells us directly how to feel" (Martin and White 2005: 62).[55]

In the analyzed corpus, many of the acts expressed by consumers can be interpreted as instances of complimentary behaviour. Compliments constitute

---

[55] Evaluation is strictly associated with the persuasive function of language, the use of language to influence the addressee's beliefs and attitudes. As Laskowska (2000: 342) claims, every evaluative statement induces a change in behaviour or attitude. By evaluating an object as good or bad, we not only inform the addressee about our thoughts or feelings towards this object, but we also persuade the addressee to accept similar beliefs and feelings. This aspect of evaluation is particularly meaningful in the analyzed context of word-of-mouth communication in customer encounters.

evaluative speech acts that "explicitly or implicitly attribute credit to someone other than the speaker, usually the person addressed, for some 'good' (possession, characteristic, skill, etc.) which is positively valued by the speaker and the hearer" (Holmes 1986: 485). They are viewed as manifestations of solidarity through the expression and acknowledgement of admiration (Herbert 1989). Compliments are described as "formulaic speech acts" with recurrent patterns occurring in the acts (Holmes and Brown 1987: 529). The most frequent formulae used in complimentary behaviour comprise the following structures: NP V (is/looks, etc.) ADJ; I V (verb of liking/loving) NP; PRO is ADJ NP or ADJ NP! (Manes and Wolfson 1981, Holmes 1986).[56]

4.2.1.1. Positive evaluation tweets – structure

Messages expressing positive evaluation typically include the following structural elements:
- factual data:
  - user-identification: username, Twitter address,
  - date and time of posting the comment,
  - addressee identification: the company's Twitter address;
- the main body of the message,
- a link to further sources concerning the review (optional),
- a multimodal component: photograph or video attachments (optional).

Comments expressing positive evaluations may take a purely textual or multimodal form. In the case of the latter, a user's comment may be supplemented by an image or video.

The above-mentioned elements are presented in the message below:

(16) user @user Feb 19
    Loving my new #[product name] ♥ @Company3

    [multimodal component – photograph of the product]

    Company3 @Company3 Feb 19
    @user A true classic. Today belongs to you [name]. (@Company3)

---

[56] Manes and Wolfson (1981) provide the following classification: NP {is/looks} (really) ADJ; I (really) {love/like} NP; PRO is (really) (a) ADJ NP; You V (a) (really) ADJ NP; You V (NP) (really) ADV; You have (a) (really) ADJ NP; What (a) ADJ NP!; ADJ NP!; Isn't NP ADJ! (Manes and Wolfson 1981: 120-121).

4.2.1.2. Positive evaluation tweets – strategies and means of expression

4.2.1.2.1. Positive evaluation

Positive evaluation concerns different aspects associated with the company's operations. The evaluation expressed by the consumers comprises acts indicating:
- positive emotions evoked by the product/service (i.e. emotional affect) – consumers express their feelings concerning the product or service:

(17) love the display of flowers in your Arnold store, a lot of thought gone into it & very eye catching (@Company10)

(18) Guys I'm so so excited to get the [product name], Even more excited it comes in white !!! Very beautiful indeed (@Company9)

- positive attitude to the company/product (i.e. aesthetic appreciation) – tweets express consumers' attitude towards the company or offered goods:

(19) Well done @Company9 the #[product name] is amazing and puts all other devices to shame ! Absolutely in love! #[product name] (@Company9)

(20) Fantastic @Company9 #VR experience in Westfield. I've watched #VR videos before but that rollercoaster is a truly 21st century stuff! (@Company9)

- positive assessment of the service/customer care (i.e. moral judgement) – consumers express evaluation of the quality of customer care services provided by the company:

(21) [name] at your Bristol Road, Birmingham store is wonderful. She had me smiling throughout the transaction #Thankyou[name] (@Company10)

(22) Excellent customer service from [name] at @Company5 in Bury St Edmunds today. Asset to the company (@Company5)

4.2.1.2.2. Form of the messages and means of expression

The following means of expression tend to be used in the tweets expressing positive evaluation:
- the level of directness: customers address the message directly to the company, using second person pronouns or express positive evaluation using the company's name (for instance by means of @mentions) and third person forms of the verb. Consumers also positively evaluate the product without directly addressing the company or referring to the company's name:

(23) you have the nicest staff at your Truro store #proud (@Company10)

(24) love the display of flowers in your Arnold store, a lot of thought gone into it & very eye catching (@Company10)

(25) Gotta admit, I'm seriously impressed with @Company4 right now. (@Company4)

(26) Being looked after by lovely team @Company12 on my way from Nottingham to London. I love travelling First Class! (@Company12)

(27) Great customer service from @Company10 Straiton Edinburgh #[name] was awesome 👏 (@Company10)

(28) Loving my new #[product name] ♥ @Company3 (@Company3)

(29) absolutely love the #[product name] #MustHave (@Company9)

– declarative acts: tweets expressing positive evaluation may be composed of declarative clauses. Full and abbreviated clauses are used:

(30) Great customer service from @Company10 Straiton Edinburgh #[name] was awesome 👏 (@Company10)

(31) on the [product name] from London - Sheff. Coach G, staff member called [name + surname] has been excellent. V polite & nothing too much trouble (@Company12)

– exclamative acts: a positive evaluation is expressed by means of exclamatives. Full and abbreviated clauses can be found in the tweets:

(32) Being looked after by lovely team @Company12 on my way from Nottingham to London. I love travelling First Class! (@Company12)

(33) Catching up on paperwork today! Thank goodness for @Company5 Online banking!!! Saved me so much time and most of all no #badcreditscore! (@Company5)

– imperative acts: imperative clauses are used to express the consumers' wish for the company to maintain a high quality of the service. The use of imperative clauses, however, proved rather more infrequent (4 instances):

(34) Surely! And I received my card in the mail today. Honestly so impressed by the efficiency! Keep it up! (@Company5)

– further syntactic and lexical patterns recurring in the tweets:
  • the patterns frequently used in the messages expressing positive emotions (i.e. emotional affect) comprise: *(I)* (intensification) *love/like* NP, as well as: (intensification) ADJ, with a recurrent use of such terms as *pleased, impressed, excited*. For example:

(35) love the display of flowers in your Arnold store, a lot of thought gone into it & very eye catching (@Company10)

(36) absolutely love the #[product name] #MustHave (@Company9)

(37) Loving my new #[product name] ♥ @Company3 (@Company3)

(38) Well done @Company9 the #[product name] is amazing and puts all other devices to shame ! Absolutely in love! #[product name] (@Company9)

(39) Guys I'm so so excited to get the [product name], Even more excited it comes in white!!! Very beautiful indeed (@Company9)

(40) Pre-oredered the @Company9 #[product name] from @Company1 😊 very excited. Big upgrade frome my [product name] #cantwait (@Company9)

- a positive emotional reaction to the product is also expressed by the pattern *(I) can't/cannot wait* (cf. Vásquez 2014). The expression underlines the consumers' impatience in anticipating the usage of the purchased product:

(41) waiting for my [product name] VR for my [product name]! Can't waaaaaaaaiiit!!!! (@Company9)

(42) I cannot wait to get a new phone on Saturday :) yassssss (@Company9)

(43) just ordered my [product name], really cannot wait!! (@Company9)

- the patterns which recur in the messages expressing positive attitude to the company/product (i.e. aesthetic appreciation) involve the following formulas: NP *is/looks* (intensification) ADJ, ADJ NP!, *You have* (a) (intensification) ADJ NP. The words used repeatedly comprise positively loaded adjectives, e.g. *excellent, amazing, fantastic, improved, great, lovely, beautiful*, the comparative and superlative forms, e.g. *faster, best*. The use of forms personalizing the product and expressing an emotional attitude can also be found. For instance:

(44) she's a real beaut! Super quick, amazing display, fantastic camera and water proof! Just need Company9 pay now to be unbeatable (@Company9)

(45) Fantastic @Company9 #VR experience in Westfield. I've watched #VR videos before but that rollercoaster is a truly 21st century stuff! 😊 (@Company9)

(46) current ads -50% faster than Company1 [company name] and [company name]. Can't wait for [product name] faster connection improved call quality (@Company2)

(47) love the display of flowers in your Arnold store, a lot of thought gone into it & very eye catching (@Company10)

(48) 😎 these babies get me through the endurance @curves fitness #bloodsweatandtears -#worthit ⭐ (@Company3)

- in acts of the positive assessment of the service/customer care (i.e. moral judgement), the consumers evaluate both the service in general as well as individual representatives of the company. The most frequent pattern identified in the messages is: NP (representative's name) *is* ADJ. The lexical items expressing attitude comprise evaluative adjectives or nouns, such as *nice, polite, helpful, excellent, friendly, credit, asset*:

(49) [name] at your Bristol Road, Birmingham store is wonderful. She had me smiling throughout the transaction #Thankyou[name] (@Company10)

(50) [name] the conductor on the [product name] Grimsby to Newark very helpful & friendly. Very Customer focused a credit to your company! (@Company12)

(51) on the [product name] from London - Sheff. Coach G, staff member called [name + surname] has been excellent. V polite & nothing too much trouble (@Company12)

- tweets expressing positive evaluation also feature instances of enumeration. Consumers tend to enumerate positive qualities and features concerning the company/representative or the evaluated product. For instance:

(52) camera looks amazing for a phone!, I love the edge. And you brought back water resistant and expandable memory yippee!!! (@Company9)

(53) she's a real beaut! Super quick, amazing display, fantastic camera and water proof! Just need Company9 pay now to be unbeatable:) (@Company9)

(54) The man who drove this train needs a pay rise-sharp, honest, funny and had carriages clapping him! (@Company12)

(55) [name] the conductor on the [product name] Grimsby to Newark very helpful & friendly. Very Customer focused a credit to your company! (@Company12)

– modification:
  - upgrading: modification encompasses the use of intensifiers upgrading the evaluation. The most frequent intensifiers comprise adverbs, such as *so, very, really, absolutely, ever*:

(56) really impressed with the vr had it a couple weeks now (@Company9)

(57) Well done @Company9 the #[product name] is amazing and puts all other devices to shame ! Absolutely in love! #[product name] (@Company9)

(58) Guys I'm so so excited to get the [product name], Even more excited it comes in white!!! Very beautiful indeed (@Company9)

(59) Just had a very pleasant shopping experience in @Company10 Newport. They had everything I wanted and more! (@Company10)

(60) Best train announcer ever by [name] today on @Company12 to London (@Company12)

(61) just ordered my [product name], really cannot wait!! (@Company9)

(62) Fantastic @Company9 #VR experience in Westfield. I've watched #VR videos before but that rollercoaster is a truly 21st century stuff! (@Company9)

(63) Shout out to @Company12 manager [name] for making my journey to #spanc16 far more entertaining! (@Company12)

(64) [name] the conductor on the [product name] Grimsby to Newark very helpful & friendly. Very Customer focused a credit to your company! (@Company12)

- downgrading: downgrading modification includes the use of hedges mitigating the expression of the evaluation, as in (65) and (66). Further means of diminishing the force of positive evaluation involve aligning positive assessment with negative evaluation, which can be seen in (67) and (68):

(65) just like to say the train manager dealt brilliantly with an abusive passenger at Leicester. She was on the [product name] Lei – Not (@Company12)

(66) just want to say #Taunton branch staff have impressed me more than once this week. Gladdens my #FacetoFaceBankingisNotDead♥ (@Company4)

(67) your @Company9UK team is awesome. Took us a few weeks but we got there in the end. Top class support. Big fan. ♥👍 (@Company9)

(68) credit to the staff on [product name] to Nottingham, delayed train but top class (and friendly) customer service. 5* (@Company12)

- interjections: the use of interjections as a means of expressing or upgrading positive affective meaning was also identified in the corpus. Interjections most frequently assume the following forms: *yeh*, *yippee*, as well as *yass* (cf. Vásquez 2014):

(69) Yeh! 4G signal with @Company1 in Eston #Middlesbrough (@Company1)

(70) I cannot wait to get a new phone on Saturday :) yassssss (@Company9)

(71) camera looks amazing for a phone!, I love the edge. And you brought back water resistant and expandable memory yippee!!!👍 (@Company9)

- paraverbal and nonverbal means: positive evaluation may be expressed and/or upgraded or upscaled (Zappavigna 2012: 67) paraverbally and nonverbally by means of acronyms, capitalization, vowel prolonging, the use of multiple punctuation marks, emoticons or emojis:

(72) I think [product name] will be.....interesting, to say the least lol (@Company9)

(73) Guys I'm so so excited to get the [product name], Even more excited it comes in white!!! Very beautiful indeed (@Company9)

(74) THANK YOU so much to our delivery driver @Company10 today, AMAZING getting through the snow to get to us even on foot in the end! (@Company10)

(75) waiting for my [product name] VR for my [product name]! Can't waaaaaaaaiiit!!!! (@Company9)

(76) Fantastic @Company9 #VR experience in Westfield. I've watched #VR videos before but that rollercoaster is a truly 21ˢᵗ century stuff!😄 (@Company9)

(77) 👊these babies get me through the endurance @curves fitness #bloodsweatandtears -#worthit⭐ (@Company3)

- hashtags;

It is worth noting the use of hashtags as components of the tweets due to their medium-specific nature. The tags perform different pragmatic functions and comprise different structural forms, i.e. one-word or clause-based structures. Hashtags with an evaluative meaning usually constitute tags following the message, placed as extrasentential modifiers to the main statement. The tags may express the following meanings:

- name of the company's employee/service/product: #[name], #[product name], *#VR*, *#Company11*,
- slogans: #[company slogan],
- expression of appreciation: *#Thankyou*[name],
- expression of positive evaluation: *#mustcelebrateexcellencewhenfound, #FacetoFaceBankingisNotDead, #amazebites, #greatjourney, #welldone, #MustHave, #proud, #cantwait, #loveit, #bloodsweatandtears, #worthit, #whowantstodietanyway.*

For example:

(78) Well done @Company9 the #[product name] is amazing and puts all other devices to shame ! Absolutely in love! #[product name] (@Company9)

(79) Fantastic @Company9 #VR experience in Westfield. I've watched #VR videos before but that rollercoaster is a truly 21ˢᵗ century stuff!😊 (@Company9)

(80) Loving my new #[product name] ♥ @Company3 (@Company3)

(81) #[company slogan] FAB (@Company3)

(82) Beautiful morning for some @_GBHockey training #[company slogan] @Company3 (@Company3)

(83) we're ready for next season's away days. Can't wait. #[company slogan] (@Company3)

(84) [name] at your Bristol Road, Birmingham store is wonderful. She had me smiling throughout the transaction #Thankyou[name] (@Company10)

(85) Pre-oredered the @Company9 #[product name] from @Company1😊very excited. Big upgrade frome my [product name] #cantwait (@Company9)

(86) you have the nicest staff at your Truro store #proud (@Company10)

(87) I'll be writing to the branch manager too. Impressed. #mustcelebrateexcellencewhenfound (@Company4)

(88) just want to say #Taunton branch staff have impressed me more than once this week. Gladdens my #FacetoFaceBankingisNotDead♥ (@Company4)

(89) #homemade @Company11 #flowers #gardening #loveit #chocolatecake (@Company11)

(90) I NEED to try those #amazebites by #Company11! brownies are the best thing ever! Do any have caramel in? #whowantstodietanyway @Company11 (@Company11)

(91) Have to say I am in love with camera! Was worried about it being only a 12mp compared to s5 16mp! Really impressed! #welldone (@Company9)

Hashtags assigned to product names and slogans may further promote the company and its offer, but, owing to the searchable potential of the tags, they also position the author of the message in the community of other consumers of the product or service. Hashtags expressing evaluation and emotions, rather than searchable ideas, represent metacomments which enhance the illocutionary force of the assessment.

– simple and complex tweets;

Tweets expressing positive evaluations may be phrased in the form of simple tweets, comprising one speech act:

> (92) Best train announcer ever by [name] today on @Company12 to London (@Company12)

> (93) Loving my new #[product name] ♥ @Company3 (@Company3)

The messages may also include several acts in a single tweet, thus forming complex tweets:

> (94) Well done @Company9 the #[product name] is amazing and puts all other devices to shame ! Absolutely in love! #[product name] (@Company9)

> (95) Pre-oredered the @Company9 #[product name] from @Company1 😊 very excited. Big upgrade frome my [product name] #cantwait (@Company9)

In the collection of tweets analyzed, complex messages proved more frequent, with 30 percent of the tweets in the simple and 70 percent in the complex form. In 11 percent of the complex messages, acts accompanying the expression of evaluation comprise acts of appreciation in the form of thanks:

> (96) Thank you Street @Company10 your sandwich platters this afternoon were excellent; please pass on a big thanks to the deli counter (@Company10)

> (97) Thank you so much @Company3 these are beautiful (@Company3)

> (98) THANK YOU so much to our delivery driver @Company10 today, AMAZING getting through the snow to get to us even on foot in the end! (@Company10)

> (99) Informative & amusing on train announcement. Thanks [name] for bringing a smile to everyone's face. 😊 (@Company12)

In the acts, the consumers thank the company for a specific product or service. The thanks are addressed to the company or to the praised representative of the company.

4.2.2. Positive review management

Compliments and compliment responses represent an example of an adjacency pair or "action chain event" (Pomerantz 1987: 109-110). Most studies on compliment responses rely on the taxonomies developed by Holmes (1986) and

Herbert (1989). Holmes' (1986) taxonomy includes such responses as compliment acceptance, rejection, evasion or no acknowledgement. In Herbert's (1989) classification, compliment responses may comprise the following: comment acceptance, comment history, return, praise upgrade or reassignment.[57]

4.2.2.1. Strategies of positive review management

In the analyzed context, the responses encompass, among others, acts of acceptance/acknowledgement in the shape of a positive evaluation of products, acts of appreciation in the form of thanks and expressions of positive feelings, as well as compliment return in the shape of a positive evaluation and approval of the customer's performance. The acts are designed to attend to and meet consumers' interactional goals, show recognition of the evaluation, gratitude and appreciation.

4.2.2.1.1. Appreciation: expression of positive feelings

Positive evaluation expressed by consumers concerns specific products, but also the company's service or customer care procedures. Company representatives respond to customers' evaluation by expressive messages in which they share the customer's positive feelings.

Table 2. Appreciation: expression of positive feelings

Type of act	Number
Appreciation: expression of positive feelings	49
Form of act simple complex	8 41

Source: own work.

The messages take the form of personal statements, expressed in the first person singular or plural (e.g. *I'm/we're glad*), or of impersonal statements (e.g. *it's/that's great*). The complements to the expressive acts comprise a restatement of the positively evaluated service or a repetition of the positive emotions experienced and expressed by the consumer. For instance:

(100) Thank you for the wonderful ladies at your #Rhyl branch for helping me sort out my app. Always helpful.
Company5 @Company5
@user Hi [name], it's great to hear that our staff were able to help you sort out your app :) ^[initials] (@Company5)

---

[57] The subchapter, with modifications, has been included in a separate publication (Tereszkiewicz 2018).

(101) I actually did appreciate it. @Company5 sends a text with "reply 1 if valid, 2 if fraud."
I replied 2 and went back to sleep!
Company5 @Company5
@user Hi [name], I'm glad we were able to spot this for you and make it easier!
^[initials] (@Company5)

(102) She's a real beaut! Super quick, amazing display, fantastic camera and water proof! Just
need Company9 pay now to be unbeatable:)
Company9 @Company9
@user She sure is a beauty. It's great to know that you're loving your #[product name]
(@Company9)

(103) Fantastic @Company9 #VR experience in Westfield. I've watched #VR videos before
but that rollercoaster is a truly 21st century stuff 😊
Company9 @Company9
@user The world of #VR is pretty awesome, glad to hear you had a great experience
with it. (@Company9)

(104) Hi there, Cool stuff with lunch deals.
Company1 @Company1
@user Hi [name], thanks :) We're glad you're enjoying our Priority offers. (@Company1)

In the complements, the representatives underline the company's active
role in assisting consumers, in efforts undertaken specifically for the individual
(e.g. *our staff were able to spot for you, we were able to sort out for you*). The
complements to the acts also tend to name the customer's feelings in a strongly
evaluative way, promoting the company's product (e.g. *you're loving your, you
had a great experience, you're enjoying our Priority offers*). The strategy and the
use of the complements has a clearly persuasive and promotional function. Since
it is the reply that is visible on the profile and the consumer's message remains
hidden unless the reader opens a specific thread of a conversation, the company
repeats the statement with the compliment to make it public, so that other users
can see it and learn about the positive customer care provided by the company.
In this way, the acts perform an important image boosting function and serve
as a persuasive strategy enforcing the positive image of the company and the
positive evaluation. The acts underline the company's customer-orientation.
The authors express positive feelings concerning successful customer care and
the company's being able to meet customers' needs and offer satisfying service.
The company may thus enhance its image as attentive and successful in solving
customer issues, expressing its concern for the customer.

4.2.2.1.2. Appreciation: expressing thanks

The acts used in response to customers' positive feedback also comprise thanks.
By thanking, the companies attend to consumers' interactional goals and indicate that the positive evaluation has been acknowledged and appreciated. The

thanks represent positive politeness acts, enhancing customer engagement and interactional closeness.

Table 3. Appreciation: thanks

Type of act	Number
Appreciation: thanks	31
Form of act simple complex	 2 29

Source: own work.

The acts have the form of a more formal *thank you* and a less formal *thanks* extended to include the object of thanks, predominantly comprising thanking the customer for the feedback, for the time and effort of contacting the company to share the appraisal:

(105) Excellent customer service from [name] at @Company5 in Bury St Edmunds today. Asset to the company
Company5 @Company5
@user Hi [name], thank you for taking the time to share this with us :) ^[initials] (@Company5)

(106) hi. Just wanted to say a big thank you for the passenger assistance given today for my disabled mother from GY To BDM.
Company12 @Company12
@user Hi [name], your very welcome. Thank you for taking the time to get in touch. (@Company12)

(107) Gotta admit, I'm seriously impressed with @Company4 right now.
Company4 @Company4
@user Hi, I'm SO. Thanks for your positive comments! Please don't hesitate to tweet if there's anything we can do. (@Company4)

The complements stating the object of thanks tend to underline the positive nature of the evaluation, e.g. *your positive comments, wonderful feedback.*

4.2.2.1.3. Compliment return: complimenting the consumer

In reaction to the positive comments expressed by the consumers and to tweets in which users share their experience connected with the product, companies also tend to return the compliment and praise the consumers.

Table 4. Compliment return: complimenting the consumer

Type of act	Number
Compliment return: complimenting the consumer	29
Form of act simple complex	 9 20

Source: own work.

Company representatives compliment the consumers, their achievements, looks and performance (cf. Tereszkiewicz 2017a). The acts have the form of declarations evaluating the consumer and/or the consumer's actions in a positive way:

(108) your @Company9 team is awesome. Took us a few weeks but we got there in the end. Top class support. Big fan. ♥📦
Company9 @Company9
@user You're the best, [name]! We're glad it's all sorted for you, we hope you're having a great weekend! ^[initials] (@Company9)

(109) Loving my new [product name] ♥ @Company3
Company3 @Company3
@user A true classic. Today belongs to you [name]. (@Company3)

(110) #homemade @Company11 #flowers #gardening #loveit #chocolatecake
Company11 @Company11
@user Wow this is a beautiful cake! Almost too good to eat😋 (@Company11)

Acts positively evaluating the consumers also assume the shape of motivational messages in the form of imperative acts, encouraging and inspiring the consumers to maintain and improve their performance, thus implicating their future use of the product:

(111) And wearing them today I just equalled my fastest ever 10k time. Set in 2013!
Company3 @Company3
@user You're on fire in #[product name],[name]. Keep up that good work. Looking forward to reading your review. 👏📖 (@Company3)

(112) 👟these babies get me through the endurance @curves fitness #bloodsweatandtears -#worthit⭐
Company3 @Company3
@user keep it up, [name]! 💪💪💪 (@Company3)

(113) Sunday 10k, recovery shake time. Love running in my @Company3 https://twitter.com/namefashionvest. #runlikethewindblows
Company3 @Company3
@user glad to have you in three stripes, [name]. Keep on running. 👟 (@Company3)

(114) all cool from your end, I just want RM to act up 😅im like a child at Xmas with new
Company3 @Company3
@user We hear you! It'll be worth the wait [name]. Bring on the [product name]. (@Company3)

The use of the imperative indicates a less formal, more direct and closer relationship with the consumer. The use of first name terms of address was also found, which mitigates the imperative, but also personalizes the act and individualizes the message.

Compliments and motivational messages express appreciation of the consumer and reinforce their positive face. The acts indicate that the companies take notice of the consumers and their use of the products (Tereszkiewicz 2017a).

4.2.2.1.4. Requests for further information/contact

Acts frequently exploited in the exchanges comprise requests addressed to the consumers encouraging them to share further details concerning the products they use and further positive experiences with the products.

Table 5. Requests for further information/contact

Type of act	Number
Request for further information/contact	28
Form of act simple complex	1 27

Source: own work.

The requests most often have the form of interrogative and imperative acts.

Table 6. Requests for further information/contact

Type of act	Number
Interrogative acts – direct questions	16
Interrogative acts – ability questions	4
Imperative	8

Source: own work.

Modification of the acts is rather infrequent and includes the use of first names (example (116)), which mitigates the request and individualizes the act:

(115) Guys I'm so so excited to get the [product name], Even more excited it comes in white !!! Very beautiful indeed
Company9 @Company9
@user We can sense your excitement, which is understandable. The #[product name] is awesome. What excites you the most about it? (@Company9)

(116) Excited to get @Company7 tomorrow
Company7 @Company7
@user Eee exciting!!! What package have you gone for [name]? [initials]
@Company7 the big [product name] movies!!
Company7 @Company7
@user Good choice! Pop back and let us know how it all goes tomorrow :) ^[initials] (@Company7)

(117) Well done @Company9 the #[product name] is amazing and puts all other devices to shame ! Absolutely in love! #[product name]
Company9 @Company9
@user Thanks for the love, [name]! What's your favourite feature so far? ^[initials] (@Company9)

The use of more direct forms of requests, such as interrogative acts and imperatives, may be aimed at marking a close relationship with the consumer. The acts directly ask the consumers to express more positive evaluation and name the best qualities of the products (e.g. *What excites you, What's your favourite feature*).

The requests used in the handling of positive evaluation have a slightly different purpose than in the case of complaint handling, which will be shown in the subsequent subchapter. Though in both situations the acts indicate attention awarded to an individual consumer, in the case of positive evaluation management, their role appears to be oriented more towards promotion and rapport enhancement.

4.2.2.1.5. Compliment acceptance: positive evaluation of the offer/product

Company responses to positive eWOM also contain messages expressing a positive evaluation of the product (cf. Tereszkiewicz 2017a).

Table 7. Compliment acceptance: positive evaluation of the offer/product

Type of act	Number
Compliment acceptance: positive evaluation	21
Form of act simple complex	 1 20

Source: own work.

The tweets comprise an evaluation of the product, often by means of strongly evaluative vocabulary and intensification (e.g. *true classic, sure, beauty, pretty awesome, so many things to love*). The responses exemplify the process of accepting and additional upgrading of the assessment (Herbert 1989) or upscaling of the appraisal (Zappavigna 2012) provided by the consumer:

(118) Loving my new #[product name]♥ @Company3
   Company3 @Company3
   @user A true classic. Today belongs to you [name]. 🌊 (@Company3)

(119) She's a real beaut! Super quick, amazing display, fantastic camera and water proof! Just need Company9 pay now to be unbeatable:)
   Company9 @Company9
   @user She sure is a beauty. It's great to know that you're loving your #[product name] (@Company9)

(120) Fantastic @Company9 #VR experience in Westfield. I've watched #VR videos before but that rollercoaster is a truly 21st century stuff!😃
   Company9 @Company9
   @user The world of #VR is pretty awesome, glad to hear you had a great experience with it. (@Company9)

(121) camera looks amazing for a phone!, I love the edge. And you brought back water resistant and expandable memory yippee!!!👍
   Company9 @Company9

@user Loving the excitement! There's so many things to love about the #[product name] (@Company9)

The shape of the act may be dictated by the context and may be interpreted as a deliberate promotional strategy. Since, as indicated above, the customer's initial message remains covered and it is only the response that is initially visible on the profile, the company expresses a positive evaluation of the product to promote it among other users.

Previous research indicated the use of such evaluations with prospective customers and pointed to their considerable impact on the sales. The exchanges help to create an affiliative relation with the customers (Clark et al. 2003: 24) and may thus influence their decisions on the purchase.

In the analyzed interaction, however, these assessments occur as acts following the purchase. Their primary aim, therefore, may be to reaffirm the consumer's right decision, to maintain a sociable relation with the consumer with the prospect of future transactions. More importantly, however, these acts have a clearly persuasive and impressive function, and, though addressed to a specific individual, since they have a public character, they may appeal to other viewers of the message.

4.2.2.1.2. Reporting feedback to the relevant party

Reactions to positive comments include acts of reporting the consumer's evaluation further.

Table 8. Reporting feedback to the relevant party

Type of act	Number
Reporting feedback to the relevant party	19
Form of act simple complex	 - 19

Source: own work.

The responses comprise acts in which the authors state that the feedback obtained from the consumer was or will be forwarded to the relevant party, such as the employee praised by the customer or the management of the company. For example:

(122) Thank you Street @Company10 your sandwich platters this afternoon were excellent; please pass on a big thanks to the deli counter
Company10 @Company10
@user Hi [name], I've passed your feedback on to the store manager to review. Thanks for letting us know! Have a great day! [name] (@Company10)

(123) Shout out to @Company12 manager [name] for making my journey to #spanc16 far more entertaining!
Company12 @Company12
@user Hi [name]. That's great to hear. We've passed on your lovely feedback to [name] and his manager. Thanks. (@Company12)

(124) just want to say #Taunton branch staff have impressed me more than once this week. Gladdens my #FacetoFaceBankingisNotDead♥
Company4 @Company4
@user Hi, I'm [initials]. Thanks for your wonderful feedback. I'll ensure it's passed on to the branch directly. Thanks & take care. (@Company4)

The statements, analogically to the previous acts, show attention to the consumer, are designed to satisfy consumers' interactional goals and show that feedback is meaningful, having been recognized and acknowledged.

4.2.2.1.7. Wishes

The responses also comprise wishes addressed to the consumer.

Table 9. Wishes

Type of act	Number
Wishes	16
Form of act	
simple	-
complex	16

Source: own work.

The messages include conventional acts, such as wishes of a great day, weekend, pleasure and enjoyment:

(125) oh my god I love your new stuffed mushrooms. I've eaten two packets in 2 days.
Company10 @Company10
@user Glad you're a fan [name]! Have a great day! [name]. (@Company10)

(126) great team on today's [product name] Lei-She in First. Particular thanks to [name] for her excellent service & keeping me topped up with tea
Company12 @Company12
@user Hi [name]. That's great to hear. We will be sure to feed this back. Enjoy your brew! (@Company12)

(127) your @Company9 team is awesome. Took us a few weeks but we got there in the end. Top class support. Big fan. ♥📷
Company9 @Company9
@user You're the best, [name]! We're glad it's all sorted for you, we hope you're having a great weekend! ^[initials] (@Company9)

4.2.2.2. Positive evaluation response speech act sets

Replies to consumers' positive evaluation, as could be seen in the examples, rarely have the form of simple/individual acts and tend to occur predominantly in the shape of complex responses. Nearly 83 percent of the messages in this corpus take the form of complex tweets. The combination and patterning of the acts performs the function of increasing the illocutionary force of the message and/or enhancing rapport with the customers.

Company responses to positive evaluation expressed by the consumer most frequently comprise tweets with the following patterns of move combination:
- acts expressing appreciation (thanks and/or positive feelings) extended to include a commissive or declarative act of reporting feedback to the relevant party
  - acts of appreciation: expression of positive feelings/thanks + report of feedback to the relevant party (20 instances);
- acts with a confirmation of the positive evaluation extended to include a request for further feedback from the consumer
  - compliment acceptance + request for further feedback/evaluation (12 instances);
- acts with a confirmation of the positive evaluation extended by compliment return, acts evaluating consumer's experience
  - compliment acceptance + compliment return (10 instances);
- acts expressing appreciation extended by a request for further feedback from the consumer
  - acts of appreciation: expression of positive feelings/thanks + request for further feedback/evaluation (6 instances).

The compositional units of the tweets often involve an act of appreciation in the form of thanks and/or expression of positive feelings combined with a declaration or offer of reporting the feedback further. This patterning is clearly designed to satisfy the consumers' interactional goals, i.e. show gratitude and recognition, enhance rapport by sharing positive emotions, show that the feedback is not disregarded, but meaningful and considered relevant for the company.

Another recurring pattern involves an act of compliment acceptance or an act of appreciation extended by a request for further information and contact. Questions following the evaluation or appreciation, as indicated previously, may be designed to maintain interaction and encourage the consumer to expand the evaluative message. Recurring patterns also comprise a combination of compliment acceptance and compliment return. In such cases, an evaluation of the product and/or sharing a positive feeling on the customer's choice of the offer is further supported by an expressive act complimenting the customer, encouraging them to pursue using the product. The patterning also involves a combination of acts of appreciation in the form of thanks or an expression of positive feelings with a request for further feedback or evaluation. The companies wish to prolong the interaction, encourage the consumer to reveal more positive features of a product and thus share more promotional content.

The patterns found in complex tweets work simultaneously to enhance the promotional tone of the message by means of acknowledging and/or upgrading the positive evaluation expressed by the consumer, on the one hand and, on the other, to establish or strengthen the positive relationship with the consumer. It is in these acts that the relational orientation of the encounters is the strongest.

External modification of the acts by emoticons is also frequent in the case of positive evaluation management. The emoticons expressing positive affective meaning as well as emojis indicating respect and enthusiasm are placed at the end of the evaluation or the message. The emoticons enhance rapport and the positive motivational content of the message, and strengthen the positive evaluation (Placencia and Lower 2013: 635).

The responses in the category of positive evaluation management outlined above represent relationally-oriented strategies of positive politeness, associated with expressing and sharing emotions. The expressions in this context have an important contact and rapport building function (ibid.: 642, Carratero et al. 2014), help to establish and increase solidarity with the customers (Placencia and Lower 2013: 622). The strategies also reflect an interactionally proactive approach of the companies (Bailey 1997). By interacting with customers about the use of the products, the companies have a chance to trigger or strengthen the relationship with the customer, try to persuade the customer to share more experiences with the company and thus tie the individual to the brand. The acts have a clear function of creating a positive atmosphere and triggering positive energy associated with the company and its product. They also construct the image of the company as spontaneous, emotional, enjoying the cooperation with the customer, sharing their excitement and being pleased with the customer's evaluations. The interaction exemplifies one of the primary purposes of social media, that is "ambient affiliation" (Zappavigna 2012), the use of social media to share emotions, reactions, evaluations, likes and dislikes. It reflects the focus on affinity seeking and the wish to indicate that one is a part of a community of users with similar experiences. The influence of the context of social media can be observed not only in the affiliation-oriented purpose of the messages but is also reflected in the shape of the tweets. Such expressiveness, the use of paraverbal (e.g. interjections *wow, whoopwhoop, eee*) and nonverbal means of expression (e.g. emoticons), rather unlikely in other channels of customer encounters, is clearly dictated by the medium, whose defining features comprise spontaneity and emotionality.

Positive evaluation of products and compliments addressed to customers are also far from rare in face-to-face communication, where they often help to finalize a transaction and encourage the customer to purchase a product. In the analyzed material, however, expressions of positive evaluation appear as acts following the transaction. Such responses and comments produced in reaction to the customer's positive feedback and evaluation can be regarded as instances of "post-transaction" promotion. The messages build on consumer-initiated positive evaluation and comprise acts of self-praise and a confirmation of the assessment of products expressed by the consumers. The evaluative and expressive acts make the positive evaluation public and thus promote the positive image of the company. The messages confirm the good choice that the customer had made or support the customer in his/her decision. In this way, the positive evaluation acts can indirectly persuade others to purchase the evaluated product.

The responses to positive evaluation show how relational and transactional, rapport-building and promotional content can be strategically combined. The company successfully uses the potential offered by the medium to get closer to its customers, to engage with the customer at a personal level. Yet, bearing in mind the generally low degree of familiarity between the customers and providers, and the transactional rationale underlying the interaction, the exchanges may be regarded as evidence of the conversationalization of public discourse, the spread of informality and pseudo-intimacy (Fairclough 1989, 1993, 1995a). The messages can be perceived as only superficially phatic, as they have a clear promotional purpose behind and constitute a "tactical strategy" employed by the company enhancing their professional face. The focus, namely, is not solely on interaction and strengthening the relation with the consumer, but on the transactional aspects of the interaction as well. Such acts are designed to maintain interaction, to encourage the reader to enter into a conversation with the company with further praise of the product, to continue spreading positive eWOM and, as a result, to raise and/or strengthen the positive associations about the company in the consumer's and other readers' minds, enhance the satisfaction derived from the choice or use of the company's product, and to create a more personal experience.

4.3. Consumer complaint and negative evaluation management on Twitter

This chapter comprises a discussion of complaint management on selected Twitter profiles. The investigation of companies' management strategies is preceded by a short overview of the structure and content of consumer complaints and messages expressing negative evaluation.

4.3.1. Consumer complaints on Twitter

Within linguistic research, complaints encompass acts in which "the speaker (S) expresses displeasure or annoyance – censure – as a reaction to a past or ongoing action, the consequences of which are perceived by S as affecting her unfavourably. This complaint is usually addressed to the hearer (H) whom the S holds, at least partially, responsible for the offensive action" (Olshtain and Weinbach 1993: 108).

Meinl (2010), in turn, defines a complaint as an act in which the complainer "expresses his/her disapproval of a past or ongoing action which does not conform with [his/her] expectations and interests. The consequences of this action are at cost to the speaker, who holds the hearer at least partly responsible for or capable of remedying the perceived offence" (Meinl 2010: 14).

Based on the previous definitions of the act, Decock and Depraetere (2018) propose to define complaining as a speech act situation in which "the complainer disapproves (B) of a past or ongoing action or occurrence (A) which does not conform to her expectations and interests. The consequences of this action or occurrence are at cost to the complainer, who holds the complainee (at least partly) responsible for the perceived offence (C) and who wants the complainee to remedy the perceived offence in some way (D)" (Decock and Depraetere 2018: 38).

This definition points to the four main constituents of a complaint, the statement of the complainable, the disapproval or negative evaluation of the complainable, the assumed negative involvement of the complainee and the wish for the offence to be remedied (ibid., cf. Wyrwas 2002).

Complaints are characterized by low formulaicity. The acts do not have a "predetermined form" (Chen et al. 2011: 258) and tend to utilize different means of expression. The following strategies of expressing a complaint have been identified, among others: explicit complaint, expression of annoyance, disapproval or disappointment, expression of anger, negative judgement, accusation, insult, warning and threat (House and Kasper 1981, Olshtain and Weinbach 1987, 1993, Trosborg 1995, Meinl 2010, Vásquez 2011, Decock and Spiessens 2017, Decock and Depraetere 2018). Moreover, complaints rarely occur in the form of a single speech act and tend to assume the form of a speech act set (Vásquez 2011, Decock and Depraetere 2018).

Most of the definitions of complaints arrange the acts along a continuum pointing to a different level of directness, ranging from explicit (on-record) complaints to implicit acts. House and Kasper (1981) locate the acts along a continuum ranging from implied attribution of the complainable, explicit assertion of the complainable, of negative feelings, explicit attribution of blame, explicit evaluation of the complainee's actions as negative, to an explicit negative evaluation of the complainee. In Trosborg's (1995) framework, complaints range from hints (the complainer does not mention the complainable), expression of disapproval, through accusation (direct and indirect), to the act of assigning blame (modified and explicit) to the complainee. Decock and Depraetere (2018), based on a corpus of messages derived from different channels of computer-mediated interaction, propose a novel approach, in which the directness of the complaint is associated with the number of the constituents in the complaint. The range encompasses an implicit complaint (the elements of a complaint are implicated), an explicit complaint (with the use of a verb/noun that names the speech act, i.e. *complain/complaint*), followed by acts comprising a number of constituents, i.e. from one to four constituents communicated on-record/explicitly. The directness of the acts increases with the number of the elements.

Customer complaints include messages in which consumers report problems and faults in the service or a lack of service, express anger and/or dissatisfaction with the company's services, warn other consumers and demand corrective measures (cf. Meinl 2010, Vásquez 2011, Tereszkiewicz 2015a, 2017b, forthcoming-b, Ho 2017b). Interactional goals underlying a complaint on the consumer's part may involve receiving an apology, explanation, some form of compensation, recovery of a positive state of affairs or an acknowledgement of their comments (Ho 2017b: 6). Consumers may also express complaints online in order to satisfy their need for a public recognition of their feelings by other customers or by the company (cf. Tereszkiewicz 2015a).

4.3.1.1. Complaints: structure of the messages

Consumer complaints posted on Twitter, analogically to positive reviews, may have a textual or a multimodal form, with textual content accompanied by an image or a video.

Complaints may include the following elements:
- factual data:
  - user-identification: username, Twitter address,
  - date and time of posting the comment,
  - addressee identification: the company's Twitter address;
- the main body of the message;
- a link to further sources concerning the complaint (optional);
- a multimodal component: photograph or video attachments (optional).

The pictorial content serves as supplementary material confirming the occurrence of the complainable, constitutes evidence of the reported infraction.

An example of a tweet expressing a complaint and negative evaluation of a company's product is provided below.

(128) user @user Dec 6
     @Company3 this is not on! 3rd pair in the past months with issues. Contacted your customer care…no response…

[multimodal component – photograph of the product]

Company3 @Company3 Dec 6
@user hi [name], where did you purchase these boots? (@Company3)

4.3.1.2. Consumer complaints

4.3.1.2.1. Constituents of the complaint

Complaints expressed by the consumers comprise the constituents identified for complaint situations in the previous research:

- expression of the complainable: the consumer presents the negative state of affairs. The complainable reported in the messages refers to the following areas:
  - lack of due service/product,
  - inadequate/poor quality of the service/product, i.e. quality not in line with expectation/promise/cost,
  - inadequate quality of customer care, i.e. quality not in line with expectation/convention. For example:

(129) Why are replacement coaches now the norm? No plugs or no plugs & no toilets. Delays waiting for passengers from late coaches. (@Company8)

(130) @Company6 have lost my mum's mother's day flowers!! .. not "on front porch" & no calling card.. web chat unavailable!! (@Company6)

(131) stopped card with no warning in USA. 76 mins to sort out on mobile #disgraceful (@Company5)

(132) travel currency not delivered to branch next day as per guarantee and no communication #poorcustomerservice (@Company4)

- expression of dissatisfaction/disapproval and/or negative evaluation of the complainable: the consumer implies or directly expresses his/her emotional reaction to the complainable and negative evaluation of the infraction. As part of this constituent, consumers express:
  - negative emotions evoked by the company/product/service (i.e. emotional affect) – consumers express feelings caused by the complainable,
  - negative attitude to the company/service/product (i.e. aesthetic appreciation) – consumers negatively evaluate the product/the company,
  - negative assessment of customer care (i.e. moral judgement) – consumers express evaluation of the quality of customer care services provided by the company. For instance:

(133) Disgusted by the @Company6 News driver who cut us up and then bombards us with disgusting verbal abuse. #appalled (@Company6)

(134) #Company6 is rubbish. Been waiting all day for a delivery. Very disappointed and angry. (@Company6)

(135) You need to get back to me ASAP in regards the funds taken from my account. Collection calls for such practice is unacceptable (@Company4)

(136) My @Company9 [product name] is the worst phone I've ever had. Slow, laggy and the battery lasts 4 hours. Shocking. Give us vanilla [product name]. (@Company9)

(137) AWFUL SERVICE FROM Company7. 😠wifi still not working after 3wks of excuses and broken promises. (@Company7)

(138) To add insult to injury..Super hub 2 still not connecting...now Company7 mobile data is either at minimum or NO connection (@Company7)

- assumed agentive involvement of the complainee: the customer either explicitly or implicitly attributes blame for the infraction to the complainee:

(139) Another failed delivery from @Company6 surprise surprise! #crapservice (@Company6)

(140) here we are on a beautiful sunny April day heading down to London. Just a shame Company12 can't be bothered to clean the Windows!😠 (@Company12)

(141) @Company5 actively sabotaging my biz account taking more than a month, 3 branch visits & 10 billion phone calls to make changes #stillstalled (@Company5)

- the wish for the offence to be remedied: the customer expresses a request for repair, for remedial action and corrective measures aimed at solving the infraction and restituting a positive state of affairs. In the analyzed corpus, the acts most frequently comprise requests for contact from the company, requests for a refund or requests to sort out the complainable:

(142) Please give me the email address I could write to to stop getting junk mail from your bank. (@Company5)

(143) You need to get back to me ASAP in regards the funds taken from my account. Collection calls for such practice is unacceptable (@Company4)

(144) Seriously, one hour on hold?! Please can someone call me back! (@Company4)

(145) No signal at all with @Company1 it's been over a week. I'm paying for a service I can't use! Keep being fobbed off Not happy at all & want a refund (@Company1)

(146) have lost my order, ?25 Mother's Day flowers are dying god knows where. Think I deserve my money back frankly. (@Company6)

(147) Sort it out half my loaf is missing.,, (@Company10)

4.3.1.2.2. Form of the messages and means of expression

In presenting complaints, consumers resort to different syntactic and lexical means of expression.

- The level of directness: complaints are expressed either in a direct or an indirect manner (Monzoni 2008, cf. Tereszkiewicz 2015a). The continuum encompasses the more direct forms, acts of accusation and attributing blame, in which the consumers directly accuse the company of contributing to the complainable, blame the infraction on the company, as well as the more indirect forms, in which the consumers express disapproval or name the complainable. In direct complaints, the company is addressed by means of second person pronouns (examples (151), (152)) as well as by means of third person forms, the name of the company (for example by the use of @mentions) and the third person singular or plural form of the verb (examples (153)-(155)):

(148) stitching came loose on my [product name]!!!! (@Company3)

(149) size of these [product name] bars is an absolute joke (@Company11)

(150) Just bought these and very disappointed with the amount of [product name] bites in here. Not even half a bag :((@Company11)

(151) thank you Company1 for two extortionately high bills. My son won't be getting birthday celebrations this year. DW I will be leaving you in sep (@Company1)

(152) You need to get back to me ASAP in regards the funds taken from my account. Collection calls for such practice is unacceptable (@Company4)

(153) here we are on a beautiful sunny April day heading down to London. Just a shame Company12 can't be bothered to clean the Windows!😠 (@Company12)

(154) @Company6 have lost my mum's mother's day flowers!! .. not "on front porch" & no calling card.. web chat unavailable!! (@Company6)

(155) items ordered and not received. Company3 opened a case and then closed it without giving answers. Still no items! Appalling! (@Company3)

- Declarative acts: complaints are expressed by means of declarative statements, in a full or abbreviated form. This syntactic form may be used to express all the constituents of a complaint, e.g. the complainable, expression of dissatisfaction or the statement of an agentive involvement of the complainee (cf. Decock and Depraetere 2018):

(156) just opened a [product name] to find a pathetic stick. Weighed it and it is underweight. Not happy #needstobulkup (@Company11)

(157) every single one of these biscuits has been broken 😭😭#breakingmyheart (@Company11)

(158) Massive reduction in #girth @Company11. Poor. (@Company11)

(159) My @Company9 [product name] is the worst phone I've ever had. Slow, laggy and the battery lasts 4 hours. Shocking. Give us vanilla [product name]. (@Company9)

 – Interrogative acts: interrogative acts are used to communicate requests for information (cf. Monzoni 2008, Decock and Depraetere 2018). Similarly to declaratives, interrogative acts are used to express all the components of a complaint, i.e. to name the complainable, express the consumer's annoyance, accuse the complainee of causing the complainable, point out that the consumer considers the complainee's behaviour improper and challenges him/her (Monzoni 2008), or to request remedial action:

(160) is there a problem with the website safety certificate? I can't make a payment (@Company8)

(161) Is your website down at the moment? Crashed halfway through my grocery order! (@Company10)

(162) Hi I'm trying to topup my new pay&go sim&the phone system gave a msg that there's a system error you're fixing.When will this be sorted? (@Company1)

Interrogative acts are very often used in the function of rhetorical questions as a means of naming the complainable and expressing negative evaluation. As such, the acts express incredulity and constitute a form of indirect assessment (Vásquez 2014). The use of a series of questions is frequent, which confirms previous observations concerning patterns of evaluation in online reviews (ibid.). One of the most frequent patterns found in the complaints comprises the *wh*-interrogative in the form: *why are you/why is (are)* NP + negative evaluation:

(163) why are you always so understaffed in Balham?? Queues out the door. Always. #customerservice #terrible (@Company5)

(164) why are you so stingy with the nuts?? 😖 (@Company11)

(165) Why is the [product name] from Alfreton to Norwich consistently late on a Friday? It's ridiculous! 😖 (@Company12)

(166) why are your deals so much more expensive than carphone warehouse for exactly the same deal?? (@Company2)

(167) where is the bus from newbury to Cheltenham??? Cannot track it??? Should have been here at 820??? (@Company8)

(168) No internet data at CO3 0PW too. 4G never picked up when It was meant to there. Want anymore postcodes? @Company2 how bad is this? (@Company2)

The acts may assume the form of the so-called aggressive interrogatives, emphasized verbally by swear words or insults, and/or paraverbally or nonverbally by multiple punctuation marks and emoticons (cf. Tereszkiewicz 2015a, Decock and Spiessens 2017, Decock and Depraetere 2018):

(169) Why the fk is @Company1 so shit??? (@Company1)

(170) what is this???? No caramel and only one twisted?!?!? (@Company11)

(171) still waiting to hear and still cannot get a hold of the driver??!! (@Company6)

(172) can you please explain how on earth ive used 3 gb of data in 16 days when i have wifi at home! Your an absoulte joke&rip off!! (@Company2)

(173) still after 15mins train not yet departed. What's the delay??? (@Company12)

- Exclamative acts: complaints are expressed by exclamative clauses. Full and abbreviated clauses can be found in the messages. Analogically to the syntactic forms mentioned above, exclamatives may express all the components of a complaint, e.g. the complainable or negative evaluation, exemplified below (cf. Tereszkiewicz 2015a, Decock and Depraetere 2018):

(174) stitching came loose on my [product name]!!!! (@Company3)

(175) Why is the [product name] from Alfreton to Norwich consistently late on a Friday? It's ridiculous! (@Company12)

(176) Only one caramel in my @Company11 hero, what's going on?! Terrible!! (@Company11)

(177) What's happened to your chocolate? There's hardly any cocoa in it... and it's plain sugar! Rubbish quality. It used to be so good (@Company11)

(178) Worst Wednesday ever...Company11 [product name] minus the [product name] centre my Wednesday treat has been ruined!!!! @Company11 (@Company11)

A recurrent use of the pattern *what a* can be seen in the tweets: *what a joke, what a shame, what a shocker, what a rip off, what rubbish, what a palaver*:

(179) what a shame! A sticker that doesn't peel off a gift bag! #poor #badidea #shouldhave-wenttopoundland (@Company10)

(180) what a joke. Fraud reported on the 15 Feb and still not sorted (@Company5)

(181) again, no one in business team to help! What a shocker.. You need to take better care of your customers (@Company4)

(182) Company4 just charged me ?56 to spend ?1900 in USA ... What a rip off (@Company4)

- Imperative acts: imperatives are most frequently used to express the expected remedial action (cf. Tereszkiewicz 2015a). Imperative acts are also used to refer the addressee of the message to the evidence confirming the complainable (example (186)). The acts tend to be used in an unmitigated form. The most frequent form of mitigation comprises the use of the politeness marker *please* (14 instances):

(183) Sort it out half my loaf is missing.,, (@Company10)

(184) trying to set up rewards and not letting me! I know how to spell my name and I'm not a new customer. Sort it out! (@Company5)

(185) How do I get hold of someone regarding access to my mobile account? It's been a nightmare. Someone please help. (@Company7)

(186) Opened up this [product name] egg that's got a best before date of 31/7 but look at the state of it (@Company11)

– Statements of obligation/need/want: expressions of strong recommendation or necessity, as well as want statements are used to express a description of the expected remedial action:

(187) Dear @Company7 This had better be fixed by 7. 😠 (@Company7)

(188) You need to get back to me ASAP in regards the funds taken from my account. Collection calls for such practice is unacceptable (@Company4)

(189) ????? Hello? Its urgent I need to know where the coach is and why is an hour late?! (@Company8)

(190) No signal at all with @Company1 it's been over a week. I'm paying for a service I can't use! Keep being fobbed off Not happy at all & want a refund (@Company1)

(191) Not happy with the quality of my [product name]! I worked hard for this, I want a box full. :((@Company11)

– Warning: the complainers resort to the use of warnings or threats as a reaction to the complainable and as an expression of dissatisfaction, as well as a means of forcing the complainee to undertake remedial action (Vásquez 2011):

(192) sorry to say that [product name] is appalling your customer service team is rude I or my family will never use you again (@Company10)

(193) what the fuck is wrong with your website, having problems art your end? Sort it out or I'm not paying another penny.😠 (@Company1)

(194) Bough a ?1 bar of milk choclate and its horrible Not what it used to be . Why was the reciepe changed ? Wont buy Company11 again (@Company11)

– Accusation: consumers directly or indirectly blame the company for the complainable. They also resort to insults (cf. Trosborg 1995, Decock and Spiessens 2017):

(195) @Company5 didn't tell me moving my loan date would mean you take it twice in a week!! Fucking joke. Thanks for screwing my account up!! (@Company5)

(196) Company5 actively sabotaging my biz account taking more than a month, 3 branch visits & 10 billion phone calls to make changes #stillstalled (@Company5)

(197) ur all liers one if the advisirs tell me 9.30 for parcel then10pm but now told drivers finished at 9pm! Company6 were is my parcel😠 (@Company6)

- Negation: negation is one of the most frequent means of expression used in the complaints. Negation serves to express a lack of a desired state of affairs, to portray the situation as contrary to expectations (cf. Wyrwas 2002, Tereszkiewicz 2015a):

(198) @Company6 have lost my mum's mother's day flowers!! .. not "on front porch" & no calling card.. web chat unavailable!! (@Company6)

(199) Disappointed with @Company10 home delivery. Delayed and no one came, and the day after, after promising they'd come - not even a phone call (@Company10)

(200) as all the others are saying. No reply and no parcel. Not impressed. (@Company6)

(201) sorry to say that [product name] is appalling your customer service team is rude I or my family will never use you again (@Company10)

(202) Why are replacement coaches now the norm? No plugs or no plugs & no toilets. Delays waiting for passengers from late coaches. (@Company8)

- Negative evaluation – negative emotions evoked by the infraction (i.e. emotional affect): customers explicitly express their feelings, point to their emotional state caused by the complainable. The patterns which recur in the tweets include: *(I am)* (modification) ADJ, ADJ N, with the most frequent terms comprising adjectives: *not happy, livid, beyond annoyed, disgusted, far from satisfied, angry, appalled, shocked, fed up*, as well as *(It is)* (modification) ADJ: *so disappointing, very frustrating*:

(203) No signal at all with @Company1 it's been over a week. I'm paying for a service I can't use! Keep being fobbed off Not happy at all & want a refund (@Company1)

(204) rang 7 different numbers trying to get hold of someone regarding my credit card, no luck. I am beyond annoyed please help! (@Company4)

(205) just opened the [product name] I got for my birthday and there's one missing!! Not a happy bunny :((@Company11)

(206) worst Internet customer service I have ever had the misfortune of contending with!!! An absolutely livid customer!!!😠 (@Company3)

(207) Disgusted by the @Company6 News driver who cut us up and then bombards us with disgusting verbal abuse. #appalled (@Company6)

- Negative evaluation – negative attitude to the company/product (i.e. aesthetic appreciation): consumers express a negative attitude towards the product purchased or service provided. The means valuing the products or services negatively include for instance: *worst, worse, slow, lower, more expensive, problem, pricey, poor, worthless, rip off, rubbish*:

(208) My @Company9 [product name] is the worst phone I've ever had. Slow, laggy and the battery lasts 4 hours. Shocking. Give us vanilla [product name]. (@Company9)

(209) Company7 s a pile of wank (@Company7)

(210) having broadband problems today? getting lower download speeds then upload and unplayable gaming on this fibre :((@Company2)

(211) Is your website down at the moment? Crashed halfway through my grocery order! (@Company10)

(212) why are your deals so much more expensive than carphone warehouse for exactly the same deal?? (@Company2)

(213) what's happened to your chocolate? There's hardly any cocoa in it… and it's plain sugar! Rubbish quality. It used to be so good 😣 (@Company11)

(214) Massive reduction in #girth @Company11. Poor. (@Company11)

(215) Your signal is atrocious regardless of where i go.. #Company2 #bumped (@Company2)

- Negative evaluation – negative assessment of the service/customer care (i.e. moral judgement): consumers negatively appraise the quality of customer care and the approach expressed or shown by the company representatives. Consumers explicitly or implicitly evaluate employees' behaviour as being below the expected standard. Evaluative terms typically comprise: *rude, unhelpful, arrogant, fraudulent, pathetic, unacceptable, disgrace*. For instance:

(216) your fraud team very rude putting phone done on me! Because we can't not get to a bank to sort out the problem! #rude (@Company5)

(217) ur all liers one if the advisirs tell me 9.30 for parcel then10pm but now told drivers finished at 9pm! Company6 were is my parcel 😡 (@Company6)

(218) Top marks to [name] @Company10 in Barnes. Verbal abuse day 1 for your customer service training is it? (@Company10)

(219) are the worst bank I have ever dealt with terrible customer service completely unhelpful staff in your beckenham branch (@Company4)

(220) sorry to say that [product name] is appalling your customer service team is rude I or my family will never use you again (@Company10)

(221) clever tactic. Crap service from insurance so I give up before cancelling my insurance policy. 30 mins and counting! (@Company4)

(222) you are a disgrace. New customer and you couldn't connect landline and broadband on day set. You then said it would be 2 more weeks. (@Company2)

(223) your customer service is about as good as your ability to prevent fraud. Not only have you fucked that up, no one has rang me about it. (@Company2)

- Negative evaluation: additional examples of negatively evaluative lexical items comprise: *problem, trouble, issue, spam, fault, failure, delay, late, down, ruined, lost, crashed, failed, blocked, wasted, broke, broken, abuse*:

(224) never have i had so many issues disputing fraudulent charges with @Company5... @[company name] here i come. (@Company5)

(225) Disgusted by the @Company6 News driver who cut us up and then bombards us with disgusting verbal abuse. #appalled (@Company6)

(226) Why are replacement coaches now the norm? No plugs or no plugs & no toilets. Delays waiting for passengers from late coaches. (@Company12)

(227) my phones broke and my signal is shit (@Company1)

(228) Hi, what's going on with the signal in the Reading area? Texts won't send/intermittent signal/no 4G. Fault for at least a week #help (@Company1)

Further means of negative evaluation:
- statement of contrast to expectations: complainers explicitly state that the situation complained upon is contrary to their expectations and/or contrary to the complainees promises (cf. Vásquez 2011). Recurrent expressions include: *not what I expect/expected, not what it used to be*:

(229) my tvs gone dark at the bottom half of the screen it's a 5series it not what I expected from Company9 (@Company9)

(230) why have i still not got #wifi Its never gone live since the date you said it would! #sick-fedup #whatajoke #8weekswithoutinternet (@Company2)

(231) Bough a ?1 bar of milk choclate and its horrible Not what it used to be . Why was the reciepe changed ? Wont buy Company11 again (@Company11)

(232) 6 out of 12 mini rolls are not sealed properly, shoddy, not what I expect from Company11! (@Company11)

- provision of factual details: in describing the complainable, consumers resort to the presentation of very detailed factual information, which strengthens the righteousness of the complaint and emphasizes the negative nature of the complainable (cf. Wyrwas 2002, Tereszkiewicz 2015a):

(233) No response to my email 2 weeks ago & already another "unfortunate" incident on the 7:15 from St Pancras @Company12 (@Company12)

(234) stopped card with no warning in USA. 76 mins to sort out on mobile #disgraceful (@Company5)

(235) ur all liers one if the advisirs tell me 9.30 for parcel then10pm but now told drivers finished at 9pm! Company6 were is my parcel😡 (@Company6)

(236) rang 7 different numbers trying to get hold of someone regarding my credit card, no luck. I am beyond annoyed please help! (@Company4)

(237) Company5 actively sabotaging my biz account taking more than a month, 3 branch visits & 10 billion phone calls to make changes #stillstalled (@Company5)

(238) shameful! Only 2 x [product name], 2 x dairymilk, 3 x [product name] but 12 x eggs and 8 x eclairs! (@Company11)

  – enumeration: the means emphasizing the negative character of the complainable and the consumer's disappointment comprise the use of enumeration. Consumers list negative actions or disadvantages of the service/product:

(239) my issue is not being listened too. My account has been overcharged. My service has been suspended and I'm generally unhappy! (@Company2)

(240) My @Company9 [product name] is the worst phone I've ever had. Slow, laggy and the battery lasts 4 hours. Shocking. Give us vanilla [product name]. (@Company9)

(241) First cheap instant coffee in bolognese, then horseradish in macaroni, now desiccated coconut in chili. Go home @Company10, you're drunk. (@Company10)

  – irony and sarcasm: complaints are expressed by means of irony. The use of irony has been interpreted as a means of upgrading the force of the complaint (cf. Meinl 2010, Tereszkiewicz 2015a, Decock and Spiessens 2017). Ironic and sarcastic statements involve the use of positive evaluation of the negative state of affairs, the use of conventional politeness, salutations, expression of congratulations and thanks for the infraction. For example:

(242) just got on train in London. Couldn't you find one with an older interior? Or one less clean? French train this morning? Lovely. (@Company12)

(243) Dear @Company7 STOP SENDING ME YOUR SHITTY POST TO MY HOUSE I AM WITH TALK TALK AND DO NOT WANT Company7. Thanks. (@Company7)

(244) There's a hole in my [product name] dear @Company11 dear @Company11… (@Company11)

(245) Top marks to [name] @Company10 in Barnes. Verbal abuse day 1 for your customer service training is it? (@Company10)

(246) clever tactic. Crap service from insurance so I give up before cancelling my insurance policy. 30 mins and counting! (@Company4)

(247) Well done @[company name] and @Company5 for messing up my account transfer, missed all payments made on 01/03, late payments everywhere (@Company5)

(248) thank you Company1 for two extortionately high bills. My son won't be getting birthday celebrations this year. DW I will be leaving you in sep (@Company1)

  – positive evaluation aligned with a complaint: consumers juxtapose a positive assessment of the company or service with a report of the complainable and a negative evaluation of the occurrence of the reported infraction. The strategy downgrades the force of the complaint (Trosborg 1995, Vásquez 2011):

(249) I kinda like @Company12 but why offer passengers chicken tikka to eat in such a confined space and stink the place out - #ihadtomoveseats (@Company12)

(250) Central Southampton. They were professional, but not helpful. And polite, but not understanding. Thanks (@Company5)

— preparators: references to previous actions or communication with the company. The expressions prepare the addressee for the speech act or the content of the complaint (Trosborg 1995, Decock and Spiessens 2017):

(251) just opened the [product name] I got for my birthday and there's one missing!! Not a happy bunny :((@Company11)

(252) just got on train in London. Couldn't you find one with an older interior? Or one less clean? French train this morning? Lovely. (@Company12)

— modification: further strategies:
   • downgraders;

Other means used to downgrade the force of the complaint comprise the use of such syntactic and lexical means of expression as indirectness, agent avoiders, politeness markers (e.g. *please*), conventional politeness acts (e.g. apologies, thanks), understaters (e.g. *a bit, virtually, basically, generally*), downtoners and hedges (*you might, not sure, can't seem to*), emoticons expressing irony or positive emotions (cf. House and Kasper 1981, Trosborg 1995, Decock and Spiessens 2017):

(253) my issue is not being listened too. My account has been overcharged. My service has been suspended and I'm generally unhappy! (@Company2)

(254) sorry to say that Company10 energy is appalling your customer service team is rude I or my family will never use you again (@Company10)

(255) Not having much luck with @Company10 at the minute… Not sure it should be quite so… green 😒 (@Company10)

(256) How do I get hold of someone regarding access to my mobile account? It's been a nightmare. Someone please help. (@Company7)

(257) Please give me the email address I could write to to stop getting junk mail from your bank. (@Company5)

(258) can we expect an answer about where these flowers are at any time? And what state there'll be in? #rubbish (@Company6)

(259) little bit annoyed I've only had this contract phone 3 days and no network error all day bit annoying as I need it for work :((@Company7)

(260) why do you have ~15 different bottles of Pinot Grigio, a few Chardonnay and S. Blanc and basically no other varieties?! (@Company10)

(261) Had virtually no service for the last 24 hours. What's happening in L9 area of Liverpool? Not a great start to the year?! (@Company1)

(262) Are these SO #organic that you just get the stems and no no tomatoes? ;) (@Company10)

(263) not sure if the persistent app notification for contactless payment is good security practice (@Company5)

(264) I can't seem to see my PAYPAL four digit code, does it normally show up online for people or you (@Company5)

(265) hey there! Both platform 1's displays are playing up at HNK! You might wanna send someone out to fix em :) (@Company12)

- upgraders;

The means serving to intensify the complaint and upgrade the force of the act involve the use of emphatic syntactic and lexical structures, such as inversion, adverbial intensification (*still, so, absolutely, always, again*), swear words, interjections, repetition or exaggeration (*10 billion calls, bombards*) (Trosborg 1995, Meinl 2010, Decock and Spiessens 2017):

(266) never have i had so many issues disputing fraudulent charges with @Company5... @[company name] here i come. (@Company5)

(267) why are your deals so much more expensive than carphone warehouse for exactly the same deal?? (@Company2)

(268) still waiting to hear and still cannot get a hold of the driver??!! (@Company6)

(269) why are you always so understaffed in Balham?? Queues out the door. Always. #customerservice #terrible (@Company5)

(270) Why is the [product name] from Alfreton to Norwich consistently late on a Friday? It's ridiculous! 😫 (@Company12)

(271) still no service 😵 shite network!!! (@Company2)

(272) Company5 actively sabotaging my biz account taking more than a month, 3 branch visits & 10 billion phone calls to make changes #stillstalled (@Company5)

(273) absolutely disgusting behaviour from a [name + surname] claiming to be the head of your complaints department. Moving funds asap. (@Company4)

(274) are the worst bank I have ever dealt with terrible customer service completely unhelpful staff in your beckenham branch (@Company5)

(275) Disgusted by the @Company6 News driver who cut us up and then bombards us with disgusting verbal abuse. #appalled (@Company6)

(276) Once again 1 of the 2 cashiers tills is out of action in @Company4 Ruislip. Getting fed up of this. Long queues yet again! (@Company4)

(277) fkn freezing on this @Company12 i don't know how i have coped with it for over an hour! (@Company12)

(278) can you please explain how on earth ive used 3 gb of data in 16 days when i have wifi at home! Your an absoulte joke&rip off!!😫 (@Company2)

(279) What the hell's this ludicrously tiny [product name] about @Company11? Thumb for reference. It's half the size it used to be! (@Company11)

- acronyms: consumer's negative emotions and evaluation of the complainable, as well as the expectation of a remedial action may be expressed by means of acronyms and abbreviations:

(280) ?823.23 for Buildings Insurance Renewal loooool Are you having a laugh after the way we've been treated…!!!! (@Company5)

(281) Wtf have @Company11's done to their crunchies?! (@Company11)

(282) You need to get back to me ASAP in regards the funds taken from my account. Collection calls for such practice is unacceptable (@Company4)

- paraverbal and nonverbal means: similarly to positive evaluation, complaints are expressed or upgraded paraverbally and nonverbally by means of capitalization (which has been interpreted as shouting in CMC communication), the use of multiple punctuation marks (e.g. multiple exclamation and question marks), suspension dots and emoticons or emojis denoting negative feelings, as well as onomatopoeic expressions. The devices serve as a means of expressing consumers' disapproval and dissatisfaction (cf. Meinl 2010, Decock and Spiessens 2017, Decock and Depraetere 2018):

(283) Dear @Company7 STOP SENDING ME YOUR SHITTY POST TO MY HOUSE I AM WITH TALK TALK AND DO NOT WANT Company7. Thanks. (@Company7)

(284) WHAT THE HELL IS THIS PATHETIC EXCUSE OF A CHOCOLATE BAR ITS TINY MULTIBAR CHOCOLATE SIZES ARE A JOKE (@Company11)

(285) was told on a previous tweet that I would get reimbursed just been told over the phone "no I won't" DISGRACEFUL! (@Company7)

(286) Why is NOBODY answering the phone in stores😫😫😫@Company3 (@Company3)

(287) AWFUL SERVICE FROM Company7. 😡wifi still not working after 3wks of excuses and broken promises. @Company7 (@Company7)

(288) stitching came loose on my [product name]!!!! (@Company3)

(289) still waiting to hear and still cannot get a hold of the driver??!! (@Company6)

(290) worst Internet customer service I have ever had the misfortune of contending with!!! An absolutely livid customer!!!😡 (@Company3)

(291) still after 15mins train not yet departed. What's the delay??? (@Company12)

(292) Took out home insurance ref MPH803911XXX. No confirmation arrived. Spent 40 mins on helpline, email promised. Nothing… ?? (@Company5)

(293) having broadband problems today? getting lower download speeds then upload and unplayable gaming on this fibre :((@Company2)

(294) Been waiting to see someone at Company5 for an hour after being promised a wait of 40 mins max. And still have someone in front of me :((@Company5)

(295) just opened the [product name] I got for my birthday and there's one missing!! Not a happy bunny :((@Company11)

(296) Wow – you can now send more annoying, useless SPAM even quicker! #please STOP (@Company2)

(297) Argh! Just wanna pay for a gift card! @Company10 till sent me to Cust Serv, Cust Serv sent me back to a till. Just let me pay! #exaspersted (@Company10)

– hashtags;

Tweets expressing negative evaluation and complaints also feature hashtags (cf. Tereszkiewicz 2015a). The tags exhibit considerable variation as to their pragmatic and structural properties. Structurally, hashtags may have the form of one-word tags, phrases or clauses. Pragmatically, the hashtags may express all of the respective constituents of the speech act of a complaint. For example:

– name of the company/product: #Company2, #Company10, #[product name],
– expression of the complainable: #8weekswithoutinternet, #kosher #empty, #stuck, #ColdAndWaiting, #antsinmyegg, #nochocolate,
– expression of negative evaluation: #disgraceful, #fraud, #whatajoke, #poorcustomerservice, #notcool, #rude, #crapservice, #customerservice #terrible, #disgrace, #ripoff, #breakingmyheart, #sad, #weeps, #sickfedup, #sodisappointing, #feelsick,
– expression of remedial action: #needstobulkup, #please STOP, #BringBackThe[product name].

Examples:

(298) Dear @Company10 pls make your packaging easier to open; it's taken me 5mins to peel plastic off #[product name] #Snacks (@Company10)

(299) Apocalypse now at Company10 Bromley. 8:30 on a Saturday and no bread. #Company10 #wakeup (@Company10)

(300) Got a 4G 7mbps #mobile #phone signal on the course here at #Bowood. Shame the #data signal in #Avoncliff is rubbish. #NextProject (@Company1)

(301) Another failed delivery from @Company6 surprise surprise! #crapservice (@Company6)

(302) It really annoys me when @Company10 garage closes the entire forecourt when the tanker comes to refuel. Been waiting 40m now. #stuck (@Company10)

(303) your fraud team very rude putting phone done on me! Because we can't not get to a bank to sort out the problem! #rude (@Company5)

(304) what's up with the kosher section in Fallowfield Manchester? I need my biscuits! :(#kosher #empty #sad (@Company10)

(305) On the 10th working day of awaiting a refund from @Company10, to now be told I have to wait another 3-7 working days. #shit (@Company10)

(306) every single one of these biscuits has been broken🙈🙈 #breakingmyheart (@Company11)

(307) Your signal is atrocious regardless of where i go.. #Company2 #bumped (@Company2)

(308) travel currency not delivered to branch next day as per guarantee and no communication #poorcustomerservice (@Company4)

(309) is your [product name] Stratford to Norwich bus running late? 🥶#ColdAndWaiting (@Company8)

(310) why are you always so understaffed in Balham?? Queues out the door. Always. #customerservice #terrible (@Company5)

(311) how come UK [product name] pre-orders don't get the vr headset? We're paying more than the US after conversion too! #notcool (@Company9)

(312) why have i still not got #wifi Its never gone live since the date you said it would! #sickfedup #whatajoke #8weekswithoutinternet (@Company2)

(313) Thanks to #Company4 for your text alerts. Someone has been having a swinging time overseas with my debit card today! #fraud (@Company4)

(314) stopped card with no warning in USA. 76 mins to sort out on mobile #disgraceful (@Company5)

(315) Wow – you can now send more annoying, useless SPAM even quicker! #please STOP (@Company2)

(316) I kinda like @Company12 but why offer passengers chicken tikka to eat in such a confined space and stink the place out - #ihadtomoveseats (@Company12)

(317) just bought a [product name] and none of the caramels have caramel in them😡 #sodisappointing (@Company11)

The hashtags may constitute internal components of the main body of the complaint. In this case, the tags most frequently mark factual data concerning the complainable, such as the company's name, localization or affected phenomena (e.g. (300), (312), (313)). More frequently, however, hashtags are introduced as external modifiers in the form of metacomments to the preceding message. The components function as a concise summary and evaluation of the circumstances. The hashtags serve as further means of venting negative emotions and assessment of the company (cf. Erz et al. 2018: 52).

– simple and complex tweets;

In the analyzed material, complaints comprise messages including simple tweets with one speech act and one complaint constituent, as exemplified in:

(318) Company7 s a pile of wank (@Company7)

(319) IMessage unavailable since yesterday . (@Company2)

Such acts constitute 24 percent of the messages in the corpus. More often (76 percent of the messages), the posts assume the form of complex tweets, which represent speech act sets. For example:

(320) just had a horrible experience at one of your stores, sort this out. (@Company10)

(321) items ordered and not received. Company3 opened a case and then closed it without giving answers. Still no items! Appalling! (@Company3)

(322) No signal at all with @Company1 it's been over a week. I'm paying for a service I can't use! Keep being fobbed off Not happy at all & want a refund (@Company1)

Complex tweets may embrace different constituents of the complaint. In the messages quoted above, the posts include the complainable, negative evaluation, expression of dissatisfaction and disapproval, as well as a request for remedial action.

As mentioned above, in Decock and Depraetere's (2018) approach, the number of constituents may reflect a different degree of explicitness of the complaint. A greater number of messages featuring a number of constituents in the analyzed material constitutes a further confirmation of the observations by Meinl (2010) as well as Decock and Depraetere (2018) concerning the preference for the more direct form of complaints in online interaction. The more explicit and direct form of the complaints expressed online was attributed to anonymity and brevity of the communication (Meinl 2010). On Twitter, however, anonymity may not constitute the primary reason for the form of the complaints, since the profiles may reveal the consumer's true identity, and other considerations seem to underlie the form of the tweets. The use of direct strategies in the comments may constitute evidence of a task-oriented form of consumers' messages, the focus placed primarily on transactional aspects of the encounters and attending to one's professional face needs, i.e. obtaining the due/expected service (cf. Decock and Spiessens 2017).

4.3.2. Complaint management – responses to complaints and negative evaluations

The purpose of the company's response is, among others, to apologize, acknowledge and validate the customer's opinions, and, consequently, to maintain or repair the relationship with the consumer (cf. Zhang and Vásquez 2014). The company may also decide to repudiate the evaluation and complaint, in which case it risks damaging future relations with the consumer.

4.3.2.1. Strategies of complaint and negative review management

In the analyzed context, responses produced in reaction to customers' complaints comprise the following acts:
- request for information/contact and/or for action,
- apology:
  - Illocutionary Force Indicating Device (IFID),
  - empathy expression,
  - acknowledgement of the complainable,
  - explanation of the complainable,
  - denial of the complainable,
  - offer of help and repair;
- thanks (cf. Page 2014, Tereszkiewicz 2017b, forthcoming-b).

The structure of these acts will be investigated below.

4.3.2.1.1. Requests

As the previous research has shown, requests constitute one of the most significant speech acts used in customer encounters. Studies on the use of this act in face-to-face and mediated telephone encounters have indicated considerable variation in the form of the act, both on the part of the customer and the company. It is therefore worth investigating the structure of the act in the online context.

Requests are face-threatening to the hearer's negative face. The form of the request may increase or diminish the face-threatening potential of the act. Shaping the request in an appropriate manner is particularly significant especially in the context of complaint management, i.e. a highly face-threatening situation.

Page (2014) observed that requests of a different kind belong to the most frequent acts accompanying apologies on corporate profiles. The analyzed corpus shows that such acts, in addition to supporting other acts, also constitute individual strategies of responding to complaints and problems reported by consumers. The acts comprise requests for information, for further contact through a different channel and requests for action. A high number of requests shows that they constitute one of the most important types of responses to customer complaints.

Table 10. Requests in the interaction

Type of act	Number
Requests	564
Form of act: simple complex	76 488

Source: own work.

(1) Types of requests
– Requests for information/contact

Requests for information may be interpreted as insertion sequences (Schegloff 2007) before a response with a solution to the consumer's problem is provided. The aim of this act is to gather the information necessary to verify the problems, check if the information provided is correct and/or suggest appropriate corrective actions (cf. Page 2014).

Requests for information involve an inquiry about the issue which the customer is reporting. In the case of complaints and messages reporting problems, the reactions usually involve a question concerning the circumstances in which the negative state occurred. The companies ask for clarification, for details concerning the problems encountered by the customers (Tereszkiewicz 2015b, 2017b, forthcoming-b). Tweets with requests for information comprise a single question or a series of questions. The use of a series of questions helps to emphasize interest and concern for the customer. It may also serve as a strategy of controlling the interaction, guiding it in a specific direction so as not to allow the user to continue complaining. For example:

(323) Company5 actively sabotaging my biz account taking more than a month, 3 branch visits & 10 billion phone calls to make changes #stillstalled
Company5 @Company5
@user Hi there, can I ask for more information around what's happened please? ^[initials] (@Company5)

(324) your coaches constantly leaving early is really starting to annoy me. A few minutes does make a difference at an airport.
Company8 @Company8
@user Could you please let us know the full journey details, so we can look into the matter? ^[initials] (@Company8)

(325) i am trying to reply to messages but get a message saying ive insufficient funds, im on sim only including unlimited texts whats going on
Company2 @Company2
@user Good morning [name], are you on a pay monthly [product name] plan? Do you have the My Company2 app to track your plan? [name] (@Company2)

Though the use of requests for information is typical of institutional communication and constitutes a standard procedure especially in customer encounters (Drew and Heritage 1992, Varcasia 2013), in Twitter interaction, the use of such requests is particularly abundant (cf. Einwiller and Steiler 2015). As Page (2014: 40) observes, on Twitter, the use of questions is additionally dictated by the design of the medium – messages are by definition short (around 140 characters) and often incomplete, vague and imprecise. Requests for information serve as a means of obtaining information, maintaining interaction and showing attention to the customer (Tereszkiewicz 2017b). In this way, they constitute a face and rapport restoring strategy – they are a sign of feedback to the customer that the inquiry is attended to and clarification is pending (Page 2014: 39).

Responses to customer inquiries also involve requests to provide further information or to contact the company through a direct message on Twitter, through a different channel, e.g. telephone line, online chat or a face-to-face encounter in the company's branch (cf. Tereszkiewicz 2017b). The most frequent cases comprise requests addressed to the consumer to contact the company via a direct message (95 instances) or a phone call (74 instances). For example:

> (326) no network issues! Was all over edinburgh last night & still the same. Followed all your troubleshooting and still no service!
> Company1 @Company1
> @user Ok, please give our Tech team a call and they will be happy to look into this for you – http://xx.co.uk/help/get-in-touch … ^[name] (@Company1)

> (327) still waiting on my brand new fridge freezer that's never worked being fixed , don't seem to much bothered about it .
> Company9 @Company9
> @user Can you DM more information about the issues you're having with your fridge freezer, [name]? ^[initials] (@Company9)

> (328) yes only suggest was that it would be collected pronto but no suggestions that they would be able to sort it quickly so I have it back
> Company1 @Company1
> @user Okay, you would need to speak with our Insurance team for a timescale on this, sorry. (@Company1)

In the analyzed material, a request for interaction invited from the user (e.g. *call our team, give our team a call, chat with us, contact us/our team, DM us*) tends to be used, which confirms the results obtained by Page (2014). A high number of such requests across the profiles indicates that they may be considered as typical of this channel of communication. Analogically to the requests for information described above, they may be regarded as the first step towards solving the complainable. The requests, while not providing a solution to the issues, may help the company to show the customer that s/he is being attended to and if s/he proceeds with further action, appropriate assistance will be provided. A request for interaction via a different channel may be understandable concerning the open and public nature of Twitter and the need to protect personal data and process inquiries in the form of personal one-to-one communication (Page 2014, Tereszkiewicz 2017b). The invitation for further contact via a direct message or e-mail may be also seen as an evasive strategy, however. It may help the providers to avoid a public discussion concerning the complainable and thus avoid further threat to the company's image, may help to create an impression of responsiveness and attentiveness instead (cf. Lillqvist et al. 2016). The high number of the above-mentioned strategies indicates as well that Twitter serves predominantly as a channel for initiating a complaint handling process – the complaints are still largely directed to be handled through other channels. Twitter may thus be seen as a channel allowing the customers to vent anger and express their dissatisfaction, but not allowing them to fully handle the complaint.

  – Requests for action

In answer to complaints, companies also proceed with a response to the problem and provide the customers with advice and recommendation on corrective actions (Tereszkiewicz 2015b, 2017b, forthcoming-b). The representatives offer solutions and provide suggestions as to which steps the consumers might undertake to solve the complainable:

(329) still there is no way i should be using 3gb in 16 days mun! My contract was up last month,why im still with you i dont know
Company2 @Company2
@user I'd advise turning WiFi Assist off, and you should find you'll be using less data. ^[name] (@Company2)

(330) Is your website down at the moment? Crashed halfway through my grocery order!
Company10 @Company10
@user We're not aware of any issues our end. Have you tried using a different browser? [name] (@Company10)

(331) I want my money back or a replacement pair, this isn't on.
Company3 @Company3
@user We understand [name], you would need to return the shoes to store to process a refund. Please call us on Monday and we'll try to help. (@Company3)

(2) The structure of requests

The analyzed material offers a range of request patterns, involving direct, conventionally indirect and non-conventionally indirect acts (Blum-Kulka et al. 1989, Economidou-Kogetsidis 2005). Both imperative and interrogative acts involving different strategies mitigating the directive force of the act occur in the analyzed material (cf. Page 2014). The table below presents a list of the most frequent requesting patterns in the corpus.

Table 11. Requests

Type of act	Number
Interrogative acts – direct questions	228
Interrogative acts – ability questions	123
hearer-oriented	99
can you	71
could you	28
speaker-oriented	24
Imperative acts	169
Declarative acts – need statements	15
hearer-oriented	12
speaker-oriented	2
Declarative acts – performative acts of advice	9
advise	6
recommend	2
suggest	1
Declarative acts – ability statements	4
Other	16

Source: own work.

The use of the respective strategies will be discussed below.

— Interrogative acts – direct questions

Requests for information in the form of interrogative acts proved the most frequent in the analyzed corpus. The acts are used to express general questions asking consumers to clarify the issues they have encountered as well as more specific questions concerning the services used (cf. ibid.: 40):

(332) your website having problems?
Company1 @Company1
@user Hi there, what seems to be the issue? (@Company1)

(333) I've just had a delivery of a [product name] and there was supposed to be a 3 months trial from Now TV. No sign of this in the box???
Company2 @Company2
@user Hello there, [name]. How did you order the tablet initially? ^[name] (@Company2)

Interrogative acts are also employed in responses suggesting which actions could be undertaken to resolve the problem (cf. ibid.). The exchanges below show the use of questions the aim of which is to help the customer to deal with the reported issues:

(334) trainers ordered on the 29th June, still not even packed! Awful services!
Company3 @Company3
@user hi [name], have you contacted our team for an update on this? Contact info here: http://xxxs/6019BvXXX (@Company3)

(335) Is your website down at the moment? Crashed halfway through my grocery order!
Company10 @Company10
@user We're not aware of any issues our end. Have you tried using a different browser? [name] (@Company10)

(336) fkn freezing on this @Company12 i don't know how i have coped with it for over an hour!
Company12 @Company12
@user Morning [name]. Sorry to hear its a bit chilly on the train this morning. Have you spoken with the train manager>> to see if they can adjust the temperature for you? << (@Company12)

The representatives respond to the consumer's problem by asking if the customer has already proceeded with certain actions. Such voicing of the advice may be seen as politer and less direct than the choice of, for instance, the imperative form.

— Interrogative acts – ability questions

Among conventionally indirect requests, ability questions proved to be the most frequent. A high number of such strategies indicates the representatives' willingness to decrease the imposition on the consumer and to mark the distance between the interlocutors. Two main forms of requests can be seen – in the first and in the second person. The choice of one of the respective strategies entails a different level of directness and politeness (cf. Economidou-Kogetsidis 2005, Ogiermann 2012, Page 2014).

Most of the ability questions are formulated in the first person singular. This, in contrast to other acts which are more frequently expressed in the first person plural to underline an institutional perspective, lends the request a more personal character. Using the author's perspective also reduces the directive force of the request and the imposition on the addressee, which is important in the case of negative politeness cultures (Ogiermann 2012: 42). *Can I ask...* is the most frequent phrase used in the requests:

(337) Company5 actively sabotaging my biz account taking more than a month, 3 branch visits & 10 billion phone calls to make changes #stillstalled
Company5 @Company5
@user Hi there, can I ask for more information around what's happened please? ^[initials] (@Company5)

(338) not an error message as such but keeps telling me that it's available only to Company5 customers blah blah blah
Company5 @Company5
@user Can I ask how you're trying to sign up for the rewards? ^[initials] (@Company5)

Hearer-oriented acts most frequently consist of ability questions involving modal verbs *can* or *could*:

(339) never have i had so many issues disputing fraudulent charges with @Company5...
@[company name] here i come.
Company5 @Company5
@user Hi [name], can you give me some more information around what has happened to make you feel this way? ^[initials] (@Company5)

(340) your customer service is about as good as your ability to prevent fraud. Not only have you fucked that up, no one has rang me about it.
Company1 @Company1
@user That isn't what we like to hear [name]:(Could you DM us some more info about what's happened exactly please? We'd like to help. (@Company1)

– Imperative acts

Imperative acts are used in requests for further contact and/or information, as well as in acts of direct advice suggesting corrective actions. The high number of imperatives might seem surprising, since previous studies on requesting behaviour in English have indicated a preference for more indirect requesting patterns, with the aim of lowering the imposition on the addressee (Wierzbicka 1985, Trosborg 1995, Ogiermann 2009b).

However, the unmitigated imperatives only include individual instances. In the majority of the cases, the acts are mitigated, as in the examples below, where the directive force is reduced by the politeness marker *please*, an address term, as well as by supportive and accompanying acts comprising reasons and grounders or acts offering further assistance:

(341) shocked by service. No card yesterday. This today, nobody tried to deliver. 2 lies. Saturday wasted
Company6 @Company6
@user Thanks for bringing this to our attention [name]. Send over your tracking details & I'll investigate this for you. #[name]Cares (@Company6)

(342) station said it's fine and a good idea to get on early. Your ticket lady just charged me an additional? 29.00
Company12 @Company12
@user How strange, let us know the details here and we'll investigate: http://xxx.do/10sXXX (@Company12)

(343) been here since 3.15 & been told every time that the next service is scheduled. now lost faith & ordered a taxi. Will cost a fortune
Company12 @Company12
@user Please keep hold of your receipt and send it to us. getintouch@xxxx.co.uk (@Company12)

(344) The new [product name] to Plymouth 23 arrival is awful; just sat at Exeter bored for 18 mins. when we could be getting home.
Company8 @Company8
@user Apologies for that [name], we can look into this for you. Please leave your comments via: http://goo.gl/GsEXXX (@Company8)

– Declarative acts – need statements

Need statements also occur in requesting patterns. Among the acts, hearer-oriented advice with the modal verb *need* is used:

(345) Your signal is atrocious regardless of where i go.. #Company2 #bumped
Company2 @Company2
@user Hi [name], you will need to contact us on 150 and speak to our technical support department, our lines open at 8AM. –[name] (@Company2)

(346) I would like to know why there has been such a large delay in the collection and how quickly I can hope to be reunited?
Company1 @Company1
@user Okay, you would need to speak with our Insurance team for a timescale on this, sorry. (@Company1)

– Declarative acts – performative acts of advice

Among the acts of advice, acts of recommending and suggesting solutions can also be found in the form of acts with the performative verbs *recommend* or *advise* in the first person singular or plural, additionally mitigated by *would*. For example:

(347) still there is no way i should be using 3gb in 16 days mun! My contract was up last month, why im still with you i dont know
Company2 @Company2
@user I'd advise turning WiFi Assist off, and you should find you'll be using less data. ^[name] (@Company2)

– Other structures

Requests for action are also phrased in an impersonal form, in which the authors avoid naming the agent performing the action, thus diminishing the face threat to the consumer. The most frequent structures used in this function comprise the use of the passive voice or suggestive hints, among others:

(348) so disappointed in your aftercare. [product name] not 1 year old and instead of replacing it you are sending out an engineer?!?!
Company9 @Company9
@user Repairs are offered to resolve the issue under warranty. Info about the warranty can be found at http://spr.ly/6016BRXXX^[initials] (@Company9)

(349) due to a mixup i ended up with 2 pairs in grey! Im guessing no chance of finding a black pair now?
Company3 @Company3
@user where did you buy them? It's worth contacting your point of purchase to see if there's anything they can do. (@Company3)

(350) Hey @Company11 why is there a sour patch kid piece in my [product name] package???
Company11 @Company11
@user Hi [name], what a great surprise! Why not ask [company name], our parent company, who own them?…1/2 please contact them here: https://www.facebook.com/ [company name] … Thanks :) 2/2 (@Company11)

– Modification of requests

Various means of the modification of acts, mainly aimed at minimizing imposition, diminishing the directive force of the act and increasing the politeness of the request can be seen in the corpus. The most frequent modifiers comprise the politeness marker *please*, softening adverbials and understaters, as well as terms of address, disarming softeners, *if*-clauses or reasons and grounders. For example:

(351) Company3 customer service is terrible @Company3
Company3 @Company3
@user We're sorry to hear this, can you please let us know what the problem is? (@Company3)

(352) not directly. I'm just surprised by the really poor state of the train!
Company12 @Company12
@user That's disappointing to hear [name]. Which train are you travelling on please? (@Company12)

(353) not sure if the persistent app notification for contactless payment is good security practice
Company5 @Company5
@user Hi there, could you kindly provide more details in regards to this? ^[initials] (@Company5)

(354) 4th tweet! and I have DM'd – please can you tell me where my parcel is??? JD0002 224400458XXX it should have come yesterday
Company6 @Company6
@user I'd be happy to take a look for you [name], please can you just confirm the full delivery address for me in a DM? (@Company6)

(355) #hessleroad staff couldn't make it anymore obvious that they could bearsed to help me
set up a basic account. #badservice #nohelp
Company5 @Company5
@user Hi there, can you give me some more information around what has happened
to make you feel this way? ^[initials] (@Company5)

(356) [product name], and it didn't work
Company5 @Company5
@user Thanks for confirming. Unfortunately, you'll need to speak to the team on
034594XXX for this to be looked into. ^[initials] (@Company5)

(357) ive upgrade to the z5 early, i used my Company1 open code on my last contract, keep
the same number and now its saying ive used all my codes
Company1 @Company1
@user Oh right, okay. How many lines have you applied the discount code on [name]?
Have you checked the terms and conditions? (@Company1)

(358) No I've tried all of the above many times and still the same problems – as soon as my
contract has finished I'm moving to something else
Company1 @Company1
@user We're sorry to hear that. Just to clarify [name], did it work fine before the update? Have you tried a backup and restore? (@Company1)

(359) let down by Company2 yet again, now my whole family can't use our phones to communicate easily without costing us a fortune, #niceone
Company2 @Company2
@user Good afternoon, what has been happening? You can send a DM for privacy
reasons if you wish. [name] (@Company2)

(360) rang 7 different numbers trying to get hold of someone regarding my credit card, no
luck. I am beyond annoyed please help!
Company4 @Company4
@user Hi, I'm [initials]. Sorry to read your tweet. Can you please provide more info on
your credit card query? DM if you prefer. (@Company4)

The use of the politeness formula *please* proved to be the most frequent
form of modification of requests (245 instances). The formula occurs in most
of the request patterns and serves the function of downgrading the force of the
request. Among adverbials diminishing the directive tone of the act, adverbs
such as *just* (15 instances) or *some more* (12 instances) tend to be used. *Just*
used in the requests clearly performs the function of mitigating the threat to
the consumer's face and diminishes the effort the consumer needs to make
to perform the requested activity. The directive tone of the request or advice-giving
acts also tends to be mitigated by the use of *if*-clauses (14 instances). The use of
terms of address in the requests constitutes a further component diminishing
the directive force of the act. First names used in the messages mitigate the force
of the act and personalize the request.

The analyzed material shows a considerable diversification of requesting strategies used by the representatives. A relatively high number of ability questions
and other conventionally indirect requesting strategies reflects a wish to lower

the imposition on the customer and make the acts politer. A high number of requests in the form of interrogative and imperative acts is worth noticing, as it does not comply with the conventions of a negative politeness culture and the need to attend to the consumer's negative face. As mentioned before, previous studies on requesting behaviour in English have shown that it is conventionally indirect acts that tend to be the most frequent (Wierzbicka 1985, Trosborg 1995, Ogiermann 2009b). A higher number of imperatives and interrogative acts functioning as requests in the analyzed material, however, may be dictated by the context and character of the interaction. The use of these strategies may result from the constraints on the length of the message imposed by the medium itself. Moreover, since many of the customers' messages are requests for help following the infraction, advice on corrective measures in the form of a clear and direct act may seem suitable and understandable in the circumstances (Tereszkiewicz 2015b, forthcoming-b). The choice of this requesting strategy marks a shift towards a more task-focused interaction, the focus on solving the consumer's problem and providing assistance in a short time. The use of such direct strategies may enhance the efficiency of the encounter. A high number of the politeness formula *please* represents a further feature characterizing the analyzed requests. Previous studies devoted to the use of this formula have produced contrasting results, e.g. a study by Economidou-Kogetsidis (2005: 264) showed that *please* is used predominantly in conventionally indirect strategies, preferably in query preparatory requests, while research by Marquez Reiter (2000: 139) indicated that this formula is not commonly used in requesting strategies whatsoever. The use of this formula in the analyzed context, with its flexibility and possibility to be used in a range of contexts, allows the representatives to introduce a component of politeness into a predominantly task-focused interaction and thus to diminish the imposition posed by the directive.

A high number of requests in the messages may be interpreted as a sign of a dialogic orientation and a problem-solving approach to the encounters (cf. Coyle et al. 2012, Romenti et al. 2014). The requests constitute a "tactical move," an important first-step in the process of attending to consumers, establishing and maintaining contact, and showing willingness to help in this context.

Requests may constitute an individual turn constructional unit or may be a part of a complex tweet with other accompanying acts in the response. Most of the acts of request are used in complex messages.

4.3.2.1.2. Apology

It has been observed that Twitter's affordances allowing for real-time communication make it the perfect space for the expression of an apology. As Page (2014) states, "Twitter's affordances of immediacy and directness are well suited to the timely and sincere characteristics associated with a successful apology" (Page 2014: 31).

Apologies represent remedial acts which occur following offensive behaviour done to the hearer for which the speaker holds some responsibility (Blum-Kulka et al. 1989, Marquez Reiter 2000). In service encounters, apologies constitute a strategy which is to compensate the customer for the fault in the service (Marquez Reiter 2008: 5). The purpose of the apology is to redress damage done to the customer's negative face (Scollon and Scollon 1983, Holmes 1990, Marquez Reiter 2008: 14). The companies acknowledge the fault and express understanding of the customer's situation (Marquez Reiter 2008: 16).

Apologies are considered as face-threatening acts for the speaker. In an act of apology, the speaker "accepts a certain degree of moral responsibility for the offence" (ibid.: 5) and thus admits that some offensive behaviour took place. However, apologies may also be considered as face-supportive acts for the speaker (Scollon and Scollon 1983, Holmes 1990, Lubecka 2000: 146, Marquez Reiter 2008: 3). Although apologies pose a threat to the speaker's negative face, they may support their positive face at the same time. Through an act of apology, the speaker may both redress damage done to the hearer's negative face and also enhance his/her own positive face (Marquez Reiter 2008: 3). This is particularly important in the case of service encounters, where apologies may help to support the company's professional face (ibid.: 5).

According to Blum-Kulka et al's (1989) typology, which served as the basis for the classification, the expression of apology may be realized by five strategies: expression of apology, i.e. Illocutionary Force Indicating Device (IFID), expression of the speaker's responsibility for the offence, explanation or account of the cause of the offence, offer of repair/restitution, promise of forbearance. The strategies may be used individually or in a combination (Blum-Kulka et al. 1989: 289). In this approach, acts of explanation or account may be used to accept or deny one's guilt and may constitute a full apology act.[58]

In the analyzed corpus, the following apology strategies were identified:
- expression of apology, i.e. Illocutionary Force Indicating Device (IFID),
- empathy device,
- acknowledgement of the complainable,
- explanation of the complainable,
- denial of the complainable,
- offer of repair (cf. Page 2014, Tereszkiewicz 2017b, forthcoming-b).

Apologies more frequently tend to be extended and accompanied by other speech acts (ibid.). In the corpus, with just two exceptions, the acts occur in the

---

[58] A similar approach, suggesting that the category of accounts comprises acts which may be placed along a continuum ranging from acceptance to denial of blame, was proposed by Ogiermann (2009a). In Goffman's (1967) view and approach to apologies, by contrast, the act of apology cannot contain an explanation which justifies or denies the offender's acts, as it would change the function of the act, i.e. recognition of blame and subsequent repair.

form of complex tweets, in which the message is extended to include accompanying acts. Respective categories of apologies are discussed below.

- Illocutionary Force Indicating Devices

Table 12. Illocutionary Force Indicating Devices

Type of act	Number
Apology	254
IFID: Apologies Performative verb: to apologize Expression of regret: sorry	 35 9 210
Form of act: simple complex	 2 252

Source: own work.

The major component of an explicit apology is the Illocutionary Force Indicating Device (IFID). The IFIDs used in the corpus comprise the performative verb *to apologize*, the noun *apology*, often in the plural form of *apologies*, and the expression of regret in the form of (*I am/we are*) *sorry*, the latter being considerably more frequent (cf. Tereszkiewicz, forthcoming-b). Apologies, as was the case with other acts, are expressed in the first person singular or plural form of the verb. The acts assume different levels of complexity, comprising both simple acts involving a sheer expression of an apology or regret, and acts in which the apology is further extended to include a complement stating the offence. The structure of the act thus may be as follows:

IFID +/– the complainable

- The perfomative

The following structural forms of apologies were identified in the corpus:

• the performative verb or noun

I/we apologize

Apologies

• the performative + the complainable

I/we apologize for X

Apologies for X

The use of the noun in an elliptic form, which proved more frequent than the verbal form of the apology, is considered less formal (Ogiermann 2009a: 95). Both structures are exemplified in the following messages:

(361) Shocking service! 1 week so far without access to my debit card and now I have to wait until Monday for further help.
Company4 @Company4
@user Hi, I'm [initials]. Apologies for this. I can confirm your query has been passed to your complaint handler & they'll contact you ASAP. (@Company4)

(362) Booked a ticket from London to Bristol, but the transaction stopped in between, but my debit card showing successful transaction.
Company8 @Company8
@user Apologies for that, please can you DM us with the email address you used to book [name]? (@Company8)

(363) stopped card with no warning in USA. 76 mins to sort out on mobile #disgraceful
Company5 @Company5
@user I do apologise for the wait and length of the call, is it now resolved; [name]? ^[initials] (@Company5)

The use of the first person singular form in the acts proved considerably more frequent, with eight of the acts expressed in this form and only one apology expressed in the first person plural. The preference for the use of the first person singular form in the apology individualizes and personalizes the act, decreasing its institutional tone. Intensifying devices involve the use of emphatic auxiliary *do* (6 occurrences) or determiners, such as *many* (2 instances):

(364) didn't tell me moving my loan date would mean you take it twice in a week!! Fucking joke. Thanks for screwing my account up!!
Company5 @Company5
@user Hi, I do apologise, this should not happen please contact us so we can discuss this for you, 03457345XXX (24/7), thanks! ^[initials] (@Company5)

(365) been on hold for 20 mins now, service is shocking
Company2 @Company2
@user It can be busy at this time on the weekend many apologies. [name] (@Company2)

– Expression of regret

The expression of regret occurs both in an isolated form and in the form accompanied by the statement of the complainable:

- the expression of regret

(*I'm*/*we're*) *sorry*

- the expression of regret + the complainable

(*I'm*/*we're*) *sorry about X*

(*I'm*/*we're*) *sorry for X*

(*I'm*/*we're*) *sorry to hear*/*to read X*

The apology occurs in the full and in the elliptical form, with the latter being more frequent (68 and 142 instances, respectively). In the case of the full form, the use of the singular form of the pronoun proved slightly more frequent, with 37 instances of this form, and 31 occurrences of the use of the first person plural. The choice of the form, as indicated above, may lend the apology a different tone, personalizing the act or marking its corporate character, respectively. For example:

(366) Why are replacement coaches now the norm? No plugs or no plugs & no toilets. Delays waiting for passengers from late coaches.
Company8 @Company8
@user I am sorry to hear about your journey. Can u plz DM your ticket number so we cn get this fedback? (@Company8)

(367) just opened a [product name] to find a pathetic stick. Weighed it and it is underweight. Not happy #needstobulkup
Company11 @Company11
@user Oh dear, sorry about that [name]! Please call our team on 0800 818XX & they'll be able to help. :) (@Company11)

(368) what a joke went to the Broadway branch this morning Tacky sign on the door closed due to fault no I can't pay a bill!!!!
Company4 @Company4
@user Hi, I'm [initials]. Sorry to read your tweet. Were you able to visit a different branch to do this? DM if you'd prefer. (@Company4)

(369) Company7 s a pile of wank
Company7 @Company7
@user Hey! Sorry to hear you feel this way! What's happened? Let me know, here to help. [initials] (@Company7)

(370) fkn freezing on this @Company12 i don't know how i have coped with it for over an hour!
Company12 @Company12
@user Morning [name]. Sorry to hear its a bit chilly on the train this morning. Have you spoken with the train manager>> to see if they can adjust the temperature for you? << (@Company12)

(371) No response to my email 2 weeks ago & already another "unfortunate" incident on the 7:15 from St Pancras @Company12
Company12 @Company12
@user Hi [name]. Sorry to hear you've not had a response from our team yet. If you can DM us your e-mail address, we can check >>that we have received it successfully.<< (@Company12)

The choice of the short variant over the full form may also lend the message an alternative tone and indicate a different force of the act. The short elliptical form, namely, has a lower illocutionary force and it also decreases the degree of formality of the act. The preference for the short form in the interaction may also be dictated by the structural limitation on the length of the message.

Intensification devices with the expression of regret comprise the use of boosters in the form of adverbs (e.g. *very, so, really, terribly*) (20 instances). The components serve to increase the effectiveness of the act (Kozicka-Borysowska 2009: 172):

(372) thank you but I'm still stranded!
Company12 @Company12
@user The next train is at 18.36. We are really sorry for today's delays. (@Company12)

(373) that's there first time in 15 years of working in banks that I've heard of anyone being refused to pay money into an account!
Company4 @Company4
@user I'm terribly sorry to hear about your experience. I'll certainly ensure your comments are recorded for feedback. ^[initials] (@Company4)

As indicated above, the act of apology in the case of both apology formulas may be extended to include the statement of the complainable in the form of a complement to the IFID specifying the reason for the apology (cf. Tereszkiewicz 2017b). In 38 of the cases, the complainable is named, referring directly to the customer's message. In the complements naming the offence, the representatives explicitly refer to the occurrence of the complainable and thus openly admit that the issues took place (e.g. *for the wait and length of call, for the delay, that the call hasn't come*). This may be interpreted as a sign of the company's honesty. However, even in the cases where the companies admit to the infraction, they try to diminish the force of the customer's complaint, as in examples (370) or (371) (*a bit chilly, yet*). The apology is also expressed by means of a conventional statement *apologies for the issue* (18 instances) or *apologies/sorry for the inconvenience* (8 instances), which concedes that a negative state of affairs did take place, but does not explicitly name the complainable.

In 58 apology tweets, the complainable is referred to deictically as *this/that*. Such a restatement, as Page (2014) observes, constitutes a strategy helping to protect the image of the company, as the infraction is not shown to the public view. A brief apology may also be seen as a strategy used to minimize the complainable.

In the complements, the representatives also refer to the customers' complaints in more vague terms as *your journey, your experience* (5 instances) or *your tweet* (9 instances). This may reflect a customer-oriented and a personalized approach towards the consumer. However, it also individualizes the complaint uttered by the customer and may indirectly point to a single and uncommon character of the state of affairs complained upon by the customer. Moreover, the complements do not name the complainable and do not point to the company's responsibility for the reported issues. They do not value the complainable in a negative way and may similarly be a means of protecting the company's face and covering the negative feelings expressed by the consumer.

The high occurrence of IFIDs in the analyzed corpus may be explained by the public context of the interaction and the need to attend to the consumer, a need which is especially significant in negative politeness cultures.

4.3.2.1.3. Expression of empathy

A significant number of expressions of empathy uttered in response to customer complaints and negative feedback concerning products or services can be seen in the messages.

Table 13. Expressions of empathy

Type of act	Number
Expression of empathy	125
Form of act: simple complex	 - 125

Source: own work.

The acts express a recognition of the customer as deserving an apology (cf. Lubecka 2000: 161) and have the intention of an apology. The expressions focus on the representative's feelings and his/her evaluation of the customer's situation and reported issues. The function of empathy expressions is to show that the representative shares the customer's feelings (ibid.: 176) and understands the customer's disapproval of the obtained service or product. The expressions, however, do not point to the company's blame for the infraction. The table below lists the most frequent expressions used in this function.

Table 14. Expressions of empathy

Form	Number
Oh no/oh dear	47
I/we understand/appreciate [your frustration/how frustrating]	22
That/this doesn't sound/look right/is disappointing / That's not good/great to hear	20
[That's] Odd/not good/not cool/not ideal	15
[That's/how] Strange	10
[Oh] Crumbs, Blimey, Eck, Gosh, Goodness	8
This isn't what we like to hear	3

Source: own work.

The empathic expressions can be grouped into three categories based on structure.

The first group comprises evaluative acts concerning the consumer's message and the state of affairs described. The representatives refer deictically to the customer's tweet and the complainable:

That/this doesn't sound/look good/right.
That's not good/great (to hear).
That is/seems odd/strange/bizarre.
It's/that's disappointing.
For instance:

(374) what the hell? Total gel sole disintegration on one trainer. Like some weird alien slime attack!
Company3 @Company3
@user Hi [name], that doesn't look right. Where did you get your shoes from? (@Company3)

(375) hi, you've debited my account for this months bill but are still chasing me for money
Company1 @Company1
@user That doesn't sound right [name]. So we can check into this, please chat with us here: http://bit.ly/XyeXXX (@Company1)

(376) here we are on a beautiful sunny April day heading down to London. Just a shame Company12 can't be bothered to clean the Windows! 😖
Company12 @Company12
@user Hi [name]. That's disappointing. Which train are you travelling on please? (@Company12)

The statements comprise simple evaluations in the form of negated adjectives *right, good,* with fewer instances of intensified negative evaluations, such as *extremely unforunate.* The acts also point to an uncommonness of the complainable, for instance by the use of evaluative adjectives such as *bizarre, odd, strange*:

(377) still doesn't work! Spelt my name exactly how it's spelt so assume your records hold my dob incorrectly...
Company5 @Company5
@user That does seem bizarre. If possible can you DM me your full name and post code and I'll take a look for you. ^[initials] (@Company5)

(378) Well [product name] issues with Internet connectivity saying can't connect right now even though I have 4G and Wi-Fi
Company1 @Company1
@user That's odd. Do all your other apps work okay? Do you have the latest version of the app installed? (@Company1)

The above-mentioned acts are less personal and more indirect, which might indicate the representative's willingness to distance him/herself from the problem.

The acts also assume the form of a personal statement, an expression of feelings, in which the representatives express understanding for the customer's negative emotions. The act usually has the following frame:

I/we understand/appreciate your e.g. frustration.
This/That isn't what we like to hear.

For example:

(379) anyone. When I could clearly see the manager not helping anyone. I felt like I was nothing. My money not good enough clearly
Company5 @Company5
@user I do understand your frustration, did they offer to arrange you an appointment for a more suitable time? ^[initials] (@Company5)

(380) [product name] service from Leicester to London StP. Coach C windows are awful-both sides.
Company12 @Company12
@user Thanks for letting us know [name]. We understand this is not the view you were hoping for. This train will be cleaned tonight. (@Company12)

(381) your service would be laughable if wasn't so pathetic.
Company6 @Company6

@user Hi [name]. This isn't what we like to hear – if you have a parcel query, please DM the address & I'll look into this for >> you. Please just tweet once you've DM'd. [name] (@Company6)

In the case of expressions of empathy, intensifying devices are used in a similar manner to the above-mentioned apologies in the form of, for instance, auxiliary *do* (2 instances), which strengthens the illocutionary force of the message.

Expressions of empathy also assume the form of interjections. The acts most frequently have the following form:

Oh no (!)
Oh dear (!)
Oh eck/Crumbs/Oops/Whoops (!)
How strange (!)
What a surprise (!)

For example:

(382) My @Company9 [product name] is the worst phone I've ever had. Slow, laggy and the battery lasts 4 hours. Shocking. Give us vanilla [product name].
Company9 @Company9
@user Oh no, [name]! How long has this been happening? Did you recently update the software on your phone? ^[initials] (@Company9)

(383) Not happy with the quality of my [product name]! I worked hard for this, I want a box full. @Company11
Company11 @Company11
@user Oh dear sorry about that [name], please give us a shout here: http://bit.ly/YCp - XXX & we'll look into this (@Company11)

(384) So. This is what MY @Company7 #[product name] onscreen guide mostly looks like this evening.
Company7 @Company7
@user Oh eck! Doesn't look like there's much on tonight. Have you tried resetting the box at the power to see if that helps? ^[initials] (@Company7)

(385) yep and it's not worked for 14 days
Company7 @Company7
@user Oh crumbs! What was advised when you contacted our technical support team about this issue? ^[initials] (@Company7)

(386) guessing that is like talking to you on the phone. Gibberish from your end
Company7 @Company7
@user Blimey [name]. Is there something we can help you with? ^[initials] (@Company7)

(387) just got cold called by someone from Company1… Who then hung up on me… Awkward and bad customer service
Company1 @Company1
@user Hi [name], How strange! Did you get a number they called from so we can check if it was us? Let us know so we can take a look. (@Company1)

Interjections are placed in the initial position, opening the message, marking the spontaneous character of the reaction to the consumer's post, lending the response an emotional tone and marking its speech-like and informal character.

Interjections are used individually and as devices strengthening direct apology expressions. Though, as Lubecka (2000: 156) observes, they represent a maximally reduced form, the acts can perform the role of an expression of apology. The expressions indicate the author's emotional engagement – they do not carry any significant substantial content, but rather express an emotional stance of the representative (Kozicka-Borysowska 2009: 164). They express regret, compassion, dislike or surprise, and an unexpected character of the message received (Ogiermann 2009a: 124).

Interjections constitute a frequent component of face-to-face apologies among the speakers of English (Suszczyńska 1999: 1060). As Lubecka (2000: 156) observes, such emotionally toned apologies tend to be triggered by an informal character of the situation, emotional involvement of the offender and intimacy between the participants. The use of the acts in the analyzed data exemplifies a transfer of the conventions typical of everyday interaction, may be designed as a means of marking emotionality, expressiveness and spontaneity, and a means of reducing distance with consumers.

The use of empathy devices may seem unconventional, as these devices have not been typically associated with the context of customer encounters. A high number of empathy devices in the encounters may be triggered by the context. The acts reflect one of the main purposes and uses of social media, that is sharing emotions and feelings, the focus of interaction on building relationships. Such acts serve to empathize with the customer, to express the company's understanding of the negative feelings concerning the state of affairs, understanding of the consumer's anger and disappointment (cf. Lubecka 2000: 161, Tereszkiewicz, forthcoming-b), and, in this way, reflect the company's attentiveness and care.

Acts of empathy may be used to add a human touch to the interaction and to make the interaction more emotional and genuine. The acts may have a persuasive role as well (Kozicka-Borysowska 2009: 166). They may help the representatives to convince the consumers that they share their feelings and share the negative perception of the situation. However, the high occurrence and a repetitive nature of such acts lends them a formulaic character and diminishes their emotional force. It is here that their use as "a conventional device aimed at 'being nice' to the addressee rather than any spontaneous and unrestrained outburst of the heart" (Wierzbicka 1985: 163) is particularly clear.

The acts of empathy are rarely independent and in most cases are accompanied by other acts, mainly requests for further information or for further contact, suggesting further actions which customers may take to solve the problematic issue, and commissives, in which the providers offer support. Both acts can be considered as strategies helping the company to save face, show their customer care and thus redress damage done to the customer.

As the data show, a high number of IFIDs and empathy acts characterizes the interaction in the analyzed context. However, as indicated above, the use of the acts has a somewhat routine nature, as very often the same pattern of an apology is used repeatedly within a single profile. The analyzed corpus appears to confirm a highly conventionalized use of apologies in English (Ogiermann 2015: 4), the production of apologies without "much reflection" (ibid.).

By resorting to an apology, the representatives attend to the consumer's interactional goals and diminish the face threat posed by the infraction. At the same time, however, the apologies are face-threatening for the company as the representatives admit that the complainable took place. Still, it needs to be noted that the sheer expression of the act does not indicate that the company takes responsibility for the negative state of affairs (Ogiermann 2012: 31).

4.3.2.1.4. Acknowledgement of the complainable

Apology expressions also comprise acts in which companies acknowledge the infraction (cf. Tereszkiewicz 2017a, 2017b, forthcoming-b).

Table 15. Acknowledgements of the complainable

Type of act	Number
Acknowledgement	11
Form of act: simple	1
complex	10

Source: own work.

Acts in which the companies admit to the complainable are rare in the analyzed corpus, as only 11 instances of this act were identified. Nevertheless, the form in which the companies acknowledge that there occurred a fault in their services is worth noting due to a highly face-threatening potential of such acts. The acts in which companies admit to the complainable, however, though posing a threat to the company's image, may also help the company to improve their image as honest, as a company that takes responsibility for the faults in the service (Tereszkiewicz 2017b).

There occurred only one message in which the representative openly agrees with the customer and admits to a fault in the company's campaign:

(388) Route [product name] fails power socket guarantees :/
        Company8 @Company8
        @user I agree, we should not be advertising information, if we cannot guarantee this facility. We will get this investigate ^[initials] (@Company8)

In the majority of the cases, the representatives admit to the occurrence of the complainable but somewhat evasively. They do not name the nature of the complainable, but rather mitigate the acknowledgement (cf. Ogiermann 2009a), resorting to distancing strategies, devices downgrading the infraction, describing the complainable in vague and general terms (e.g. *some issues, some disruption*), and/or underline its singular occurrence (e.g. *today*), all of which is to diminish the face threat to the company's image and professional face posed by the acknowledgement. The acknowledgements have the form of personal statements, expressed in the second person plural forms, and an impersonal form of existential clauses:

(389) little bit annoyed I've only had this contract phone 3 days and no network error all day bit annoying as I need it for work :(
Company7 @Company7
@user Sorry about this [name]. We're aware of some issues. Have you tried a reboot? This is helping some customers. >[initials] (@Company7)

(390) Why is the [product name] from Alfreton to Norwich consistently late on a Friday? It's ridiculous!😡
Company12 @Company12
@user We are sorry for the inconvenience today, there has been some disruption today but i will pass on your comments. (@Company12)

Most of the acts of acknowledgement are phrased in the form of complex tweets. The acts tend to be accompanied by offers of repair promising a pending solution of the issue or further corrective actions. Phrasing the acknowledgement in this manner constitutes an image-saving strategy for the company.

4.3.2.1.5. Explanation

In response to customer complaints and negative opinions, the companies also resort to acts of explanation. The acts can be interpreted as evasive strategies of diminishing responsibility and reducing the offensiveness of the infraction. In these acts, the companies admit to the occurrence of the complainable and may accept a degree of responsibility for the infraction, but try to justify or account for it (cf. Trosborg and Shaw 1998: 75, Page 2014: 37). In the analyzed corpus, the companies justify the complainable by referring to external circumstances, events, as well as regulations or company's aims, or the influence of a third party (cf. Tereszkiewicz 2016, 2017b, forthcoming-b). The acts are designed to help the company to dissociate from guilt, make their actions more acceptable (Ogiermann 2009a) and their behaviour less offensive. As such, the acts constitute examples of face-saving strategies for the company. Similar strategies were identified also in Benoit's (1995, 1997) and Coombs' (1998) classifications.[59]

---

[59] The subchapter concerning the acts of explanation and denial, with modifications, and from a contrastive English-Polish perspective, has been planned as a separate publication (Tereszkiewicz, forthcoming-a).

Table 16. Explanations

Type of act	Number
Explanation	92
Form of act:	
simple	9
complex	83

Source: own work.

A number of sub-strategies among the acts can be singled out.

– Referral to regulations

Explanation and the denial of the righteousness of the complaint is expressed in the form of factual statements concerning the company's practices and terms of service. The companies evade blame and refute the accusation by informing customers of the practices in force in the company, pointing out that the company is acting in accordance with appropriate procedures, showing that the issues and situations which the consumers are complaining about comply with the regulations governing the company's operations. In this way, the company protects its image and indicates that no blame can be attributed to it. In these messages, the representatives indirectly criticize the customer for not being familiar with the terms (cf. Page 2014):

(391) so disappointed in your aftercare. [product name] not 1 year old and instead of replacing it you are sending out an engineer?!?!
Company9 @Company9
@user Repairs are offered to resolve the issue under warranty. Info about the warranty can be found at http://spr.ly/6016BRXXX ^[initials] (@Company9)

(392) I'm receiving this SPAM every day #pleaseSTOP
Company2 @Company2
@user These are automated as you are abroad. –[name] (@Company2)

(393) Doesn't help when you get to the train before allotted departure time&cant get on it yet it sits still for further 30 secs!!! Grrr
Company12 @Company12
@user We apologize for any frustration this has caused. Train doors are closed up to one minute before the departure >>time to ensure a safe despatch from the platform. << (@Company12)

(394) hi we just got off holiday but was disappointed going as we had to sit in different parts of bus now small children separated awful
Company8 @Company8
@user Apologies [name] but our seats are offered on a first come first served basis though we try to accommodate where possible ^[initials] (@Company8)

(395) Just bought these and very disappointed with the amount of [product name] bites in here. Not even half a bag :(
Company11 @Company11
@user Hi [name], they're sold by weight, not volume. If you feel undersold, contact us here: http://bit.ly/YCpXXX . :) (@Company11)

– Referral to limitations

The companies also excuse themselves by pointing out the limitations they are under including a lack of capacity, resources and/or a lack of formal ability or permission to act according to customers' suggestions (cf. Tereszkiewicz 2016). For example:

(396) No signal at all with @Company1 it's been over a week. I'm paying for a service I can't use! Keep being fobbed off Not happy at all & want a refund
Company1 @Company1
@user We understand your frustration [name], but we're unable to guarantee a fault free service. (@Company1)

(397) Highly annoying there's only one carriage working on [product name] @Company12 Lincoln to Leicester service. Ridiculously crowded, so had to get off.
Company12 @Company12
@user Hi [name], we appreciate how frustrating this must be, unfortunately we are limited in how many different >> services we can strengthen as we do not have an in-finite number of carriages available. << We are sorry about this, this has been reported already and will be fixed as soon as possible. (@Company12)

(398) ?637 to sit on the floor @Company12 sort it out, this is insane
Company12 @Company12
@user Hi [name], We are sorry that you have been unable to locate a seat this evening. We do try to strengthen >>our busier services but we do not have the availability with-in our fleet at the moment. << (@Company12)

– Underlining the company's aims and mission

The responses to negative opinions concerning the services comprise acts in which the companies underline their aims, mission and commitment. The repre-sentatives emphasize the company's practices directed at providing high quality services or confirm that actions to introduce the desired services or solutions have already been undertaken (cf. Tereszkiewicz 2016, 2017b). A frequent form of the act encompasses statements in the first person plural, present tense, indi-cating that the company is working on the advancement of the services and that appropriate actions to satisfy the consumers' needs are in progress. For instance:

(399) WHAT THE HELL IS THIS PATHETIC EXCUSE OF A CHOCOLATE BAR ITS TINY MULTIBAR CHOCOLATE SIZES ARE A JOKE
Company11 @Company11
@user Hi there, we've introduced a new smaller bar of some of our most popular [product name] bars which will be available widely in..1/3…grocery, convenience and discounter stores. You can still purchase your favourite [product name] bars in the traditional…2/3…sizes, these bars are just a way to increase variety in stores and add something new for consumers. :) 3/3 (@Company11)

(400) I kinda like @Company12 but why offer passengers chicken tikka to eat in such a con-fined space and stink the place out – #ihadtomoveseats
Company12 @Company12
@user Good afternoon [name]. We try and offer a wide variety of meals and snacks to ensure we cater to our customers >> needs. We are sorry you don't enjoy the smell. << (@Company12)

(401) First class windows are so overrated. Surprisingly it's only my window that seems to
be a mess.
Company12 @Company12
@user Hi [name], we are sorry for the window. They are cleaned on a regular basis but
with the damp conditions they soon become dirty. (@Company12)

In explaining the occurrence of the complainable, the representatives also
refer to a necessity of performing certain actions on a given occasion, a need to
conduct service works, to assist consumers in specific situations:

(402) Just noticed both my accounts are saying my balance is at ?0. Is there someone I can call
asap if I think its fraudulent??
Company4 @Company4
@user Hi, I'm [initials]. We're currently undertaking some essential system maintenance & this should be completed very (1/2) shortly. Please check again later & I'm
sorry for any inconvenience caused. Thanks. (2/2) ^[initials] (@Company4)

(403) you switch to a voyager for [product name] to Liverpool from Nottingham, everyone
is confused
Company12 @Company12
@user Hi [name]. We're using this train today to support our customers travelling to/
from the #GrandNational. (@Company12)

The form of the acts expresses a strong customer-orientation and emphasis
on diminishing the face threat posed to the company's image and constructing
a positive image of the company. The representatives underline that all the
activities are undertaken to the benefit of the customers, emphasize practice or
mission (Ho 2017b: 6), the commitment of the company to meet consumers'
preferences and highlight the value of their services. This can be seen in the
examples above, where the companies point to *trying and offering, strengthening*,
as well as *supporting customers, catering to customers' needs, adding something
new for consumers*. In the acts providing an explanation, the companies underline positive aspects concerning their services, their attempts to improve and
maintain a high quality of services (e.g. *to increase variety, a wide variety, on
a regular basis*), the company's effort to meet customers' demands (e.g. *we try/
we do try*) and point to external factors inhibiting the undertaken attempts
(cf. Tereszkiewicz 2016, 2017b). Strategies mitigating the threat to the company's
face also comprise vague statements concerning the complainable (e.g. *some
essential system maintenance*), underlining an isolated or temporary nature of
the infraction (e.g. *currently, today*). As such, the acts help the company to protect their image. The justifications tend to underline the positive aspects of the
regulations which are in force in the company and which have been introduced
to the benefit of the consumers.

A frequent use of *but* clauses in the acts (e.g. (396), (398), (401)) reflects the
contrast between the company's aims and the external factors inhibiting the achievement of these aims. By phrasing the justification in this manner, the companies

try to minimize the offence and undermine the need to take responsibility for it. The means mentioned above perform an important face-saving function for the company, downgrading the offence.

   – Referral to external factors and circumstances

Among the reasons justifying the occurrence of the complainable, the representatives point to external events and objective factors which contributed to the occurrence of the infraction. For instance:

(404) is your [product name] Stratford to Norwich bus running late? 😬#ColdAndWaiting
     Company8 @Company8
     @user Hello, sorry the coach gut stuck in traffic. It's currently in Mile End so shouldn't be too long now. ^[initials] (@Company8)

(405) been on hold for 20 mins now, service is shocking
     Company2 @Company2
     @user It can be busy at this time on the weekend many apologies. [name] (@Company2)

(406) 10-11 delivery booked, driver arrives 10:02 and won't wait 10 mins for me to get home "wait a reasonable time" disappointing
     Company10 @Company10
     @user Hi [name], our online service is quite popular and as such our drivers are very busy. Did you receive your order at all? [name] (@Company10)

The representatives explain the complainable by referring to different circumstances, such as traffic, the time (e.g. *the weekend*) or, finally, to the popularity of the company's service. By resorting to such justifications, the companies dissociate themselves from guilt and create a picture of the company as the party which is affected by external conditions.

   – Negation of company's involvement/shifting blame to third party

The representatives evade responsibility for the offence also in acts in which they negate their involvement in the complainable. In the responses, the authors openly point out that the infraction did not occur as a result of the company's activity, negate their contribution to the problems and explain the causes of the complainable, pointing to a third party as a primary agent causing the infraction. The acts are face-saving for the company, as they show that the company is not the source of the problems and thus is not to be blamed for the complainable:

(407) same here no reply.
     Company2 @Company2
     @user Good morning, we have been advised that this is an [product name] issue, therefore we aren't able to raise a complaint I'm afraid. ^[name] (@Company2)

(408) Could you warn people about WiFi assist in the text you send about nearing your data limit. I didn't realise it's switched on by default
     Company1 @Company1
     @user Hi there, we're sorry about that, as it's a phone feature it's not something included in our text. (@Company1)

The acts in the category of explanation are very often characterized by a high degree of formality, visible on the lexical and syntactic levels in the use of formal vocabulary items, nominalizations and impersonal structures, among others. These means lend the tweets a formal and institutional tone, and perform an important face-saving function for the company, designed to decrease an agentive role of the company in the infraction and to increase the level of objectivity of the statements.

A relatively high number of acts of explanation may result from the public context of the interaction and the need to undertake steps to protect the company's image. By resorting to explanations, as described above, the representatives rationalize the state of affairs complained upon by the consumers, point out the positive aspects of their activities and underline an impossibility of introducing desired solutions.

4.3.2.1.6. Denial of the complainable

The responses to customers' complaints and negative opinions involve acts in which the companies directly or indirectly deny the occurrence of the complainable, reject criticism and disagree with the opinion voiced by the consumers (cf. Tereszkiewicz 2015b, 2017b, forthcoming-b).

Acts rejecting complaints, analogically to the above-mentioned acts of explanation and evasion, have the aim of diminishing the threat posed to the complainee's face, who thus refutes the accusation concerning the complainable. The acts, however, while face-saving for the company, may pose a threat to the consumer, whose complaint is rejected or denied, and whose interactional goals are thus ignored. As Ho (2017b: 5) observes, a denial of an infraction poses a threat to the consumer's face since it devalues and diminishes the credibility of the reviewer. Consequently, the acts may damage companies' rapport with customers. Due to this face-threatening potential, such acts are considered risky and should be avoided in the context of customer encounters in order not to threaten future customer relations (Tereszkiewicz 2015b, 2017b). Still, they do occur in various channels of interaction and it is worth noting their form in the context of online customer encounters.

Acts in which companies refute the righteousness of the complaint comprise 24 messages, which shows that the strategy is rather infrequent.

Table 17. Denial of the complainable

Type of act	Number
Denial	24
Form of act: simple complex	2 22

Source: own work.

The following sub-categories of the acts of denial were identified in the analyzed material:

– Statement of unawareness of the complainable

In answer to complaints and opinions expressing a negative evaluation of their services and offers, representatives resort to acts in which they admit their unawareness or lack of knowledge concerning the problems reported by the consumers (cf. Tereszkiewicz 2016), which corresponds to Benoit's (1997) strategy of defeasibility, which, in this case, encompasses acts admitting to a lack of information about the problem.

The acts do not deny the complainable in a direct manner and do not explicitly negate the occurrence of the negative state of affairs. Rather, the authors indirectly refute the customer's claims by admitting to a lack of personal awareness of or knowledge about any issues. In this way, the representatives diminish the threat posed to the customer's face, do not exclude the possibility of the occurrence of the complainable on the customer's part, but rather point to a lack of confirmed information concerning the infraction. For instance:

(409) went to withdraw some money last night and card swallowed, look online said there was an error, same issue with me mate
Company4 @Company4
@user Ok. We're not aware of any issues. This may have been an ATM fault. Have you spoken with our PhoneBank team (01733 347 XXX)? ^[initials] (@Company4)

(410) is there a problem with the website safety certificate? I can't make a payment
Company8 @Company8
@user Hi [name], not that I'm aware of. Payments do seem to be going through fine. Maybe retry with a different browser. ^[initials] (@Company8)

(411) what's going on with the poor signal in Dorking Surrey at the moment? I have 5 bars usually but am down to no service or 1 bar at best
Company1 @Company1
@user Hi [name], we're unaware of any issues in the general area. Do these steps help: http://xxlin.kr/1PCaXXX (@Company1)

Acts in which the representatives admit to a lack of knowledge or an unawareness of the complainable constitute an indirect denial of responsibility (Ogiermann 2009b: 140). As Ogiermann (2009b) claims, the strategy does not exclude the author's involvement in the offence.

– Explicit denial of the complainable

The strategies also involve an explicit denial of the occurrence of the complainable, a strategy typical of the process of complaint and crisis management, also found in Benoit's (1995, 1997) and Coombs' (1998) classifications. In these acts, the representatives deny the existence of the negative state of affairs presented by the customers. The acts comprise personal statements in the first person plural or impersonal statements. The acts make frequent use of negation by means of *no*, the negative particle *not* negating the verb, as well as the determiner *any*, modifying the nouns *problem* or *issue*, and strengthening the negation of the complaint:

(412) Please fix your website. This is unacceptable. On the phone you told me that there is no issue with your website but there is.
Company8 @Company8
@user We haven't any online issues, what was it that you where struggling to do? (@Company8)

(413) trying to order a [product name] and keep getting "Error. An error occurred while processing your request."
Company9 @Company9
@user We haven't experienced any problems, [name]. Have you tried a refresh and trying again? Let us know how you get on! ^[initials] (@Company9)

(414) Can u check? Gprs network slow ammanford sa18 3hg tonight. Took me 6 mins to let u know
Company1 @Company1
@user Not good [name]:(No issues show at the moment. Do these steps help at all: http://xxlin.kr/1PCaXXX ? Let us know please. (@Company1)

The acts denying the complaint pose a threat to the customer's face. Therefore, in selected cases, representatives resort to strategies mitigating the denial and softening the tone of the message, for instance by means of modification (e.g. *known issues*). Mitigation is also achieved by means of accompanying acts of offers of help and requests for further contact and information. The aim of these strategies is to diminish the threat to the customer's face posed by the denial and enhance the image of the company as customer-oriented (Tereszkiewicz 2015b, forthcoming-b).

– Statement of the opposite

The denial of the complainable also assumes the form of an indirect denial and an implicit rejection of the customer's complaint in the shape of an assertion of the contrary to the consumer's claim.

In the example below, the representative explicitly states the contrary to the consumer's accusation:

(415) Bough a ?1 bar of milk choclate and its horrible Not what it used to be . Why was the reciepe changed ? Wont buy Company11 again
Company11 @Company11
@user Hi [name], we can assure you that our recipe remains unchanged & is the same [product name] recipe that we all know & love! (@Company11)

The statement is directly addressed to the consumer in an emphatic way by employing a performative verb (i.e. *we can assure you*). The denial of the consumer's claim is additionally underlined by an emphatic statement of fact concerning the quality of the product and consumers' preferences, additionally emphasized by the use of inclusive *we* (i.e. *we all know & love*).

More often, however, the representatives avoid making a statement of fact, but express an assumption as to the positive state of the services and a lack of any issues instead. For example:

(416) still no delivery! Yet I walked past a [company name] van nearby like 3 hours ago
Company6 @Company6
@user Hi [name], It looks like your parcel has now been delivered. Please can you confirm this for me. [name] (@Company6)

(417) is there a problem with the website safety certificate? I can't make a payment
Company8 @Company8
@user Hi [name], not that I'm aware of. Payments do seem to be going through fine. Maybe retry with a different browser. ^[initials] (@Company8)

(418) Got a 4G 7mbps #mobile #phone signal on the course here at #Bowood. Shame the #data signal in #Avoncliff is rubbish. #NextProject
Company1 @Company1
@user That's not great. The general area looks fine. Does it help if you follow these steps: http://bit.ly/1PCaXXX (@Company1)

(419) website down? Also phone mast that is faulty in WC1V area. Is this due to be fixed? My 3/4g connection here is rubbish
Company1 @Company1
@user That's not great, website seems OK this end though [name]. We're working on a mast near WC1V. What's your full post code please? (@Company1)

The acts frequently make use of mitigating strategies, softening the statement (e.g. *it looks like, it looks fine, everything looks to be working/seems OK, this end*). In this way, the authors diminish the threat posed to the customer's face, express uncertainty and do not exclude the possibility of the occurrence of the complainable on the customer's part.

   – Criticism of the consumer

Apart from the above-mentioned denials of the complainable, more personally-oriented acts in the form criticism of the consumer can be found in the analyzed corpus (cf. Tereszkiewicz 2017a, 2017b). These acts correspond to the strategy of attacking the accuser identified by both Benoit (1995, 1997) and Coombs (1998).

Such acts are infrequent (cf. Tereszkiewicz, forthcoming-b), however, with only individual instances of tweets belonging to this category. The representatives avoid strong criticism addressed to the consumers and tend to mitigate the words of disapproval. This approach can be noticed in the example below:

(420) Your signal is atrocious regardless of where i go.. #company2 #bumped
Company2 @Company2
@user Hi [name], you will need to contact us on 150 and speak to our technical support department, our lines open at 8AM. –[name]
user @user
@Company2 Shut Up [name]
Company2 @Company2
@user Bit harsh [name]. I'm only trying to help –[name] (@Company2)

The message constitutes an answer to a response provided by the company to the consumer's complaint in an earlier exchange. The user sends a general comment criticizing the services of the company, negatively evaluating the communication signal offered by the provider. In response to this comment, the representative advises the consumer to contact customer services regarding the reported problems, to which the user reacts with a highly face-threatening insult, directly addressed to the assistant, thus underlining a personalized tone of the message and increasing the impact and force of the insult. The representative replies with a message negatively evaluating the user and criticizing the consumer's behaviour. The criticism of the behaviour, however, which, in this case, is highly offensive, is diminished by a softening adverbial *a bit* and by an additional justification of the assistant's previous activity, i.e. providing assistance.

A low number of the above-mentioned acts in the corpus proves that even in the cases of aggressive or strongly insulting messages published by the consumers, the representatives try to maintain a customer-oriented approach to the interaction and refrain from entering into strong arguments with the consumers.

The structure of acts of explanation and denial of the complainable may be dictated by the context and the public character of the exchange. The form of many of the tweets reflects the need to apply strategies which would help the company to protect the customer's face and diminish the threat to the consumer's face posed by the rejection. This approach is reflected in a low occurrence of the strategies, in their indirect, elaborate form, in the use of mitigation devices and accompanying acts. The majority of the messages are accompanied by other speech acts with a different illocutionary force, aimed at toning down the force of the explanation or denial. Among the accompanying acts, apologies, empathy devices, requests for information and recommendations suggesting solutions to the problem are the most frequent (cf. Tereszkiewicz 2015b). These acts indicate a greater politeness, distance and an institutional tone of the interaction.

Nevertheless, a lack of supportive acts diminishing the force of the denial/evasion may also be meaningful, as an act composed solely of a straightforward rejection of the complaint increases the force of the statement and underlines the company's stance.

4.3.2.1.7. Offers of help and repair

Offers of help and repair comprise responses in which the representatives offer assistance, express readiness to help the consumer, promise to undertake corrective actions, as well as confirm and assure consumers that appropriate corrective steps to resolve the complainable have already been undertaken (cf. Tereszkiewicz 2017b, forthcoming-b).

As Ogiermann (2009a) observes, "offers of repair assume responsibility for compensating for the offence but not for committing it" (Ogiermann 2009a: 213). The company may emphasize agentive involvement in offering repair and undertaking corrective measures actively, rather than accept the blame (cf. Page

2014: 38). In this way, the company may project its image as attentive and willing to assist, without accepting responsibility for the infraction.

The acts are to assure the customer of pending high quality assistance. The strategy may serve to diminish the face threat to the customer's face caused by the infraction and placate the consumer (Page 2014: 38, Tereszkiewicz 2017b). More importantly, the act may also fulfil a face-redressive potential for the company and create its image as ready and willing to help. It is this function of the act that seems to prevail in the analyzed interaction.

Offers of help and repair constitute accompanying acts to the acts of requests, apologies as well as thanks, but may also represent individual acts, that is the main compositional unit of the tweet. The use of this act as an individual component of the message, however, proved exceptionally rare.

Table 18. Offers of help and repair

Type of act	Number
Offer of help and repair	262
Form of act: simple complex	14 248

Source: own work.

Acts offering help and repair comprise the following types of strategies:
– Conventional declaration of help – *How can I help you?*

The offers of help in the form of the question *How can I help you?* constitute a conversational routine eliciting the customer's request, equivalent to the more formal question *What can I do for you?*, which is frequently used in face-to-face or telephone encounters and has been identified as a genre marker of customer encounters (Biber and Conrad 2009, Friginal 2009).

In the analyzed corpus, only individual instances of the offer of help in the form of a conventional question were observed. The function of the act also proved different if compared with other channels of interaction. Unlike in other service encounters, the question is used not to initiate an exchange with the consumer, but rather in response to the message posted to the company's profile by the consumer (Tereszkiewicz 2015b). The question is usually used as a routine answer to vague questions or comments on the company's services expressed by the consumers, as exemplified below:

(421) your service is ridiculously shit
Company6 @Company6
@user Hi [name]. Is there anything I can help you with? [name] (@Company6)

(422) just got on train in London. Couldn't you find one with an older interior? Or one less clean? French train this morning? Lovely.
Company12 @Company12
@user Hi [name]. Is there anything we can help with? (@Company12)

(423) guessing that is like talking to you on the phone. Gibberish from your end
Company7 @Company7
@user Blimey [name]. Is there something we can help you with? ^[initials] (@Company7)

The use of this act may be dictated by the context. The function of the offer of help may be to demonstrate attentiveness to the consumer. Due to the anonymity of the medium, reduced cues and the public character of the interaction, a quick reaction on the part of the company, expressing interest and offering assistance may help to enhance the company's reputation as customer-friendly and customer-oriented (Tereszkiewicz 2015b).
  – Promises of reporting the complainable further to appropriate departments of the company
Commissive acts comprise offers by the representatives to forward the consumer's complaint to an appropriate department of the company. The use of such acts, as Page (2014: 39) observes, may be dictated by a lack of formal ability of the representative to undertake appropriate measures. For example:

(424) do you realise how loud the speakers are in Derby station, isn't great for some of us who have tinitus, far too loud
Company12 @Company12
@user I will get this reported immediately. Thank you for making us aware. (@Company12)

(425) tracking number: 8XT210512143AXXX
Company6 @Company6
@user Thanks [name]. I'm going to raise this with the depot now and see what's going on. I'll get back to you asap. [name] (@Company6)

(426) that's there first time in 15 years of working in banks that I've heard of anyone being refused to pay money into an account!
Company4 @Company4
@user I'm terribly sorry to hear about your experience. I'll certainly ensure your comments are recorded for feedback. ^[initials] (@Company4)

  – Offers and promises of investigating and solving the complainable by the company
In the acts, most of which constitute acts accompanying requests for contact and information, the representatives promise to undertake appropriate corrective actions to satisfy the consumer's expectations or to investigate and verify the occurrence of the infraction. The acts are expressed in the first person plural or singular form of the verb:

(427) [product name] service from Leicester to London StP. Coach C windows are awful--both sides.
Company12 @Company12
@user Thanks for letting us know [name]. We understand this is not the view you were hoping for. This train will be cleaned tonight. (@Company12)

(428) from the cafe wifi I'm using I can't take that with me
Company7 @Company7
@user Okay, I assure you we will get this sorted out as quick as we can ^[initials] (@Company7)

(429) my rearranged delivery didn't turn up!
Company6 @Company6
@user Hey [name], I'd be happy to get this looked into for you. Please could you DM the tracking information over and drop me (@Company6)

(430) I wouldn't mind so much if they sent as emails, but he received these messages as texts. So I've been charged for messages being sent
Company1 @Company1
@user Hi [name], we would love to take a look at this for you, can we chat here http://bit.ly/9W4XXX (@Company1)

Instances of acts in which companies offer consumers immediate compensation in the form of a refund or other tangible goods also occur in the corpus, yet are infrequent (4 instances), in contrast to Page's (2014: 39) observations. For example:

(431) I bought them from the Company10 local on Askew Road, London
Company10 @Company10
@user Thanks, DM us your Nectar number and we'll get some points added as an apology. [name] (@Company10)

– Promises of third-person commitment

These messages comprise acts in which the representatives promise assistance provided by a third party responsible for particular issues:

(432) no damage to adapter or cable
Company9 @Company9
@user We would recommend visiting one of our face to face stores with both your phone and charger, [name]: http://spr.ly/6017BRXXX 1/2 Our tech guys can take a closer look at what the problem seems to be. Hope this helps. 2/2 ^[initials] (@Company9)

(433) I was told yesterday that there was no work being carried out in my area and the lines fine. Could've checked this last wk!
Company7 @Company7
@user Sorry about that [name]. I'm confident our engineer will get this sorted out for you ^[initials] (@Company7)

(434) no network issues! Was all over edinburgh last night & still the same. Followed all your troubleshooting and still no service!
Company2 @Company2
@user Ok, please give our Tech team a call and they will be happy to look into this for you – http://xx.co.uk/help/get-in-touch … ^[name] (@Company2)

– A confirmation of undertaken repair

Remedial acts also comprise messages in which the representatives assure consumers that appropriate actions to solve the infraction have already been undertaken (Tereszkiewicz, forthcoming-b). The authors confirm that the complaint is being investigated, that it has been forwarded to an appropriate department or that corrective steps to solve the issues have been implemented:

(435) Hi [name] thanks for the reply. tracking details: JD0002253166773XXX thanks [name] #[name]Cares
Company6 @Company6
@user Hi [name]. So I've raised this with our depot and currently waiting for a response. We'll get back to you asap. [name] (@Company6)

(436) Shocking service! 1 week so far without access to my debit card and now I have to wait until Monday for further help.
Company4 @Company4
@user Hi, I'm [initials]. Apologies for this. I can confirm your query has been passed to your complaint handler & they'll contact you ASAP. (@Company4)

(437) Dear @Company7 This had better be fixed by 7. 😠
Company7 @Company7
@user Apologies for the issue. The team are working to resolve ASAP. See here https://xxx.in/QXXX for updates. [initials] (@Company7)

Offers of help and repair tend to be expressed both in the first and third person plural and in the first person singular, which indicates an institutional or individual identity of the representative. The use of the first person singular increases the directness and personalization of the message, underlines a personal responsibility to attend to the customer and thus individualizes the commitment. The use of modal verbs and adjectives, such as *will, can, able to* is frequent, serving as means which underline willingness and readiness to undertake assistance and the ability to help to solve the customer's issues. Moreover, expressions emphasizing the dedication to the customer, such as *we'd love to, we'd like to, we'd be happy to* tend to be used, increasing the illocutionary force of the act. The acts also make frequent use of stance verbs and adjectives: *I can confirm, I assure you, I am confident,* which emphasize the commitment and the belief that the infraction will be dealt with. Similarly, the verbs used in the acts imply positive actions of *helping, sorting, resolving, looking into, verifying* the issues and *assisting* customers. In most of the acts, further devices strengthening the illocutionary force of the messages can be seen, such as emphatic adverbials, e.g. *definitely, just, immediately, ASAP, as quick as we can, always, more than happy.* A high number of *get*-passive and causative *have* in the acts can also be noticed. These forms may underline the positive effect of the action, a positive outcome of the remedial service and the power and authority of the representative to deal with the infraction and introduce a desired state of affairs. The acts make the statement more dynamic as well, creating an image of a swift action to be undertaken following consumers' complaints, which increases the illocutionary force of the commitment. What most of the offers of help also have in common is the use of direct references to the customers (e.g. *for you*), which shows them as beneficiaries of the company's actions. These forms reflect a customer-oriented approach, intensify the individualization of the messages and the concern for the customer, which is to enhance rapport and trust (Tereszkiewicz 2017b). The form of the reference to the complainable as *this, it* or as *your query, your comments* may be seen as a face-saving strategy for the company, in which they avoid naming the infraction, as has already been pointed out.

The acts seem to have a rather evasive character. They promise assistance, but as such do not offer the customer any specific details as to the resumption of the services and do not guarantee that the complaint will actually be managed successfully and to the benefit of the consumer. Moreover, due to their repetitive nature, the acts seem to have acquired a rather formulaic and ritual character.

4.3.2.1.8. Appreciation: *thanks*

The strategies employed by companies in reaction to consumers' complaints also comprise thanks (cf. Tereszkiewicz 2015b, forthcoming-b).

Table 19. Thanks

Type of act	Number
Thanks	41
Form of act: simple complex	6 35

Source: own work.

According to Trosborg and Shaw (1998: 79), thanks are a significant component of a company's communication with customers, a component especially important in response to customer complaints. By expressing thanks, the company shows that customer feedback, be it positive or negative, is welcome and is appreciated (Tereszkiewicz 2015b).

Showing appreciation may be more important online due to the public nature of the interaction. Uttering thanks may help the companies to show openly that they value customers' opinions and are grateful for pointing out any faults in the services. In the analyzed context, however, the act of thanks used in response to negative feedback may be interpreted as an evasive strategy (cf. Tereszkiewicz 2016). The representatives express thanks for the messages sent by the consumers, but do not express regret for the reported issues and do not take the blame for the complainable. The complaint is referred to in a vague way as *this, information, idea*, which covers up the negative value of the customer's feedback. The acts indicate that the company was not aware of the issues and, in this way, the thanks for the negative comments may constitute a face-saving strategy for the company:

(438) So @Company6 have lost my order, ?25 Mother's Day flowers are dying god knows where. Think I deserve my money back frankly.
Company6 @Company6
@user Thanks for bringing this to our attention [name]. Send over your tracking details & I'll investigate this for you. [name] (@Company6)

(439) delivered next day (another day lost to waiting). Driver didn't even apologize which dismayed us. No ownership of mistakes.
Company6 @Company6
@user Thankyou for this information, I'll get this passed back to the drivers manager for you – could you also confirm whether 1/2 your parcel contents were all intact? Thanks, [name] 2/2/ (@Company6)

The messages protect the company's professional face as they underline the importance attached to consumers' feedback and show that the company is actively involved in the interaction with consumers. The evasive tone of the messages may be diminished by accompanying acts, such as acts offering help or requests for further information/contact.

4.3.2.2. Complaint response speech act sets

Tweets constituting a response to consumers' complaints, as in the case of positive evaluation, tend to have the form of complex tweets, speech act clusters, i.e. tweets comprising different compositional units. In the analyzed collection of messages, 78 percent of the tweets have the form of complex acts. The representatives, analogically to what has been observed in telephone encounters "can perform several actions while providing the response" (Varcasia 2013: 116). The composition of the response, the patterns of incrementing and extending the response, the merger of various acts within a single tweet in a significant way influences the illocutionary force of the response and its effect on the consumer. As the length of a single tweet is limited, it was considered interesting to investigate the most frequent configuration patterns of the messages, i.e. to review how responses are packaged and how the pattern influences the expressive function of the message.

Multiple speech act tweets represent different levels of complexity, involving several speech acts, apart from additional components in the form of conventional politeness units opening and closing the message, such as greetings and thanks. An interplay and a mutual influence on the illocutionary force of the respective accompanying acts can be observed.

In the case of complaint management responses, a more frequent occurrence of repetitive combinations of speech acts was observed in the data. The most frequent patterns found in the answers to consumer complaints comprise the following sequences (cf. Tereszkiewicz, forthcoming-b):

- a request for information/contact or action accompanied by an offer of help and repair
  - request for information/contact/action + offer of help and repair (78 instances)
- an apology accompanied by a request for information/contact or action and/or by an offer of help and repair
  - apology + request for information/contact/action (154 instances)
  - apology + request for information/contact/action + offer of help and repair (82 instances)
  - apology + offer of help and repair (19 instances)
- an apology accompanied by an acknowledgement and an offer of help and repair
  - apology + acknowledgement + offer of help and repair + request for information/contact/action (4 instances)
- an explanation accompanied by a request for information/contact/action and/or an offer of help and repair
  - explanation + request for information/contact/action (19 instances)
  - explanation + offer of help and repair (5 instances)
- an apology accompanied by an explanation, by a request for information/ contact or action and/or an offer of help and repair
  - apology + explanation + request for information/contact/action (16 instances)
  - apology + explanation (8 instances)
  - apology + explanation + request for information/contact/action + offer of help and repair (5 instances)
- a denial of the complainable accompanied by a request for further information/contact or action
  - denial + request for information/contact/action (8 instances)
- acts of appreciation and thanks for feedback incremented by an offer of help and repair or a request for information/contact/action
  - thanks + request for information/contact/action (16 instances)
  - thanks + request for information/contact/action + offer of help and repair (12 instances)
  - thanks + offer of help and repair (5 instances).

As can be seen from the speech act sets in the tweets, the use of requests for information or action in the complex tweets is particularly frequent. It appears to constitute a clear strategy aimed at maintaining the interaction, creating an impression of attentiveness and approachability. By means of these acts, the company attends to the consumer's interactional goals. The acts reflect the company's wish to reduce the negative feelings arising among the consumers due to the occurring infraction.

It is worth noting that, unlike interaction in other channels, where requests for information on the complainable and repair sequences tend to be interspersed by the consumer's explanations, in the messages on Twitter, the sequences with requests for action in the function of advice on corrective steps often follow requests for information directly. For example:

> (440) @user Sorry to hear this [name] :(What were you charged for? You can view your bill here: http://bit.ly/9y3XXX (@Company1)

The offer of help and repair constitutes another frequently used speech act accompanying other acts in the responses. Moreover, the offers are usually placed finally, following acts with a different illocutionary force, such as apologies or requests. Closing the message with this compositional unit may be designed as a strategy aiming to leave the customer with the feeling that the company controls and will successfully manage the reported situation, with the conviction of the company's attentiveness and focus on providing immediate assistance.

A relatively frequent cluster in both corpora comprises a combination of both of the above-mentioned types of acts, i.e. a request for information/contact or action and an offer of help and repair. The offer of help and repair aligned with a request may be designed to decrease the illocutionary force of the request (Page 2014). A high number of such tweets indicates that the degree of attentiveness and the speed of reaction are the most vital dimensions in the handling of customer complaints in online interaction. Companies place the emphasis on a quick reaction to the complaint, attending to the customer and redressing the positive state of affairs. These dimensions seem to play such a vital role in the online context due to the public form of the interaction and a higher risk of potential damage to the corporate image (Tereszkiewicz, forthcoming-b).

The most frequent pattern found in complex speech acts, however, includes a response including three turn constructional units apart from greetings and signatures, i.e. an expression of apology, direct or indirect, accompanied by a request for contact/information and/or action and an offer of help and repair. The sequence reflects an approach which may be referred to as a "three-step assistance," comprising the most significant steps taken in the context of complaint management, i.e. expressing attention to the consumer, apologizing, expressing regret, showing interest and promising to solve the complainable. The acts express customer-orientation, attention to the customer's face, emphasis on the company's responsiveness. Acts in which the companies apologize, offer assistance, request further information, suggest actions which the consumers might undertake to solve problems and offers of help and repair confirming that appropriate actions to solve the complainable will be or have been undertaken may decrease the face threat posed to the company's and/or the consumer's face by the conflicting situation and may underline customer-orientation of the company and its wish to attend to the consumer (Page 2014). Requests and offers accompanying apologies, as Page (2014) observes, represent an expression of corrective behaviour on the part of the company. The acts constitute strategies allowing the company to show attentiveness and readiness to help the consumer, and thus to restore the image of the company impaired by the occurring complainable. The patterning of the acts reflects the company's wish to reduce the negative feelings arising among the consumers due to the occurring infractions. A repetitive use of this pattern of apology speech act sequencing can be seen across the corpus. This complex unit appears to have become a standard, formulaic sequence, a conventionalized response in the context of troubleshooting.

Complex speech acts of this shape may be regarded as politeness routines, i.e. sets of speech acts used repeatedly to save the company's face and enhance customer care, to help the company to manage their relationship with the customer (Kerbrat-Orecchioni 2006: 81). However, due to the brevity of the acts within the tweet, they appear to represent examples of telegraphic politeness. The reader may have the feeling of being given a set of corporate politeness formulas. The formulaic and institutionalized tone of the messages can be further exemplified in the messages below:

(441) @user That isn't what we like to hear [name] :(Could you DM us some more info about what's happened exactly please? We'd like to help. (@Company1)

(442) @user I appreciate your frustration. I hope you get this sorted. If there's any further issues, please let us know. ^[initials] (@Company4)

It is worth noting the function of the apology formulas as components of complex acts in the analyzed context. The apology (e.g. *apologies for this/ sorry to hear this*) appears to perform the role of a politeness marker, a discourse marker in the form of a formulaic politeness chunk (Wray 2002). The act seems to have become lexicalized and appears to have lost its primary expressive function and content. It can be noticed that the act is devoid of real involvement of the author, is rarely supported by an admission of guilt or assumption of blame. The apology is typically expressed in the initial part of the message and functions as an opening unit – this sequencing pattern strengthens the act of apology and makes it more conspicuous as a component which signals the reception of the message, initiates interaction and introduces further acts (Tereszkiewicz, forthcoming-b). The act fulfils its role as a preferred response to an act of complaint and as such may be expected by the consumer. It functions as a formulaic act, a routine, by means of which the company fulfils its institutional role and customer care requirements (cf. Lubecka 2000: 143). It appears to perform the function of showing attention and soothing the consumer. In the analyzed context, the acts may clearly be interpreted as "formalised behavioural codes" (Deutschmann 2003: 32) which serve as expressions used to "fulfil social conventions rather than expressions of concern for the hearer's damaged face" (Ogiermann 2009a: 235).

A combination of expressions of empathy with direct apologies and expressions of regret (41 instances) also deserves mentioning. This patterning can be exemplified in the following response:

> (443) @user Oh dear, sorry about that [name]! Please call our team on 0800 818XXX & they'll be able to help. :) (@Company11)

The use of an empathy device increases the illocutionary force of the apology, enhances its emotive tone, spontaneity and additionally personalizes the act. It may be designed to decrease the institutional and formulaic tone of the following conventional apology.

Previous research on apology expressions has proved that the use of intensifiers is typical for the British (Marquez Reiter 2000: 179-180). Some scholars consider the use of intensified apologies as "unmarked routine" (Ferguson 1981: 27) due to their commonality in everyday interaction, lack of "substantial" semantic content and their function as a means of phatic communion. The use of intensifiers in the analyzed corpus may reflect the convention, but it may be additionally influenced by the context, the lack of nonverbal communication and the need to express the author's intention in the textual layer only. It may constitute a persuasive component dictated by a wish to make the apology more conspicuous. The intensifiers help the representatives to empathize with the customer and show that they perceive the issues reported by the customers as regrettable (Ogiermann 2009a: 121). It shows greater attention given to customer care and attendance to the customer's face. The means may help to intensify the face-redressive potential of the message.

Acts of acknowledgement accompanying direct apologies function as external intensifiers of the apology. The accompanying acts promising corrective actions, as well as requests for further information on the customer's situation in complex tweets featuring these components constitute face-supportive strategies for the companies, by means of which they may both diminish the threat to their face posed by the complainable and attend to the consumer.

It is worth noting the use of complex acts involving acts explaining the complainable, evading or denying responsibility for the offence. In the case of these acts, the use of accompanying strategies seems to be particularly consequential. As mentioned before, any rejection of a complaint may be face-threatening for the consumer, but it may also significantly impair the company's image. In the analyzed corpus, the majority of the messages are accompanied by other speech acts, aimed at either increasing or diminishing the force of the explanation or denial.

Tweets featuring a rejection of the complainable tend to comprise an explanation or denial of a complaint aligned with an apology. Since an apology is a face-threatening act for the author, adding a justification and providing a reason for the occurring infraction or denying the occurrence of the infraction may constitute a strategy diminishing the face threat to the company's face posed by the consumer's complaint. The explanation accompanying an expression of apology downgrades the apology and minimizes the offence, and is face-saving for the speaker (ibid.: 211). Complex acts comprising an apology, explanation or denial of the complainable thus reflect a company's desire to diminish the threat to both its own image and to the consumer's face. By expressing an apology, the company attends to the consumer's interactional needs, while the rejection is to diminish the threat posed to the company's face.

In most cases, acts of evasion and denial are further expanded to include acts of offers of help and repair and inquiries in the form of requests for action and further contact/information/action. The aim of these strategies is to soften the denial/evasion, diminish the threat to the customer's face posed by the rejection, indicate willingness to solve customers' problems, underline attendance to the consumer and enhance the image of the company as customer-oriented (cf. Tereszkiewicz 2015b, forthcoming-a).

Acts of denial, however, also tend to be accompanied by a confirmation of a positive state of affairs, which increases the illocutionary force of the rejection and constitutes a face-saving device for the company. An addition of an offer of help and repair, a suggestion on actions to resolve the consumer's problem and/or request further contact may in this case be designed to lower the face threat to the consumer's face.

Finally, thanks in response to customer complaints are not typically used as individual acts, but tend to be extended to include offers of help and repair and requests for further details concerning the complainable, which would allow the company to proceed with corrective actions. The accompanying act assuring the customer of pending remedial steps may help the company to save its image and show attentiveness to the reported issues, and thus help to fulfil the consumer's interactional goals (Tereszkiewicz 2015b).

Complex tweets exemplify the process of "speech act packaging," where different speech acts are combined in a single tweet. The authors combine a greeting, identification, the main response and a closing act in a single response. The turns resemble complex formulae, "customer care politeness sets," which constitute a merger of speech acts with the aim of fulfilling a number of customer care functions in a single message. A tendency towards extending responses by British speakers has also been observed in telephone customer encounters (Varcasia 2013: 66). However, the sequential structuring and speech act packaging on Twitter seems to be more scripted and pre-planned than in telephone encounters. Complex tweets may be interpreted as generic responses

(Zhang and Vásquez 2014). The representatives to a great extent follow "shared schemas" (Varcasia 2013: 138), i.e. response patterns used regardless of the consumer's message.

A preference for the use of an extended form of the tweets may result from the context and mediated character of the interaction. The factors which may contribute to the preference of such tweets comprise the public nature of the interaction, anonymity of the users, disrupted turn-taking, lack of nonverbal cues, as well as the number of messages to which the representatives have to attend and the need to implement immediate measures to maintain or protect the company's image. The public character of the interaction underlines the need for a customer-friendly attitude and the need to prove attentiveness and willingness to cater for customers' needs. The company has limited control over the interaction and consumer's feedback, which increases the need to apply strategies which would diminish a public threat to the company and a potential loss of other consumers. Since the interaction may not necessarily be continued by the consumers, the representatives try to do all the face-work in a single message. Therefore, every tweet is designed to constitute a complete, closed entity. The use of different speech acts in the tweet may increase the atmosphere of politeness and highlight a customer-oriented approach of the company, which may be a strategy to protect the consumer's and the company's face. Moreover, unlike in face-to-face or telephone encounters, where the representatives can focus on a single interlocutor, in the context of Twitter, the brand representative usually has to attend to numerous incoming tweets. The use of a template in this situation facilitates the task of responding to the messages and improves the speed and efficiency of review management (Zhang and Vásquez 2014: 62). By providing extended answers and trying to satisfy consumer's interactional goals in a single tweet, the companies may avoid further queries from a specific customer. The expansion of the main act may contribute to the reception and acceptance of the response by the consumer, may convince the customer of attentiveness and customer care, and may help to avoid further disappointment with the company's services.

4.3.2.3. Complaint management closing

In the case of successful complaint management, customers may continue interaction by uttering tweets confirming a solution of the problems reported beforehand and/or expressing thanks and a positive evaluation of the company's services. The companies reply to such tweets with messages comprising expressive acts, wishes and offers of further assistance. The acts often function as units finalizing the interaction with the customer.

Table 20. Complaint handling closing acts

Type of act	Number
Appreciation: expression of positive feelings	45
Offer of future assistance	45
Wishes	18
Appreciation: thanks	5
Form of the act: simple	16
complex	62

Source: own work.

The turn constructional units of such acts comprise expressive acts, in which the representatives share the customer's positive feelings, and/or offers of future commitment in the form of directives encouraging the customer to contact the company in the case of future queries or problems. These two acts are often juxtaposed, which significantly increases the customer-orientation of the message and the company's aim towards enhancing interactional closeness:

(444) whatever it was seems to have been fixed now so hopefully will be no more issues
Company7 @Company7
@user Brilliant stuff! Let me know if you need anything further. [initials] (@Company7)

(445) debit card. Just spoke to a friendly lady who's sorted it all out for me. Thanks
Company4 @Company4
@user I'm happy to hear it has been sorted. If you need anything else, feel free to tweet. Take care & have a nice day. ^[initials] (@Company4)

The expression of emotions may be extended in the form of a complement or separate clause to include a description of the positively evaluated service or offer. A confirmation of a positive solution of a consumer's problem has a significant image-enhancing function for the company.

Nevertheless, the messages reflect a high degree of formulaicity. A repetitive and accumulated use of devices strengthening the illocutionary force of the messages as well as of emphatic structures is to be noticed, comprising emphatic auxiliary *do*, adverbs, such as *very, very best, ever*, pronouns, e.g. *anything else*:

(446) great, thanks for your response.
Company7 @Company7
@user Always here if you need our help :) [initials] (@Company7)

(447) makes perfect sense! Never noticed it before but then I try to avoid doing the accounts on Sundays! Thanks for the reply.
Company5 @Company5
@user Should you require any further assistance then do let us know, [name]. ^[initials] (@Company5)

(448) yes he's sending for a new NI number letter. Thanks for your quick response, much
appreciated.
Company5 @Company5
@user No problem, if you ever need any assistance we're always here. ^[initials]
(@Company5)

(449) thanks for the help
Company4 @Company4
@user You're most welcome. Please feel free to tweet us if you need help with anything
else. Enjoy your weekend & take care. ^[initials] (@Company4)

The offers of future assistance constitute the most frequent closing sequence.
Due to their repetitiveness and formulaic tone, the acts exemplify markers of
routine corporate online politeness. Though formulaic, however, the acts are
a sign of interactional cooperation and commitment to the customer and significantly enhance the level of politeness in the interaction. It is worth noting
that this atmosphere of politeness tends to be co-constructed by the customers,
who contribute to it by expressing thanks for the help provided earlier. The acts
closing the complaint management process have a clear function of creating
a positive atmosphere and triggering positive associations with the company
and its customer care.

Chapter 5. Selected politeness
and lexicogrammatical properties
of the tweets

5.1. Methods

The following chapter is devoted to the analysis of selected politeness acts and lexicogrammatical properties of the messages posted by the consumers and the companies. The investigation concerns forms of address and self-identification used in the interaction, as well as the opening and closing units in the tweets. The analysis also includes the presence of lexicogrammatical properties, such as informal and non-standard language items, language mistakes and the use of such components as emoticons, hashtags and links. The main focus is placed on the presence of these components in companies' tweets. The occurrence of the features in consumers' messages has been provided for additional illustration.

In the course of the analysis, the presence of greetings, self-identification and thanks in the tweets was identified, as well as the forms of address used in the messages. The analysis was performed with reference to the previous research on the structure of customer encounters, on openings and closings in customer encounters in particular (Aston (ed.) 1988, Schegloff 1968, 2007, Cameron 2000b, Kerbrat-Orecchioni 2005, Marquez Reiter 2008, 2009, Biber and Conrad 2009, Friginal 2009, Félix-Brasdefer 2015). In addition, the number of tweets with informal syntactic and lexical items, non-standard language and language mistakes was counted. Tweets were examined for the presence of grammatical devices typical of the casual style of communication (cf. Joos 1959)[60] and for the use of lexical items and spelling practices identified in previous studies as characteristic of online interaction, i.e. the presence of informal expressions, slang, elliptical structures, as well as non-standard language and language mistakes (ibid., Crystal 2006, Baron 2008, Page 2012, Zappavigna 2012, Dąbrowska 2013, Tagg 2015). The use of emoticons, hashtags and links was investigated as well.

The material for the analysis below encompasses consumers' and companies' tweets posted in the context of positive evaluation and complaint management. The material comprises the corpus introduced in the previous chapter, i.e. the

---

[60] Joos (1959) classifies style into five levels: intimate – used in the context of close relationships between the participants of a communicative situation, casual – used in the interaction among friends, consultative – neutral and used in semi-formal situations, in interactions with strangers, formal – applied in formal situations, characterized by limited amount of shared background knowledge among the participants, and frozen – typical of very formal settings, procedural and routine situations, such as church rituals.

total number of 2014 messages, with 1020 companies' messages and 994 consumers' tweets.

The examination of the above-mentioned properties was designed to verify the initial hypothesis concerning the reduction of conventional politeness and the use of the casual style in companies' tweets.

5.2. Conventional politeness acts: openings and closings, forms of address and self-identification in the tweets

The investigation of opening and closing units as well as forms of address and self-identification used in companies' tweets was included in the analysis, since, as indicated before, these components fulfil an important function in establishing the relationship between the interactants.

5.2.1. Address forms

Address forms, as mentioned before, play a significant role in managing social relationships (Clyne et al. 2009). Depending on the context, terms of address may serve various functions, i.e. to attract attention, maintain contact with the addressee, establish recipiency, demonstrate concern, express stance (Lerner 2003, Rendle-Short 2007) and to "determine interpersonal space" (Rendle-Short 2007: 1505). The choice of the form of address establishes the tone of interaction and the relation between the speakers as egalitarian or hierarchical. Since English does not distinguish the T- and V- forms of address, and pronouns are not used to mark hierarchical relations, it is usually personal names and titles that serve as markers of power and solidarity (Jakubowska 1999: 52). Titles *Sir, Madam, Miss* are used between partners who do not know each other or in unequal relationships by a person of a lower status to a person of a higher status. Titles also tend to be used where speakers perform face-threatening acts, as well as in greetings and attention gainers (ibid.: 45).

In service relationships in traditional encounters, neutral and respectful titles: *Sir, Madam, Miss* and the pronominal *you* occur the most frequently. Family names are used when there is a greater degree of familiarity between the customer and the provider. First names used to address customers occur especially in interaction in local shops, where anonymity tends to be reduced and relationships may become more personal or friendly (Lubecka 1993: 104-106). The use of first names in addressing customers has also been observed in telephone service encounters (Friginal 2009).

In the analyzed material, there is not much diversification as far as address forms are concerned (cf. Tereszkiewicz 2015b). The most frequent address terms involve pronominal and first name forms of address. Forms *Sir*, *Madam* or *Miss* were not identified in the corpus. In the majority of the cases, the companies and the consumers resort to the use of pronominal address terms encompassing the second person pronouns *you*, *your*. For example:

> (1) why have you made your choc [product name] bites smaller? They're only bitesize if your customer is an earwig
> Company10 @Company10
> @user Sorry [name], which store did you buy these from? Can you send me a pic of the barcode? [name] (@Company10)

Among other forms of address, the use of nominal forms encompassing the company's name and first name terms was identified in the material.

Table 21. Nominal address forms

	Company tweets	Consumer tweets
Form of address	Number	Number
First name	400	3
Company's name	-	12

Source: own work.

Nominal address forms occurring in consumers' tweets encompass the use of the company's name. In most cases, the name is used as part of a greeting (as in (2) and (3)) or in imperative acts directly addressed to the company (e.g. (4)):

> (2) Hi @Company5 I've been waiting since Wednesday for my replacement card and I've still received nothing and am at my credit card limit (@Company5)

> (3) There's a hole in my [product name] dear @Company11 dear @Company11... (@Company11)

> (4) First cheap instant coffee in bolognese, then horseradish in macaroni, now desiccated coconut in chili. Go home @Company10, you're drunk. (@Company10)

In companies' tweets, nominal address forms comprise the use of the consumer's name. The use of first name address forms in companies' tweets proved particularly frequent in the analyzed corpus (cf. Tereszkiewicz 2015b, forthcoming-b). First name address terms often constitute components of greeting sequences, where they follow a greeting initiating the response:

(5) Yet again no active kids vouchers, initial call from store last week with a promised call back which failed to happen
Company10 @Company10
@user Hi [name], if you take your order info to store, our colleagues will be happy to fix this and make sure this doesn't happen again. [name] (@Company10)

(6) Seriously, what was the point. Nothing has arrived. Great way to say Happy Mother's Day!!!
Company6 @Company6
@user Hi [name]. I am so sorry to hear that :-(Did the parcel arrive? If not, please DM me your tracking details. [name] (@Company6)

The use of first name terms of address in the opening units of the tweets may help the representative to lend the message a more individualized character.

First names are used in company tweets as acts accompanying not only greetings, but also a range of other speech acts, such as apologies, requests, as well as explanations, acts of appreciation or compliments, where they perform different functions, comprising the above-mentioned roles as attention getters, markers of recipiency and interpersonal space. The use of the terms of address as accompanying acts may significantly influence the illocutionary force of the message. For instance, in requests, the address terms may diminish the face-threatening character of these acts, while the use of the terms of address in apologies may increase the face-redressive potential of the message. In this way, the use of first name forms of address may make the messages politer and less direct:

(7) I only use it for one but that has been bad :(
Company1 @Company1
@user Hmm okay, have you been in an area with good signal when making the call [name]? (@Company1)

(8) thank you Company1 for two extortionately high bills. My son won't be getting birthday celebrations this year. DW I will be leaving you in sep
Company1 @Company1
@user Sorry to hear this [name]:(What were you charged for? You can view your bill here: http://bit.ly/9y3XXX (@Company1)

(9) @user Thank you [name], please can you also confirm the full delivery address in a DM for me?
user @user
@Company6 1 Warwick ave
Company6 @Company6
@user Your parcel is currently out for delivery to you [name], I'll keep a close ey on this for you until it has been delivered. (@Company6)

As exemplified, the position of first names in the acts varies – they are used to open and to close the message, to mark boundaries of different speech acts and as such can serve as markers of structural units in the tweets.

The terms of address are used in a repetitive manner in the case of a series of tweets addressed to a particular user. Though the use might seem redundant, the names may here serve as a means of maintaining coherence of the tweets addressed to a single addressee, in which case they function as markers of conversational progression (McKeown and Zhang 2015: 104). Apart from indicating the recipient, the use of the address term may help the representative to demonstrate a focus on the individual consumer and show their attention in the midst of tweets from other users:

(10) [name] the conductor on the [product name] Grimsby to Newark very helpful & friendly. Very Customer focused a credit to your company!
Company12 @Company12
@user Hi [name]. That's really great to hear. We will be sure to pass on the kinds words to [name].
user @user
@Company12 yes please and if you could let his manager know what great Customer Service he gives, and certainly takes pride in his job.
Company12 @Company12
@user Absolutely [name]. Thank you for taking the time to get in touch. (@Company12)

(11) is this by pressing Exit for 12 secs? If so, tried it and the Amazon app still won't start.
Company9 @Company9
@user No, [name]. Try turning your TV off by the main switch for a few minutes and back on again and see if this helps. ^[initials]
user @user
@Company9 yeah, that didn't work. Any other suggestions?
Company9 @Company9
@user Sorry for the confusion, [name]. To do a soft reset, select: Menu > Support > Self Diagnosis > Reset. ^[initials] (@Company9)

In the context of Twitter, the function of address terms to indicate recipiency is thus particularly visible – although the exchanges involve only two interlocutors, the context of the interaction is public and the communication often proceeds in an asynchronous manner. The use of the name provides identity to the recipient, clearly indicates the addressee of the message and, in that way, personalizes interaction taking place in this public, partly anonymous context (cf. Rendle-Short 2007: 1506, Page 2014, Tereszkiewicz 2015b). The name may be a cue for other users as to who the addressee is (cf. Rendle-Short 2007: 1511). The use of the customer's name attracts and activates the user's attention and may encourage the user to maintain interaction.

More importantly, the use of first name forms of address may make the messages politer. As mentioned above, since English does not make a distinction between T- and V- address forms, the use of the first name may actually decrease the level of directness and increase distance.

5.2.2. Self-identification

Companies' tweets and consumers' tweets differ considerably as far as the use of self-identification is concerned. Self-identification proved to be used only in the case of companies' messages. Instances of self-identification were not found in consumers' tweets.

Company representatives self-identify by giving initials or their personal names, often in a shortened form. Self-identification was used in 44 percent of the companies' tweets (449 tweets). Identification by means of the representative's initials was more common than identification by the name.

Table 22. Self-identification used in the interaction

	Company tweets	Consumer tweets
Self-identification	Number	Number
Initials	235	-
Name	214	-

Source: own work.

Self-identification is typically provided at the end of the tweet as a closing unit. However, instances of identification in the opening units, following a greeting, were also found. In these cases, the component involves the term of identification and a frame "I am …" (Schegloff 1968: 1078):

(12) Been waiting to see someone at Company5 for an hour after being promised a wait of 40 mins max. And still have someone in front of me :(
Company5 @Company5
@user Hi there, I'm sorry to hear that you've been waiting. Can I ask what your visit is regarding today? ^[initials] (@Company5)

(13) the communication I received did not have a expiry date. Just dissapointing
Company2 @Company2
@user I do apologize for this as even the original vouchers expired end of feb. [name] (@Company2)

(14) no network issues! Was all over edinburgh last night & still the same. Followed all your troubleshooting and still no service!
Company2 @Company2
@user Ok, please give our Tech team a call and they will be happy to look into this for you – http://xxx.co.uk/help/get-in-touch … ^[name] (@Company2)

(15) You need to get back to me ASAP in regards the funds taken from my account. Collection calls for such practice is unacceptable
Company4 @Company4
@user Hi, I'm [initials]. That doesn't sound good. Have you spoken to our PhoneBank team in regards to this? If so, what did they advise? (@Company4)

Self-identification tends to be repeated in successive tweets in the interaction with a single customer:

(16) i am trying to reply to messages but get a message saying ive insufficient funds,im on sim only including unlimited texts whats going on
Company2 @Company2
@user Good morning [name], are you on a pay monthly [product name] plan? Do you have the [product name] app to track your plan? [name]
user @user
@Company2 yes pay monthly sim only.yes checked the app 8hrs calls left unlimited texts 238 mb data left month ends 13th march
Company2 @Company2
@user Okay and are you the account holder of your contract? Is it on a [product name] plan or a [product name] plan? [name] (@Company2)

While the use of personal names has also been encountered in telephone and face-to-face service interaction (cf. Marquez Reiter 2006), the use of initials seems to derive from online communication (e.g. e-mails), dictated by the economy of space or speed of interaction. The use of initials may indicate a more institutional, rather than a personal identity of the representative.

As indicated above, the company representatives often choose to self-identify by means of shortened forms of personal names (e.g. *Kitty*, *Pete*, *Chris*). The use of shortened names has also been observed in service calls, where it has been interpreted as a personalization strategy (ibid.: 28). As Marquez Reiter (2006: 28) observes, the shortened form of personal names adds a touch of "humanness" to the call, marks an informal and friendly tone of the message, while still maintaining its institutional character. A similar function of shortened names can be observed in the analyzed tweets. In the corpus, the use of shortened forms of the names may also result from the context of social media communication, the context of Twitter as a sphere of "ambient affiliation" (Zappavigna 2012), conducive to a reduction of social distance and informality.

A high number of self-identification examples and a lack of organizational identification characterizes the contrast between social media service encounters and telephone calls. A lack of organizational identification, typical or even obligatory in other mediated service encounters, e.g. customer care phone calls (cf. Marquez Reiter 2006), may be explained by the context – the interaction takes place on the company's profile, usually verified, which guarantees that the profile is managed by company representatives and makes additional confirmation redundant. A high number of self-identification in the analyzed interaction and its repetitive fashion may result from the manner in which the interaction on the profiles is managed and its often asynchronous nature. In telephone or face-to-face encounters, customers usually interact with a single representative at a time. In online interaction, by contrast, a number of representatives may manage the same profile or representatives may change shifts during the interaction. An exchange managed by a specific representative may be taken over by another and the successive tweets sent by the customer may be responded to by a different representative, making self-identification a crucial component of the interaction, as exemplified below:

> (17) so yet again this is met with silence! If this is how you treat valued customers it's a wonder you have any
> Company2 @Company2
> @user I answered your tweet [name]?_[name] [1]
> user @user
> @Company2 and I responded
> Company2 @Company2
> @user Hello [name], is there anything we can assist you with please? [name] [2]
> (@Company2)

While organizational identification has been observed to serve mainly a transactional role, self-identification can fulfil both a transactional and a relational function (cf. ibid.: 21). Identification of the representatives makes the messages more reliable and gives them "a more personal and approachable feel" (Lillqvist et al. 2016: 74). Self-identification is a sign and confirmation for the customer that there is a real person interacting, that communication is managed by a human being, not by a bot, which is often the case in online communication. Knowing the identity of the representative may also be helpful for the customer in future communication with the company in case s/he needs to refer back to the information provided in the interaction.

At this point it is also worth mentioning the choice of pronouns in the companies' messages. The representatives resort to the use of first person singular (*I, me, my*) and plural pronouns (*we, our, us*), with a more frequent occurrence of the latter (there are 328 instances of first person singular pronouns and 536 instances of first person plural pronouns in the tweets). The use of first person plural pronouns can as well be seen in tweets featuring personal self-identification of the representatives by means of names or initials (as in example (17)). The use of *we* may be dictated by a wish to mark an institutional tone of the message, to diminish the individual responsibility of the representative and to enhance the reliability of the response (cf. Tereszkiewicz, forthcoming-c).

Being optional in this task-oriented interaction, the above-mentioned terms of address and self-identification perform predominantly pragmatic functions, managing the identity of the representatives and shaping the relationship between the interlocutors.

5.2.3. Opening sequences

The units opening the message typically comprise a greeting and an address term.

5.2.3.1. Greetings

Research on service encounters in other channels of communication (face-to-face, telephone) has shown a varied use of greetings in the interaction. While they constitute a frequent component of face-to-face encounters used both by the representatives and consumers, in telephone service calls, they are predominantly used by the consumers making the phone call (Marquez Reiter and Placencia 2004, Friginal 2009).

The number of greetings in the corpus indicates that they constitute an important element in companies' tweets (cf. Tereszkiewicz 2015b, forthcoming-b). The majority of the messages opening the encounter in all of the analyzed profiles contain greetings. The use of greetings in consumers' tweets is noticeably lower.

Table 23. Greetings

	Company tweets	Consumer tweets
Type of act	Number	Number
Hi	274	55
Hello	18	7
Hey	18	7
(Good) Morning	12	2
(Good) Evening	4	-
Hiya	4	-

Source: own work.

As shown above, in most cases, informal greetings are used, such as *Hi, Hello*, with a lower number of *Hey* or the more formal *Good morning* or *Good evening*. Individual instances of shortened forms *Evening, Morning* have also been identified. All of the above-mentioned greetings derive from the spoken register. The choice of informal greetings reflects the author's perception of the channel and the expected informality of the interaction. Greetings are used as individual components, are accompanied by address terms or have an informal *Hi there* form:

> (18) Hey @Company6 since when did 'left in secure place' = 'left on doorstep without even attempting to ring doorbell'?!
> Company6 @Company6
> @user Hi [name]. I am so sorry to hear about that. Do you have any tracking details? Could you DM these over to me please? [name] (@Company6)

(19) can you please explain how on earth ive used 3 gb of data in 16 days when i have wifi
at home! Your an absolute joke&rip off!! 😡
Company2 @Company2
@user Good morning, [name]. Do you have an [product name] with WiFi Assist
turned on? ^[name] (@Company2)

(20) you are a disgrace. New customer and you couldn't connect landline and broadband on
day set. You then said it would be 2 more weeks.
Company2 @Company2
@user Hello [name], I do apologize. Did the team advise why? –[name] (@Company2)

(21) ?823.23 for Buildings Insurance Renewal loooool Are you having a laugh after the way
we've been treated...!!!!
Company5 @Company5
@user Hi there, can I ask if you've spoken to anyone about this and what's been advised
to you? ^[initials] (@Company5)

In the case of companies' tweets, the greetings also tend to be repeated in
successive tweets with the same customer, which is exemplified below. This
may be dictated by the context – as mentioned above, the interaction with
a single individual may be managed by different representatives. Moreover,
the conversation does not always proceed in a continuous flow, but rather in
an asynchronous fashion and may be interspersed by tweets from other users.
A repetitive use of the act, however, may lend the greeting an impression of
a routine, somewhat automatic response:

(22) taken my laces out of my [product name] to find out the difference in length is 4 inches
Company3 @Company3
@user Hi [name], where did you buy your shoes from?
user @user
@Company3 from @[company name] this is the second pair of trainers I've received
with extra long laces the Cote are really long too
Company3 @Company3
@user Hi [name], please return the shoes to store if you're having issues or contact
customer care: http://xxx/6016BvXXX (@Company3)

A difference in the use of greetings in the analyzed context, in contrast to
other service encounters, can be observed. Research on face-to-face and telephone encounters has shown that speakers usually exchange greetings – both
in the case when the greeting was initiated by the company or by the customer
(Marquez Reiter and Placencia 2004).

The current analysis confirms the observations by Page (2014), who regards
the use of greetings as a feature typical of corporate messages. In the analyzed
interaction, customers' messages initiating the interaction only rarely include
a greeting. The greetings are used predominantly by company representatives,
who open the response with this act also in the cases when the consumer does
not use any greeting in the message initiating the exchange. The greetings are not
returned by the customer in the subsequent interaction. Greetings thus distinguish

company responses from the messages posted by ordinary users and indicate their organizational tone. A high number of greetings may indicate that brand representatives perceive them as necessary due to their pragmatic functions. Greetings, often accompanied by first name address terms, forming the opening units of the tweets, serve to introduce an element of politeness and decrease the directness of the message. At the same time, they perform the relational function of building interpersonal relationships, enacting a more personal frame and a friendly tone to this task-oriented interaction. A lower number of greetings in consumers' tweets, by contrast, indicates a more task-focused approach to the interaction.

5.2.4. Closing units

The closing units of the tweets involve two main expressive acts, namely thanks (cf. Page 2014, Tereszkiewicz 2015b, forthcoming-b) and, in the case of companies' tweets, acts in the form of (*I*) *hope this helps*. As can be seen from the table below, the number of closing units in contrast to greetings is rather low.

Table 24. Closing units

	Company tweets	Consumer tweets
Type of act	Number	Number
Thanks	34	21
Expressive acts: *I hope this helps*	8	-
Wishes	3	-

Source: own work.

In consumers' tweets, thanks are used as closing units in complaints (e.g. (23), (24)) as well as in acts of complaint closure, in which consumers report a successful management of the infraction, as exemplified in (25):

(23) Dear @Company7 STOP SENDING ME YOUR SHITTY POST TO MY HOUSE I AM WITH TALK TALK AND DO NOT WANT Company7. Thanks. (@Company7)

(24) reported stolen bank card last Friday. Still no replacement received. How much longer b4 I can use my money. Thanks (@Company5)

(25) all ok now for some reason my tv would not log in I logged in via pc and is working now thanks (@Company9)

While in all the cases the thanks are used as a routine closing of the tweet, in the case of complaints (e.g. (23), (24)), the act appears to additionally underline the consumer's irritation and the negative tone of the message.

In companies' tweets, thanks appear as closing units of a tweet both in positive and negative evaluation management. With regard to the form of the act, a more informal *thanks* tends to be used, with occasional intensification by *many*:

(26) Wow – you can now send more annoying, useless SPAM even quicker! #please STOP
     Company2 @Company2
     @user Hello there, [name]. What text messages are you receiving? Thanks, [name].
     (@Company2)

(27) you have the nicest staff at your Truro store #proud
     Company10 @Company10
     @user Lovely to hear! Can you DM us more info on why they were nice? We'll feed it
     back to management. Thanks, [name] (@Company10)

(28) So @Company6 delivered my mum's flowers to our porch, shame we dont have a porch..
     thanks for losing my mum's present #MothersDay #Company6
     Company6 @Company6
     @user Oh no! [name], could you DM your full address/tracking no and tweet once
     done, so we can investigate? Many thanks, [name] (@Company6)

Thanks as a closing unit may be combined with wishes:

(29) just want to say #Taunton branch staff have impressed me more than once this week.
     Gladdens my #FacetoFaceBankingisNotDead♥
     Company4 @Company4
     @user Hi, I'm [initials]. Thanks for your wonderful feedback. I'll ensure it's passed on
     to the branch directly. Thanks & take care. (@Company4)

The use of thanks to close the message can be compared to the use of this act
as a conventional marker of politeness (Sifianou 2013: 93), a formal marker of
discourse structure, especially frequent in ending service encounters, signalling
closing the encounter rather than expressing gratitude (Hymes 1969, Aston
1995, Biber and Conrad 2009). However, in contrast to the use of thanks in
traditional service encounters, the act in the analyzed interaction is also used
to close the message addressed to the company or produced in response to the
customer's tweet, but not the complete encounter. As can be seen in examples
(26) or (27), for instance, the messages contain a request for information, so it
can be presumed that the author expects the exchange to continue. The use of
thanks to close the message in this manner may result from the context of the
interaction and may be a strategy employed by the company to make the message
politer, diminishing the directive tone of a preceding request.

As has already been mentioned, another constructional unit closing the response
in the companies' tweets comprises the act: (I) hope this helps. The component
increases the level of politeness of the response, but, like the above-mentioned
thanks, it has a clearly routine character:

(30) Faster payment prob? I transferred ?500 from [company name] to my [company name]
     a/c 20 mins ago but it still not appeared in my a/c
     Company4 @Company4
     @user Hi, I'm [initials]. Don't worry; so long as the details used are correct, the pay-
     ment will credit within 2 hours. I hope this helps. (@Company4)

(31) Just got your business banking app up and running. Says I have to use the desktop to
do any transactions! Bit pointless!
Company4 @Company4
@user Hi, I'm [initials]. You can make payments to existing recipients using the app;
however, at present you need to log in… 1/2 ^[initials] via the desktop site to set-
up new payments. You'll find more info here: http://spr.ly/6019BFXXX . Hope this
helps. 2/2 ^[initials] (@Company4)

The low number of closing units may be explained by a wish to avoid imposing a closure of the conversation on the consumer and to create an impression
of approachability.

A repeated use of greetings, self-identification and the use of thanks to
close the message regardless of whether the encounter is to be continued, indicates that company representatives frame each message posted in response
to the consumer's inquiry as a single entity, encompassing components otherwise used at different stages of a customer encounter. The messages comply
with politeness and customer care conventions typical of traditional customer
encounters. These components of the messages may be regarded as markers of
routine online corporate politeness, as elements fulfilling the expectations of
"appropriate patterned behaviour" (Rothenbuhler 1998: 27), behaviour typical
and expected in the context of customer interaction, distinguishing corporate
tweets from ordinary interaction, thus marking its institutional character (cf.
Marquez Reiter 2008: 7, Tereszkiewicz 2015b, 2016). The components represent
a transfer of the conventions typical of call centre interaction, where the use
of salutations, self-identification or thanks is expected from the call takers and
is interpreted as a sign of politeness, professionalism and efficiency (Cameron
2000a: 103-104).

5.3. Selected lexicogrammatical properties of the tweets

5.3.1. Informal and non-standard language, mistakes

Previous studies devoted to different channels of online communication have
observed that interaction tends to be conducted in the semi-formal, casual or
even intimate style, with a preference for informal means of expression, modifications in spelling, the use of a range of means of expressing paralinguistic
meanings (Crystal 2006, Baron 2008, Page 2012, Zappavigna 2012, Dąbrowska
2013, Tagg 2015). The aim of this part of analysis was to investigate whether

informal and non-standard language items are present in the messages posted by consumers and companies.[61]

– Informal and non-standard language

Informality is exhibited on the syntactic, lexical and graphic levels in the use of exclamatives, ellipsis, informal lexical items and non-standard spelling (cf. Dąbrowska 2013).

Table 25. Informal language[62]

Feature	Number	
	Company tweets	Consumer tweets
Exclamatives	170	302
Ellipsis	191	598
Informal and non-standard lexical items	224	486

Source: own work.

- Exclamatives

A relatively high number of exclamative clauses was identified in the corpus of consumer tweets. The use of exclamatives can be seen both in the context of positive evaluation and complaining:

(32) waiting for my [product name] VR for my [product name]! Can't waaaaaaaaiiit!!!! (@Company9)

(33) Hi, my phone has stopped working half way through my contract and you're asking silly money to fix it! 11 years a customer for what?!?!? (@Company1)

(34) So, a new customer gets a far better deal than I'm getting.. I have to cancel my account and start again. What rubbish!! (@Company7)

A smaller number of exclamatives can be observed in company messages. Exclamative clauses are used predominantly in expressive acts, mainly in apologies, empathy expressions, thanks, offers of help and repair, as well as acts expressing wishes and positive emotions:

(35) @user Hi [name], pleased your finding your savings card useful! ^[initials] (@Company5)

(36) @user Enjoy! we like macaroons too! (@Company12)

(37) @user Thanks for the love, Becky! What's your favourite feature so far? ^[initials] (@Company9)

(38) @user Oh no, sorry about that! Please call our team on 0800 818XXX & they'll be able to help. :) (@Company11)

---

[61] Fragments of this section have been included in a separate analysis (Tereszkiewicz, forthcoming-c).

[62] The data refer to the number of tweets with at least one occurrence of the analyzed item.

A smaller number of such items in the companies' tweets points to a lower degree of spontaneity and emotionality of expression, as well as a lower degree of informality in the tweets.

- Ellipsis

Elliptical clauses comprise structures with subject ellipsis, with the deletion of the subject and auxiliary, as well as elliptical questions (Dąbrowska 2013). Such structures are particularly common in consumers' messages:

(39) Having problems signing up to [product name]. Waited for code for more than ten minutes. (@Company1)

(40) shocked by service. No card yesterday. This today, nobody tried to deliver. 2 lies. Saturday wasted (@Company6)

(41) was told on a previous tweet that I would get reimbursed just been told over the phone "no I won't" DISGRACEFUL! (@Company7)

(42) Just bought these and very disappointed with the amount of [product name] bites in here. Not even half a bag :((@Company11)

(43) hi, having problems with returns at the mo, unable to print any labels via the website – are there issues currently? can u help? (@Company3)

(44) trainers ordered on the 29th June, still not even packed! Awful services! (@Company3)

(45) You joking @Company11?! Only 5 in my 6 pack! (@Company11)

(46) your website having problems? (@Company1)

In the case of company tweets, the use of such structures proved definitely lower. The most frequent instances of ellipsis occur in the act of apology (142 instances):

(47) @user Sorry about that [name]. I'm confident our engineer will get this sorted out for you ^[initials] (@Company7)

(48) @user Crisis mode here [name]! Still having issues? ^[initials] (@Company7)

(49) @user Glad to hear it :) Enjoy your evening! ^[name] (@Company2)

- Informal lexical items and non-standard spelling

Informality is reflected in the use of colloquial or slang vocabulary, as well as non-standard spelling. The presence of such items has been identified as a feature typical of computer-mediated communication (Baron 2008, Crystal 2006, Zappavigna 2012, Dąbrowska 2013, Tagg 2015). The use of abbreviations, vowel deletion or phonetic spelling in the corpus reflects the conventions typical of social media and texting communication, dictated by the lack of visual cues, brevity and speed of interaction (Crystal 2006, Tagg 2012).

A more frequent occurrence of such items was observed in consumers' tweets. Consumers more often resort to the use of non-standard spelling items, as well as slang and colloquial expressions. The expressions comprise swear words as well as items describing the complainable or the consumers' emotional reaction in a positive or negative way.

Examples of informal lexical items and non-standard spelling in consumers' tweets comprise the following instances (cf. Dąbrowska 2013):

- colloquial phrases and words: *stuff, awesome, shite, shit, silly, shambles, bunny, take the piss, dude, cops, luvie, sweetie, bloody, kinda, wanna, gonna, gotta, scam, crap, fobbed off, cool, mummie, guy, guys, mate, stuck, gutted, fuck up, no way, blimey, what on earth, what the hell, screw up, thanx,*
- vowel deletion: *pls, plz, thx, ppl, fkn, txt, wks, wk, mgs, oppnty,*
- clippings: *pic, mo, comfy, sayin, del, tho, breky, cust serv, fav,*
- letter-word and number-word substitutions: *u, y, b4, 2day,*
- phonetic spelling: *fone,*
- prolonging of the vowel sound: *waaaaaaaaaiiit, soooo,*
- apostrophe deletion: *wont, cant, its, hasnt, doesnt, thats, ive,*
- lower-case spelling: *i, uk, australia, woodhouse, nottingham,*
- acronyms: *DM, ASAP, lol, WTF, ffs, tbh,*
- paralanguage: *wow, haha, argh, grrr, yasssss, yeh, blah.*

For example:

(50) when you guys gonna release the new United home kit to smash City's puny new kit? (@Company3)

(51) u serious? no way! But y? #gutted!! (@Company11)

(52) We all know chocolate bars are getting smaller but this takes the piss! (@Company11)

(53) Hi there, Cool stuff with lunch deals. (@Company1)

(54) waiting for my [product name] VR for my [product name]! Can't waaaaaaaaaiiit!!!! (@Company9)

(55) Another bag of shit service from @Company6 well done! Give a crap, (@Company6)

(56) I'm trying 2enter a voucher code u mailed me but its 2long 4the space u allow online help pls- trying 2order my weekly delivery! (@Company10)

(57) i want to cancel a payment how do i actually do this at this time?!! (@Company5)

(58) i would like to find out why i cant use my bank card plz contact me asap (@Company4)

(59) hi my mothers day gift still hasnt arrived and the tracking doesnt appear to be working. can yoh help? (@Company6)

Fewer instances of informal and non-standard lexical items occur in the corpus of companies messages. The following examples of shortenings and colloquial or slang vocabulary were identified in the tweets:

- vowel deletion: *pls, plz,*
- clippings: *fab, info, pic, dept, depo, mo, promo,*

- colloquial phrases and words: *give us a shout, no worries, back with a bang, stuff, awesome, fear not, blimey, crumbs,*
- acronyms: *DM, ASAP,*
- paralanguage: *eck, oh, wow, whoop, whoohoo, ooo.*

For example:

(60) @user Whoop whoop, that's great to hear :) (@Company1)

(61) @user Back with a bang [name]. Welcome back to your best. (@Company3)

(62) @user Great stuff! Stay tuned for everything you'll need to know. (@Company3)

The use of the above-mentioned colloquial and slang expressions in company tweets creates a modern and dynamic effect (cf. Tagg 2012: 65). It may serve as a marker of the company's approach and relationship with the customers. By these means, the authors try to diminish distance and mark the sense of belonging to the same discourse community (cf. Tereszkiewicz 2017a). Still, a relatively infrequent use of such items shows that representatives prefer to maintain a neutral tone of expression. Using colloquial lexical items may be deemed inappropriate in the context of customer encounters.

- Language mistakes

The two corpora of consumers' and companies' tweets differ as regards language correctness, attention paid to the avoidance of punctuation, spelling and grammatical mistakes. A greater number of mistakes can be seen in consumers' tweets.

Table 26. Language mistakes

	Number	
Feature	Company tweets	Consumer tweets
Mistakes	264	615

Source: own work.

Among consumers' tweets, most of the messages contain different language mistakes. The mistakes include spelling and grammatical mistakes, as well as a large group of messages with punctuation mistakes, i.e. lack of punctuation or non-standard punctuation (present in 523 tweets):

(63) brought box of [product name] for the pub I work in this is how 3 of the bars came,- caramel covered most bars (@Company11)

(64) Bough a ?1 bar of milk choclate and its horrible Not what it used to be . Why was the reciepe changed ? Wont buy Company11 again (@Company11)

(65) Are these SO #organic that you just get the stems and no no tomatoes? ;) (@Company10)

(66) I'm chasing yet another parcel that should of arrived today! (@Company6)

(67) Worse customer service from @Company5 ever! You wouldn't think that it will so hard to get a renewed debit card ! (@Company5)

(68) are shit for replacement phones through insurance not the first phone I've had that doesnt work properly. I need my camera it don't work (@Company2)

(69) how do deal with spam messages (@Company2)

(70) still waiting on my brand new fridge freezer that's never worked being fixed , don't seem to much bothered about it . (@Company9)

(71) do have a email address as the fault finding one on your Web site doesn't load up thanks (@Company9)

The form of the tweets reflects the spontaneous tone and a more unplanned character of the messages. The tweets indicate that consumers are to a lesser degree constrained by the institutional character of the interaction.

On the part of the company, language correctness may play an important role, as it may be interpreted as a sign of respect towards the consumer and an indication that the company cares about its image. In the analyzed corpus, not many instances of language incorrectness were found. The mistakes in companies' tweets comprise grammatical mistakes, typos and punctuation mistakes. In some cases, however, as is the case with consumers' tweets, it is difficult to establish whether the mistake is a result of a misspelling or represents a grammatical mistake. For instance:

(72) @user Hi [name], pleased your finding your savings card useful! ^[initials] (@Company5)

(73) @user I agree, we should not be advertising information, if we cannot guarantee this facility. We will get this investigate ^[initials] (@Company8)

(74) @user Apologies for that [name], I see you arrangements were made for you to travel on an alternative coach. (@Company8)

(75) @user I'm really sorry you didn't receive your call back, I assure you well be working as hard as we can to resolve things. ^[initials] (@Company7)

(76) @user Evening [name], just checking if you've been ab;e to set up your account and the install went okay? ^[initials] (@Company7)

(77) @user No to sure, have you checked this on the service status http://xxx.co/service ^[initials] (@Company7)

(78) @user Hi, yes they is maintenance fee's applied, please click the link provided for more information: http://bit.ly/1TX2XXX. ^[initials] (@Company5)

(79) @user Hi there, we're sorry to hear if your experience :(What was your call about? We'd like to help. (@Company1)

As in consumers' messages, the most frequent mistakes in companies' tweets comprise punctuation errors. In 216 of the messages, lack of segmentation or non-standard segmentation of sentences was identified. These messages comprise tweets without punctuation marks or with commas used to separate sentences. For example:

(80) @user Hi [name], they wouldn't need any identification, they'd just need to know your account details. ^[initials] (@Company5)

(81) @user We are sorry for the inconvenience today, there has been some disruption today but i will pass on your comments. (@Company12)

(82) @user This has been returned, is there anything else I can help with? (@Company6)

(83) @user Okay please let us know how you get on and have a lovely day – [name] (@Company2)

(84) @user Hello, sorry [name] we don't have any promo codes available at this time. ^[initials] (@Company8)

Lack of punctuation marks influences the syntactic form of the tweets. Non-standard segmentation or lack of segmentation by means of punctuation marks produces paratactic structures and contributes to the effect of syntactic flow, which reflects a speech-like character of the message.

Still, the low number of language mistakes in companies' tweets proves that despite the speed of interaction and the need to reply to customers' queries in the shortest time possible, the representatives try to keep their messages free from mistakes.

- Discourse markers and hedges

The presence of discourse markers and hedges was also analyzed, since they have been identified as components typically occurring in face-to-face encounters and call centre interaction (Cameron 2000b, Biber and Conrad 2009, Friginal 2009, Varcasia 2013). Discourse particles have a primarily emotive and expressive function. They do not affect the truth conditions of the message, nor do they affect its propositional content (Jucker and Ziv 1998: 3, qtd. in Varcasia 2013: 18). A range of discourse markers can be seen in the tweets (cf. Tereszkiewicz, forthcoming-b). The most frequent elements comprise: *oh*, *okay* and *I see*.

Table 27. Discourse markers and hedges

	Number	
Form	Company tweets	Consumer tweets
Oh	56	5
Okay	18	3
I see	12	-
Ah	4	-
Hmm	4	-
Right	-	1

Source: own work.

The use of discourse markers in consumers' tweets is rather infrequent, with individual occurrences of *oh* and *right* or *okay*. The items are used in interjections expressing negative and positive emotions, as well as in responses to the messages posted by the company with a request for action suggesting corrective measures to solve the complainable:

> (85) oh woe is me! Just opened a box of [product name] and after digging through it…no [product name]. How can this be?! #sosad #needa[product name] #helpme (@Company11)

> (86) oh my god I love your new stuffed mushrooms. I've eaten two packets in 2 days. (@Company10)

> (87) oh right okay, I've just got off the phone to ee, and they advised me not to open the file because I'm already on 4G (@Company2)

Discourse markers are more common in responses posted by company representatives. They may be seen to perform a similar function to their role in call centre interaction (Cameron 2000b, Friginal 2009, Varcasia 2013), where due to a lack of visual cues, verbal back-channeling is to ensure the customer that the operator is present and actively listening to the customer (Cameron 2000b: 336). In the analyzed material, this supportive role of discourse markers can be seen as well as their role marking the reception of the message. Discourse markers are used at the beginning of the message, which, as Varcasia (2013: 17-18) observes, is a strategic position, as it lends a particular tone to the message and clearly indicates the speaker's stance.

In the analyzed corpus, the discourse marker *oh* is the most frequent. A relatively frequent use of this marker has also been observed in face-to-face and telephone business encounters (Varcasia 2013: 18), which points to a transfer of the conventions typical of service encounters in other contexts to online interaction. *Oh* is referred to as an information management marker. It "pulls from the flow of information in discourse a temporary focus of attention which is the target of self and/or other management" (Schiffrin 1987: 73-74). It is used in a range of contexts to mark repair initiation, to preface requests for elaboration, to mark receipt or recall of information, to mark shifts in subjective orientation (ibid.). According to Heritage (1998: 269), who analyzed the function of *oh* in response to inquiries, it may be used to indicate that the message received is somehow problematic. Varcasia (2013: 18) similarly observes that *oh* marks "the receipt of solicited but unanticipated message."

In the analyzed corpus, *oh* is often a component of an interjection, such as *oh no* or *oh dear*, marking the receipt of a customer's complaint. Used in response to complaints, it indicates that the message was not expected or, rather, not desired. It shows that the receiver is surprised by the message and the feedback received. For example:

(88) Feel so defeated. Two hours spent trying to get internet with @Company7 only to be cut off #weeps #channelsKafka #actuallynotfunny
Company7 @Company7
@user Oh no! What's happened, [name]? :(| [initials] (@Company7)

(89) Disappointed with @Company10 home delivery. Delayed and no one came, and the day after, after promising they'd come – not even a phone call
Company10 @Company10
@user Oh no! Very sorry [name], can you DM the account holder's name and the order number please? [name]. (@Company10)

The discourse markers *okay, ah, ah okay* are used to acknowledge the message received, to show understanding or agreement with the message (Beach 1993: 338). As Beach (1993) observes, "*okay* indicates that the speaker agrees with, affirms, and/or understands what was projected prior, and perhaps even treats the talk as significant" (ibid.: 338). The discourse marker *I see* performs a similar function:

(90) that link isnt working? im requesting my code through the Company1 open page then text 2020 Company1 open with my details its requested!
Company1 @Company1
@user Okay [name], you would only be able to use your [product name] code on one of your contracts, sorry. (@Company1)

(91) Keeps kicking me offline with lag spikes and shit.
Company7 @Company7
@user I see, sorry about this! Does a reboot of the hub help at all? Is anything listed here http://xxx.co/service to explain? [initials] (@Company7)

Hedges such as *hmm* are used to distance the representative from the customer's observations or from the complainable (Page 2014), to mark the representative's doubt or hesitation before providing an answer to the consumer's query:

(92) I have tried every option for 2 seats and it says no seats found
Company1 @Company1
@user Hmm okay, have you tried using a different browser [name]? (@Company1)

The use of discourse markers, analogically to their use in texting, does not signal the author's "struggle to produce language in real time" (Tagg 2012: 103), but rather indicates how the message should be interpreted, i.e. as an acknowledgement and comprehension of the message, an expression of sympathy (ibid.). As Tagg (2012: 118) observes, their use introduces informality and expresses close attention typical of spoken interaction.

In the analyzed messages, the discourse markers imitate spoken conversation, lend the messages an emotive and spontaneous character. It needs to be noted, however, that their use is highly repetitive. In this way, as indicated before, the expressions appear to have acquired a routinized character and seem to have lost their emotional charge.

5.3.2. The use of emoticons, hashtags and links

– The use of emoticons

Lack of nonverbal cues in online communication creates a need for other means of expressing nonverbal content, intonation and gestures (Carretero et al. 2014: 263). Such means comprise, among others, emoticons and emojis. Emoticons and emojis are used for emphasis – as "attempts to recreate aspects of spoken language through graphic and orthographic means" (Herring 1996: 7, cf. Yus 2011, Placencia and Lower 2013: 629).

The function and use of emoticons in various channels of computer-mediated communication has already been the subject of numerous studies. Many of the analyses devoted to the role of emoticons have underlined that their primary function is to indicate emotional state and compensate for the lack of nonverbal cues in computer-mediated communication (Crystal 2006). Further studies, however, proved a more complex role that emoticons may play in the interaction. In addition to indicating emotions, as Dresner and Herring (2010) point out, emoticons perform an important function of indicating illocutionary force of the message. Emoticons may serve to express a "nonemotional meaning, mapped conventionally onto facial expression" (Dresner and Herring 2010: 263), e.g. using a wink to indicate a jocular intention. Emoticons may also introduce a form of gestural cue to the message and gestural cues (e.g. smiling, head nodding) are important in managing rapport in face-to-face interaction (Clark et al. 2003: 6). This extensive role of emoticons was further confirmed by Skovholt et al. (2014) in their study of e-mail messages, where emoticons were observed to express a range of additional meanings. Apart from their role to mark positive or negative attitude, jocular and ironic meanings, emoticons have been observed to function as hedges softening directive speech acts (such as requests, complaints, rejections, corrections) and strengthening expressive speech acts (such as wishes and greetings).

The number of the respective emoticons is shown in the table below.

Table 28. Emoticons and emojis

Emoticon type	Number	
	Company tweets	Consumer tweets
:) / :-)	110	5
:(/ :-(	24	96
;)	4	3
Emoji	46	118

Source: own work.

In the tweets, emoticons can be seen as serving the functions previously observed in other studies. Their function to mark a positive or negative feeling or attitude can be noticed. Emoticons and emojis, as indicated in the previous subchapters, can serve as further means of expressing evaluation in the tweets.

In the collection of consumers' tweets, 22 percent of the messages include an emoticon or emoji sign. A more frequent use of emoticons expressing a frowning or crying face is associated with a higher number of tweets expressing complaints in which such symbols are used. The emoticons underline the negative tone of the message:

> (93) Just bought these and very disappointed with the amount of [product name] bites in here. Not even half a bag :((@Company11)

> (94) Just bought my son a [product name] ice cream. Had to have it in a bowl it had no cone :(how does that even happen??? (@Company11)

The smiley face is used in messages expressing appreciation in the context of positive evaluation as well as positive complaint management, as exemplified in (95). The smiley face is also used in requests for remedial action, as in (96), in which case it may diminish the directive force of the statement. Its function to lower the illocutionary force of the message can also be seen in its use in complaints, where it accompanies acts expressed by means of ironic or sarcastic statements, as shown in (97):

> (95) everything is sorted now, someone just stayed downstairs all day. Thank you though:) (@Company6)

> (96) hey there! Both platform 1's displays are playing up at HNK! You might wanna send someone out to fix em :) (@Company12)

> (97) Are these SO #organic that you just get the stems and no no tomatoes? ;) (@Company10)

Consumers' tweets also feature a higher number of emoji signs, i.e. signs in the form of an image, more visually complex than emoticons. They serve as modifiers of the messages, adding a visual symbolic or iconic representation of the concepts expressed in the verbal message. Among the signs, those expressing negative emotions, such as anger, fury or a crying face, as well as those marking positive emotions, like love, power or thumbs up can be seen:

> (98) Why is NOBODY answering the phone in stores😤😤😤@Company3 (@Company3)

> (99) still no service 😒shite network!!! (@Company2)

> (100) camera looks amazing for a phone!, I love the edge. And you brought back water resistant and expandable memory yippee!!!📱 (@Company9)

> (101) Pre-oredered the @Company9 #[product name] from @Company1😍 very excited. Big upgrade frome my [product name] #cantwait (@Company9)

> (102) your @Company9 team is awesome. Took us a few weeks but we got there in the end. Top class support. Big fan. ❤📱 (@Company9)

In the analyzed corpus of companies' tweets, 18 percent of the messages contain emoticons. As the table shows, more smiley faces are used in the messages. Smiley emoticons most frequently accompany acts expressing offers of help and repair, acts expressing positive feedback to a customer's comment, as well as acts of wishes, greetings and compliments, in which cases they strengthen the illocutionary force of the message:

(103) @user Always here if you need our help :) [initials] (@Company7)

(104) @user No problem [name], please do let me know once your parcel is with you, I'll also keep my eye on this for you :) (@Company6)

(105) @user Hello, [name]. I've just replied to your Facebook post :-) ^[initials] (@Company7)

(106) @user Oh dear, sorry about that [name]! Please call our team on 0800 818XXX & they'll be able to help. :) (@Company11)

(107) @user Enjoy your day too :) –[name] (@Company2)

In the case of requests, emoticons are used to decrease the directive tone of the act:

(108) @user http://xx.co.uk/unlocking– Hi [name], please use this link to unlock the device :) –[name] (@Company2)

(109) @user You can use http://speedtest.net:) Give it a go and we'll see what you're getting! ^[initials] (@Company7)

(110) @user Thank you for letting us know [name], please could you DM over the tracking number for me?:) (@Company6)

Messages with a somewhat unclear use of emoticons can also be found. For instance, in the messages below, emoticons are used in the acts of rejecting consumers' complaints, in which case they may be used to diminish the face-threatening tone of the rejection and introduce a more friendly tone to the interaction, or, rather, to enhance the rejection and attribution of blame to a third party, which may be face-threatening for the consumer:

(111) @user Good morning [name], we have been advised this is an [company name] issue, please get in touch with [company name] for further information :-) [name] (@Company2)

(112) @user As advised, it is an [company name] issue :-) [name] (@Company2)

The frowning face most frequently accompanies apology acts, where the emoticon serves as a strengthener of the illocutionary force of the messages. For example:

(113) @user Sorry to hear that [name] :(Have you spoken with the retailer about this? (@Company1)

(114) @user Blimey, that's no fun :(Have you tried a speed test over wired connection to a PC or laptop to see what you're getting? ^[initials] (@Company7)

Emoji signs in companies' tweets are the most frequent in responses to pos itive evaluation. The emojis are usually used to represent a physical action of clapping, a fist bump or hands raised in the air. The emojis add to the meaning of the verbal message by highlighting the author's enthusiasm and admiration of and respect for the customer:

(115) @user Great work [name]! 🙌Glad you could join us. (@Company3)

(116) @user 🙌 – the hard work will all be worth it, [name]. #[company slogan] (@Company3)

(117) @user You're on fire in [product name], [name]. Keep up that good work. Looking forward to reading your review. 👋📱 (@Company3)

(118) @user A true classic. Today belongs to you [name]. 👋 (@Company3)

(119) @user The Boss of the Streets. 😎 #[company slogan] (@Company3)

As shown above, in companies' tweets, emoticons comprise nonverbal expressions of positive feelings, attentiveness, interest, involvement and evalu- ation, introduce a form of gestural cue and, in this way, enhance rapport with the consumer.

– The use of hashtags

The use of hashtags in companies' tweets stands in contrast to their use by consumers, both in the frequency with which the authors resort to the symbols, the degree of inventiveness in the formation of the tags and the variety of mean- ings expressed. Since the use of hashtags in consumers' messages was described in the previous subchapters, the following section exemplifies the use of these symbols only in companies' tweets.

Table 29. The use of hashtags

	Number	
Type of component	Company tweets	Consumer tweets
Hashtags	35	152

Source: own work.

Hashtags are not frequent in companies' tweets, as only 3 percent of the tweets contain this symbol. As regards the structure of hashtags, the tags comprise acronyms, noun phrases, proper and common nouns, as well as clause-based tags. With respect to the meaning and function, the following forms were observed:

– names of products, slogans and campaigns: *#VR*, *#[product name]*, *#[com- pany slogan]*,
– names of events: *#GrandNational*,

- expressive acts: *#BringBackOurMacaroons,*
- commissive acts of offering help and repair: *#[name]Cares, #[name]Here, #HereToHelp.*

For example:

(120) @user It really is. What have you be watching in #VR ? (@Company9)

(121) @user Loving the excitement! There's so many things to love about the #[product name] (@Company9)

(122) @user well ran, [name]. You're enjoying #[product name] then? (@Company3)

(123) @user Watch this space for news on all future #[product name] drops. 👍 (@Company3)

(124) @user Hi [name]. We're using this train today to support our customers travelling to/ from the #GrandNational. (@Company12)

(125) @user we think you will, [name]…#[company slogan] (@Company3)

(126) @user Glad to hear this [name]:). #HereToHelp for any other queries (@Company6)

(127) @user If you would like any further assistance with this do let me know :) #[name] Here (@Company6)

(128) @user Thanks for bringing this to our attention [name]. Send over your tracking details & I'll investigate this for you. #[name]Cares (@Company6)

(129) @user We will certainly pass on your feedback [name]- @Company12 #BringBack-OurMacaroons! (@Company12)

The above-mentioned hashtags perform different functions in the messages. Their promotional and persuasive role can be seen in the case of tags denoting names of products or companies' slogans. The hashtags serve the function of promoting and increasing the visibility of the product in the medium. The tags also fulfil an interpersonal function, associated with integrating the audience around events and products or activities undertaken by the users. Hashtags representing companies' advertising slogans, apart from performing an obviously promotional function, may also contribute to customer engagement and community building. The slogans, often motivational and inspiring to action, though generic in tone, when addressed to a specific consumer, may gain an individual reference in the tweets. The slogans enhance rapport as they give credit to the customer and compliment him/her, thus boosting their image.

The hashtags in examples (126)-(128) comprise uncommon but interesting examples of "customer care hashtags" expressing commissive and emotive meanings in a hashtag form. These hashtags do not seem to denote searchable components. They put the act into the form of a slogan and transform its content into a stable concept. Example (129) may additionally be classified as an emotional comment "invoking a possibility of an imagined audience of users who feel the same way" (Zappavigna 2015: 275). The tags can be considered as metacomments – they comprise authors' comments on the preceding offer of help and repair or an expressive act. The hashtags perform the function of strengthening the illocutionary force of the tweets, increasing the force of the commissive and expressive acts, emphasizing the author's commitment and emotions. The hashtags underline customer care and rapport, respectively.

– The use of links

Hyperlinks to other sources were identified in 9 percent of the companies' tweets and in 0.5 percent of the consumers' messages.

Table 30. The use of links

	Number	
Type of component	Company tweets	Consumer tweets
Links	95	5

Source: own work.

In the case of consumers' tweets, the links refer to photographs constituting evidence of the complainable or photographs depicting positively evaluated products:

(130) having a major jitter issue with my connection, really need this fixed as I play for a team, help! http://www.pingtest.net/result/141323XXX.png … (@Company7)

(131) Got a bit carried away this week Some amazing drops from @Company3 recently Thanks to… http://ift.tt/29noXXX (@Company3)

The links used in the companies' messages comprise references to the following sources:
– specific documentation/company procedures,
– specific department of the company/customer care chat,
– company website and products,
– other sources/companies.

The references are introduced by means of deictic expressions (e.g. *here, this page*), followed by the domain address. They are also placed at the end of the message as independent components, without any embedding phrases:

(132) @user How strange, let us know the details here and we'll investigate: http://xxx.do/10sXXX (@Company12)

(133) @user Please use the following address to send in your tickets for a refund http://www.xxx.co.uk/delayrepay (@Company12)

(134) @user Please see this page for info – https://support.xxx.com/en-gb/HT205XXX-^[name](@Company2)

(135) @user I am sorry to hear this [name], please provide feedback here http://socsi.in/x47XXXso we can investigate this for you ^[initials] (@Company8)

The links in the analyzed interaction perform a predominantly informative role, referring consumers to further sources on specific issues, as well as a promotional function, directing consumers to the company's website. The components perform an important role as far as customer care is concerned, referring consumers to an appropriate branch of the company, which may help them to deal with the reported issues.

The analyzed corpus exhibits the features of conventional customer encounters, as well as features triggered by the context of social media interaction. Consumers' and companies' tweets reflect properties of the so-called consultative and casual styles (Joos 1959). However, more instances of use of the casual style, more frequent instances of informality and non-standard language items were identified in consumers' tweets. Consumers appear to be less constrained by the conventions underlying communication in institutional encounters and more often follow the conventions of expression typical of social media interaction. The companies' messages, by contrast, reflect a preference for the consultative style, characterized by attention to grammatical correctness, the use of standard language and neutral vocabulary, with only occasional informal vocabulary and syntactic structures. Though a characteristic feature of social media interaction, emoticons, informal language, abbreviations or hashtags seem to be considered inappropriate in the context of customer encounters from the perspective of the representatives. The shape of the messages, with a low occurrence of paralanguage or verbal expression of emotions marks a relatively low degree of spontaneity of the interaction. The features of the language of the tweets indicate that the representatives to a considerable extent transfer the conventions of interaction from other channels of customer communication. Nevertheless, it can be noticed that the use of standardized constructions stands in contrast to the informality of customers' tweets and lends the messages a ritualized and institutionalized character.

Conclusions

The following chapter presents concluding observations concerning customer encounters on Twitter on English profiles. The main focus of the analysis was on companies' tweets posted in response to consumers' messages. The use of offline conventions concerning interaction strategies typical of customer encounters as well as some new tendencies can be seen in the tweets. The table below summarizes the strategies used by the companies in the context of positive evaluation and complaint management.

The investigation of the patterns found in the encounters enabled a verification of the initial hypotheses concerning the interaction.

The analysis confirmed the hypothesis concerning the focus placed on maintaining a positive image of the company and enhancing positive relations with customers. A range of rapport management strategies can be found, as well as strategies oriented towards enhancing the consumer's opinion concerning the company. Strategies which would pose a threat to the consumer are practically non-existent in the corpus.

A customer-oriented approach to the interaction is also reflected in the choice of strategies used in complaint and positive evaluation management. In the case of the former, it can be seen in a high occurrence of apologies and low incidence of denials, which confirms the initial assumption. In the case of the latter, this approach is reflected in the use of acts of appreciation and complimenting consumers.

The analysis did not fully confirm the assumption concerning a promotional-orientation of positive evaluation responses. A relatively low incidence of acts of self-praise and explicit advertising occurred in the tweets.

The study also did not fully confirm the initial hypothesis assuming that, owing to social media conventions, company representatives will be constrained by their institutional and social roles to a lesser degree than in other channels of communication. Similarly, a preference for informalization and conversationalization, or diminishing of interactional distance was not observed in corporate responses. Instead, a significant degree of conventionalization and formulaicity can be seen across the tweets.

A more detailed summary of the properties of companies' responses is provided below.

Table 31. Strategies used in the companies' tweets

Strategies	Number
The language and structure of tweets	
Simple tweets	146
Complex tweets	874
Style consistency	Preference for the consultative style across the profiles Speech act packaging
Formulaicity	High occurrence of conventional politeness acts Generic replies Customer-orientation Company's image protection strategies Positive politeness acts Low variation of persuasive strategies
Types of acts	
Greetings	330
First name address	400
Self-identification	449
Positive evaluation management	
Appreciation: expression of positive feelings	49
Appreciation: thanks	31
Compliment return: complimenting the consumer	29
Requests for further information/ contact	28
Compliment acceptance	21
Reporting feedback	19
Wishes	16
Complaint and negative evaluation management	
Request	564
Apology	254
Expression of empathy	125
Acknowledgement	11
Explanation	92
Denial	24
Offer of help and repair	262
Thanks	41

Source: own work.

- Structure and language of tweets: as far as the structure and language of the tweets is concerned, a preference for the consultative style of inter- action can be seen. A rather low incidence of signs of informality, slang and non-standard structures can be found, as well as a low occurrence of medium-specific means of expression, such as hashtags, emoticons or emojis. As regards the structure of the tweets, there is a stronger preference for complex tweets over simple and independent acts, and a tendency to condense interaction in a single message can be noticed. The speech acts have a different illocutionary force and perform different functions within the act. The most typical speech act sets comprise an apology, a request for information or action and a solution or promise to attend to the consumer (cf. Lillqvist et al. 2016: 73).

— Forms of address and self-identification: a preference for pronominal and first name address forms can be noticed. The use of the first name may be aimed at decreasing the level of directness and increasing the degree of politeness (cf. Jakubowska 1999: 47). As regards self-identification, a frequent use of personal names and initials can be observed. The use of both first person singular and plural forms of pronouns can be seen. The choice of the first person plural form can be designed to express the author's professional perspective and identity, and indicate a corporate instead of individual responsibility for the message. The forms of address and self-identification used by the representatives distinguish corporate tweets from consumers' messages.

— Use of conventional politeness acts: the assumption expecting a reduction of the degree of conventional politeness was not confirmed in the analysis. The use of selected positive politeness acts can be seen, i.e. the use of thanks, wishes, acts expressing positive emotions, as well as a frequent use of openings and closings in the form of greetings and self-identification. The use of acts of conventional politeness represents a replication of the strategies found in traditional encounters (cf. Lillqvist et al. 2016: 73). A repetitive use of greetings also in a single interaction with a consumer can be seen, which underlines the conventionality and the institutional nature of this act. The use of greetings and first name address terms, though it may seem generic, increases the level of indirectness and politeness in the tweets. The number of self-identification items reflects formulaicity and an institutional tone in the messages. Expressive speech acts, such as wishes, may be used to perform an important social function, as such acts create and maintain rapport, smooth interaction, personalize relationship and help to establish social harmony (cf. Carretero et al. 2014: 263).

— Requests: a high occurrence of requests for information and action in response to consumer complaints was observed in the interaction. Requests indicate a dialogic orientation of the encounters (cf. Romenti et al. 2014). The acts appear to represent a conventional response to the consumer's query, signalling attentiveness and a readiness to investigate the issues. The use of these strategies in complaint management exchanges may result from the context. The lack of face-to-face, direct contact with the customer, the need to react quickly to the complaint and thus save face may trigger the use of the acts, as they allow the representative to show customer care and readiness to deal with the infraction, which, in turn, may help the company to save reputation. A preference for imperative and interrogative acts in the function of requests can be seen, which results from the context and expresses a more task-focused interaction.

– Apologies: acts of apology are used repetitively, often as an opening formula signalling responsiveness and attentiveness, rather than a proper act of apology. The results confirm a conventionalized use of apologies in English and the use of the expression of regret (*I'm sorry*) as the most frequent illocutionary force indicating device. Moreover, a variety of modification and intensification devices used in the acts can be noticed in the corpus.

– Acts of denial: a low occurrence of acts denying the complainable was observed. This feature of the interaction indicates that the representatives avoid using acts posing a threat to the consumer's face.

– Positive evaluation management strategies: the most frequent strategies in the context of positive evaluation management comprise acts of appreciation expressing positive feelings, thanks and acts complimenting consumers. The acts tend to be hearer-oriented. By shaping the acts in this form, the representatives strengthen the customer-oriented focus of the exchange.

– Promotional orientation and persuasive strategies: the responses comprise a rather limited range of persuasive strategies. The interaction indicates that, in individual conversations, the companies tend to refrain from advertising and directly persuading consumers to use products, but rather focus on raising positive emotions associated with the brand and constructing rapport with the consumer, which may help the company to achieve transactional success in the future and in other contexts. Post-transaction rather than pre-transaction evaluation and promotional strategies tend to be used.

– Relational content: relational orientation of the exchanges is more clearly marked in the case of positive evaluation management. It is here that a wider variety of messages with a relational orientation can be found, i.e. the use of compliments, taking notice of the consumer, assessing their performance, acts of appreciation, acts expressing positive feelings, requests for further feedback and wishes.

– Degree of conventionality of the acts: the messages reflect a relative degree of variation as regards the conventionality of the respective speech acts. In the case of specific act types, a greater and lower degree of conventionality can be observed. Apologies, explanations, offers of help and repair, as well as acts closing the encounters inviting for a further contact comprise formulaic chunks and display a high degree of conventionalization and routine. The number and shape of the above-mentioned acts constitutes a clear evidence of an influence of the public context of the interaction. The public and mediated context requires more attention to the consumer's face and more effort on the company's side to protect or recover a positive image. An unsuccessful handling of the consumer's complaint may prove more consequential for the company in this context than in other customer encounters. By contrast, responses to positive evaluation appear to exhibit a lower degree of conventionality, tend to be less repetitive and formulaic, are more individualized and adjusted to a specific customer. Lower conventionality is also reflected by a lower number of repetitive speech act combinations in the case of complex tweets.

– Repetitive politeness, formulaic language: the tweets are to a large extent generic (cf. Zhang and Vásquez 2014) and reveal a tendency towards standardization understood as "reducing optional variation in performance" (Cameron 2006: 113). The interaction exhibits a low degree of individualization of the responses, a relatively high degree of formulaicity and a considerable degree of uniformity of the answers, which is reflected in a recurring use of ready-made scripts and formulas, in particular in the acts of apology, requests and offers of help and repair, as well as conventional politeness acts, concerned with "polite and professional behaviour" (Cameron 2008: 104), such as greetings and thanks, forms of address and self-identification. The same reply is used recurrently, regardless of the content of the consumer's message, which confirms previous observations (cf. Lillqvist et al. 2016: 74). Formulaicity is confirmed by the number of speech act combinations in a single tweet. It seems that the representatives, analogically to the conventions of call centres, need to follow a specific corporate norm, a set of rules of customer care interaction online – the rules which "prescribe how particular speech acts should be performed, the choice of address terms, salutations and the consistent use of certain politeness formulae" (Cameron 2006: 113). The responses express a preference for "simulated friendliness, scripted salutations and relentless positive politeness" (Cameron 2003: 27).

– Consumer-orientation: what may seem natural, considering the type of the profiles analyzed, the messages exhibit a customer-oriented focus. The emphasis placed on customer care and on attending to the consumer in any circumstances is reflected in the use of such speech acts as offers of help and repair or requests for further information and contact. Both positive and negative politeness acts are common, acts which attend to the customer's positive and negative face needs, i.e. their desire for approbation and the wish not to be imposed upon. Positive politeness is expressed mainly in the case of positive evaluation management strategies, as well as by means of conventional politeness acts, wishes, greetings and thanks. The negative politeness orientation of the tweets is reflected, among others, in the high occurrence of apology acts, as well as in the use of a range of mitigation strategies in the acts of requests (cf. Tereszkiewicz, forthcoming-b).

- Protection of the company's image: strategies aiming at saving the company's face and diminishing the threat to the company's image posed by the consumer's complaints or negative comments can also be found in the messages. The use of evasive terms naming the complainable in the acts of apology or thanks can be observed. The need to protect the company's image is reflected in the use of explanations, providing accounts of the complainable, referring to the company's regulations, procedures, external states of affairs influencing the company's operations. This approach is also reflected in the form of acknowledgements of the complainable, as the acts are expressed in a mitigated form, diminishing the gravity of the complainable, thus being oriented towards saving the company's image. The focus on saving the company's face is also reflected in the preference for requests for contact via a different channel. As indicated before, these requests are face-saving for the company, which, by using these acts, may avoid addressing the problems in public and still create an image of an attentive and responsive company (cf. Lillqvist et al. 2016: 74).
- Differences between profiles: as assumed, an increased homogenization can be observed across the profiles. Similar patterns and formulaic responses tend to be used, which reflects the tendency towards regulation and standardization in corporate discourse on Twitter in general.
- Differences between companies' and consumers' tweets: a clear dichotomy between the style of companies' and customers' messages can be observed, with a tendency towards uniformity and conventionalization of the responses, as well as a greater degree of formality and lower emotionality visible in the companies' messages, and a tendency towards informality, emotionality and expressiveness, and a less standardized discourse on the part of the consumers. The difference also concerns the use of conventional politeness acts, such as greetings and thanks, which proved more common in companies' tweets. A similar dichotomy was observed previously in other mediated channels of interaction, for instance in call centre interaction (Ptaszek 2008, 2009a, Economidou-Kogetsidis 2005, Friginal 2009, Archer and Jagodziński 2015). It appears that in both contexts, consumers are less constrained by the institutional character of the encounter.
- Positive evaluation versus complaint management: the discrepancy between the number of positive evaluation and complaint management tweets indicates that Twitter serves consumers primarily as a channel for negative eWOM. Posting positive information about a company proved a less frequent practice among consumers. Twitter appears to constitute a perfect medium to share disappointment with a company, to vent negative emotions instantaneously as the experience occurs. The difference in the orientation of consumers' messages confirms the need underlined in the previous research for the companies to develop an

efficient system of complaint management with the purpose of protecting the company's professional face.

As the summary provided above indicates, the hypothesis concerning the influence of the medium on the genre of service encounters was not fully confirmed. The context does not appear to have exerted much influence on the encounters, as many conventions of customer care typical of corporate practices previously observed in other channels, e.g. face-to-face or telephone customer encounters, seem to have been transferred to the online interaction.

However, selected aspects of the genre of customer encounters appear to have been affected by the online context of the interaction. The following properties characterize online encounters on Twitter.

- Public form of the interaction: the interaction is public and as such is accessible to other consumers and users of the microblog, which, on the part of the company, enhances the focus that needs to be placed on corporate image and establishing rapport with consumers, and which is reflected in a customer-oriented form of companies' responses.
- Participant roles and relations: participants may reveal their identity and status. The interaction may lead to familiarity in the case of followers regularly commenting on the company's profile. The degree of imposition of the consumer on the representative is low. The roles and obligations are similar as in other channels of customer encounters.
- Structure of the interaction: the interaction may proceed in a synchronous and asynchronous manner. Moreover, the interaction may have the form of a single- or multi-topic exchange and may represent an exchange of two or more participants. As a result, turn-adjacency may be disrupted. Move packaging and the use of complex tweets comprising speech acts with a different illocutionary force is frequent.
- Encounter management: a number of representatives may run the profiles. Consequently, a single conversation may be managed by different representatives, which may influence the course of the encounter and the strategies used in the responses.
- Purpose of the interaction: the interaction is not necessarily goal-oriented. The microblog may serve as an intermediary channel, directing consumers to other forms of communication with the company. A consumer's message may be left without a response or the management initiated by the company may not be continued by the consumer.

Twitter constitutes a significant channel of customer encounters, a fact which is confirmed by an increasing number of followers of corporate profiles, the high number of tweets addressed to companies on a daily basis, the growing number of companies joining the microblog and exploiting the medium in a variety of ways to reach new consumers. At this stage of development, many of the conventions characterizing customer encounters in other channels of communication still apply to interactions in the new channel. However, since the medium is undergoing constant technological development and consumers' use of the new technologies is changing dynamically as well, it is worth observing whether the interactional practices and communication strategies will evolve, and, if so, how this evolution will proceed.

References

Adams, A., McCorkindale, T. 2013. "Dialogue and Transparency: A Content Analysis of How the 2012 Presidential Candidates Used Twitter." *Public Relations Review* 39(4): 357-359.

Adolphs, S., Brown, B., Carter, B., Crawford, P., Sahota, O. 2004. "Applying Corpus Linguistics in a Health Care Context." *Journal of Applied Linguistics* 1(1): 9-28.

Albert, S., Kessler, S. 1978. "Ending Social Encounters." *Journal of Experimental and Social Psychology* 14: 541-553.

Al-Rawi, A. 2017. "News Organizations 2.0: A Comparative Study of Twitter News." *Journalism Practice* 11(6): 705-720.

Andrews, B. 2014. "Complaining on Twitter May Get You Better Customer Service." Retrieved from: http://miami.cbslocal.com (accessed: 5 March 2017).

Antonopoulou, E. 2001. "Brief Service Encounters: Gender and Politeness." In: Bayraktaroglu, A., Sifianou, M. (eds.) *Linguistic Politeness across Boundaries: The Case of Greek and Turkish. Pragmatics and Beyond New Series* 88. Amsterdam: John Benjamins, 241-269.

Archer, D., Jagodziński, P. 2015. "Call Centre Interaction: A Case of Sanctioned Face Attack?" *Journal of Pragmatics* 76: 46-66.

Artwick, C.G. 2013. "Reporters on Twitter: Product or Service?" *Digital Journalism* 1(2): 212-228.

Aston, G. 1988a. "Interactional Speech in Service Encounters." In: Aston, G. (ed.) *Negotiating Discourse: Studies in the Discourse of Bookshop Encounters*. Bologna: Editrice, 73-97.

Aston, G. (ed.) 1988. *Negotiating Service: Studies in the Discourse of Bookshop Encounters*. Bologna: Editrice.

Aston, G. 1988b. "What's a Public Service Encounter Anyway?" In: Aston, G. (ed.) *Negotiating Discourse: Studies in the Discourse of Bookshop Encounters*. Bologna: Editrice, 25-42.

Aston, G. 1995. "Say 'Thank You': Some Pragmatic Constraints in Conversational Closings." *Applied Linguistics* 16(1): 57-86.

Atifi, H., Marcoccia, M. 2017. "Exploring the Role of Viewers' Tweets in French TV Political Programs: Social TV as a New Agora?" *Discourse, Context & Media* 19: 31-38.

Baer, R., Hill, D.J. 1994. "Excuse Making: A Prevalent Company Response to Complaints?" *Journal of Consumer Satisfaction, Dissatisfaction, and Complaining Behavior* 7: 143-151.

Bailey, B. 1997. "Communication of Respect in Interethnic Service Encounters." *Language in Society* 26(3): 327-356.

Bailey, B. 2000. "Communicative Behavior and Conflict between African-American Customers and Korean Immigrant Retailers in Los Angeles." *Discourse & Society* 11(1): 86-108.

Baker, C. 1997. *Foundations of Bilingual Education and Bilingualism*. 2nd ed. Clevedon, Avon: Multilingual Matters, Ltd.

Baker, C., Emmison, M., Firth, A. 2005. "Calibrating for Competence in Calls to Technical Support." In: Baker, C., Emmison, M., Firth, A. (eds.) *Calling for Help. Language and Social Interaction in Telephone Helplines*. Amsterdam: John Benjamins, 39-62.

Baker, C., Emmison, M., Firth, A. (eds.) 2005. *Calling for Help. Language and Social Interaction in Telephone Helplines*. Amsterdam: John Benjamins.

Baron, N. 2008. *Always On. Language in an Online and Mobile World*. Oxford: Oxford University Press.

Barton, D., Lee, C. 2013. *Language Online. Investigating Digital Texts and Practices*. London: Routledge.

Bastos, M.T., Galdini Raimundo, R.L., Travitzki, R. 2013. "Gatekeeping Twitter: Message Diffusion in Political Hashtags." *Media, Culture & Society* 35(2): 260-270.

Bayyurt, Y., Bayraktaroglu, A. 2001. "The Use of Pronouns and Terms of Address in Turkish Service Encounters." In: Bayraktaroglu, A., Sifianou, M. (eds.) *Linguistic Politeness: A Case of Greek and Turkish*. Amsterdam: John Benjamins, 209-240.

Beach, W. 1993. "Transitional Regularities for 'Casual' 'Okay' Usages." *Journal of Pragmatics* 19: 325-352.

Bednarek, M. 2006. *Evaluation in Media Discourse: Analysis of a Newspaper Corpus*. London: Continuum.

Bednarek, M. 2008. *Emotion Talk Across Corpora*. London: Palgrave Macmillan.

Bednarek, M., Caple, H. 2012. *News Discourse*. London: Continuum.

Belt, T.L. 2018. "Can We at Least All Laugh Together Now? Twitter and Online Political Humor During the 2016 Election." In: Galdieri, C.J., Lucas, J.C., Sisco, T.S. (eds.) *The Role of Twitter in the 2016 US Election*. London: Palgrave Macmillan, 97-117.

Benoit, W.L. 1995. *Accounts, Excuses, and Apologies: A Theory of Image Restoration*. Albany, NY: State University of New York Press.

Benoit, W.L. 1997. "Image Repair Discourse and Crisis Communication." *Public Relations Review* 23: 177-186.

Berry, R., Tanford, S., Montgomery, R., Green, A.J. 2018. "How We Complain: The Effect of Personality on Consumer Complaint Channels." *Journal of Hospitality & Tourism Research* 42(1): 74-101.

Biber, D. 1988. *Variation across Speech and Writing*. Cambridge: Cambridge University Press.

Biber, D., Conrad, S. 2009. *Register, Genre, and Style*. Cambridge: Cambridge University Press.

Biber, D., Finegan, E. 1988. "Adverbial Stance Types in English." *Discourse Processes* 11(1): 1-34.

Biber, D., Finegan, E. 1989. "Styles of Stance in English: Lexical and Grammatical Marking of Evidentiality and Affect." *Text* 9(1): 93-124.

Biber, D., Johansson, S., Leech, G., Conrad, S., Finegan, E. 1999. *Longman Grammar of Spoken and Written English*. Harlow: Longman.

Bickart, B., Schindler, R.M. 2001. "Internet Forums as Influential Sources of Customer Information." *Journal of Interactive Marketing* 15(3): 31-40.

Bitner, M.J., Booms, B.H., Tetreault, M.S. 1990. "The Service Encounter: Diagnosing Favorable and Unfavorable Incidents." *Journal of Marketing* 54: 71-84.

Blitvich, P. 2015. "Setting the Linguistic Research Agenda for the E-Service Encounters Genre: Natively Digital Versus Digitized Perspectives." In: Hernández-López, M. de la O, Fernández-Amaya, L. (eds.) *A Multidisciplinary Approach to Service Encounters*. Leiden: Brill, 15-36.

Blommaert, J. 2005. *Discourse: A Critical Introduction*. Cambridge: Cambridge University Press.

Blommaert, J. 2010. *The Sociolinguistics of Globalization*. Cambridge: Cambridge University Press.

Blum-Kulka, S. 1997. "Discourse Pragmatics." In: Dijk van, T.A. (ed.) *Discourse as Social Interaction*. London: Sage, 38-63.

Blum-Kulka, S., House, J. 1989. "Cross-Cultural and Situational Variation in Requesting Behaviour." In: Blum-Kulka, S., House, J., Kasper, G. (eds.) *Cross-Cultural Pragmatics: Requests and Apologies*. Norwood, NJ: Ablex, 123-154.

Blum-Kulka, S., House, J., Kasper, G. (eds.) 1989. *Cross-Cultural Pragmatics: Requests and Apologies*. Norwood, NJ: Ablex.

Blum-Kulka, S., House, J., Kasper, G. 1989. "Investigating Cross-Cultural Pragmatics: An Introductory Overview." In: Blum-Kulka, S., House, J., Kasper, G. (eds.) *Cross-Cultural Pragmatics: Requests and Apologies*. Norwood, NJ: Ablex, 1-34.

Blum-Kulka, S., Olshtain, E. 1984. "Requests and Apologies. A Cross-Cultural Study of Speech Act Realization Patterns (CCSARP)." *Applied Linguistics* 5(3): 196-213.

Bolkan, S., Daly, J.A. 2009. "Organizational Responses to Consumer Complaints: An Examination of Effective Remediation Tactics." *Journal of Applied Communication Research* 37: 21-39.

Bouvier, G. 2019. "How Journalists Source Trending Social Media Feeds: A Critical Discourse Perspective on Twitter." *Journalism Studies* 20(2): 212-231.

Bowles, H. 2006. "Bridging the Gap between Conversation Analysis and ESP – An Applied Study of the Opening Sequences of NS and NNS Service Telephone Calls." *English for Specific Purposes* 25: 332-357.

boyd, d. 2006. "A Blogger's Blog: Exploring the Definition of a Medium." *Reconstruction* 6(4). Retrieved from: http://www.danah.org/papers/ABloggersBlog.pdf (accessed: 14 January 2017).

boyd, d., Ellison, N. 2008. "Social Network Sites: Definition, History, and Scholarship." *Journal of Computer-Mediated Communication* 13(1): 210-230.

boyd, d., Golder, S., Lotan, G. 2010. "Tweet, Tweet, Retweet: Conversational Aspects of Retweeting on Twitter." *43rd Hawaii International Conference on System Sciences, Honolulu, HI, 2010*, 1-10.

Bradley, G.L., Sparks, B.A. 2009. "Dealing with Service Failures: The Use of Explanations." *Journal of Travel and Tourism Marketing* 26: 129-143.

Bradley, G.L., Sparks, B.A. 2012. "The Use of Explanations Following Service Failure: If, When and How They Aid Recovery." *Journal of Services Marketing* 26: 41-51.

Breeze, R. 2013. *Corporate Discourse*. London: Bloomsbury.

Broersma, M., Graham, T. 2013. "Twitter as a News Source: How Dutch and British Newspapers Used Twitter in Their News Coverage, 2007-2011." *Journalism Practice* 7(4): 446-464.

Brown, G., Yule, G. 1983. *Discourse Analysis*. Cambridge: Cambridge University Press.

Brown, J., Broderick, A.J., Lee, N. 2007. "Word of Mouth Communication Within Online Communities: Conceptualizing the Online Social Network." *Journal of Interactive Marketing* 21(3): 2-20.

Brown, P., Levinson, S. 1987. *Politeness. Some Universals in Language Usage*. Cambridge: Cambridge University Press.

Brown, R., Gilman, A. 1960. "The Pronouns of Power and Solidarity." In: Sebeok, T.A. (ed.) *Style in Language*. Cambridge, MA: MIT Press, 253-276.

Bruns, A., Burgess, J. 2011. "The Use of Twitter Hashtags in the Formation of Ad Hoc Publics." *6th European Consortium for Political Research General Conference (ECPR 2011)*. Reykjavik: University of Iceland.

Bruns, A., Burgess, J. 2012. "Researching News Discussion on Twitter: New Methodologies." *Journalism Studies* 13: 801-814.

Bruns, A., Moe, H. 2014. "Structural Layers of Communication on Twitter." In: Weller, K., Bruns, A., Burgess, J., Mahrt, M., Puschmann, C. (eds.) *Twitter and Society*. New York: Peter Lang, 15-28.

Buccoliero, L., Bellio, E., Crestini, G., Arkoudas, A. 2018. "Twitter and Politics: Evidence from US Presidential Elections 2016." *Journal of Marketing Communications*. Retrieved from: https://doi.org/10.1080/13527266.2018.1504228 (accessed: 8 December 2018).

Burton, S., Soboleva, A. 2011. "Interactive or Reactive? Marketing with Twitter." *Journal of Consumer Marketing* 28(7): 491-499.

Buttle, F.A. 1998. "Word-of-Mouth: Understanding and Managing Referral Marketing." *Journal of Strategic Marketing* 6(3): 241-254.

Callahan, L. 2006. "English or Spanish?! Language Accommodation in New York City Service Encounters." *Intercultural Pragmatics* 3(1): 29-53.

Callahan, L. 2009. *Spanish and English in US Service Encounters*. New York: Palgrave Macmillan.

Cameron, D. 2000a. *Good to Talk? Living and Working in a Communication Culture*. London: Sage.

Cameron, D. 2000b. "Styling the Worker: Gender and the Commodification of Language in the Globalized Service Economy." *Journal of Sociolinguistics* 4: 323-347.

Cameron, D. 2003. "Globalizing 'Communication.'" In: Aitchison, J., Lewis, D., Jenkins, S. (eds.) *New Media Language*. London: Routledge, 27-35.

Cameron, D. 2006. *On Language and Sexual Politics*. London: Routledge.

Cameron, D. 2007. "Redefining Rudeness." In: Gorji, M. (ed.) *Rude Britannia*. London: Routledge, 127-138.

Cameron, D. 2008. "Talk from the Top Down." *Language & Communication* 28: 143-155.

Canter, L. 2015. "Personalised Twitting: The Emerging Practices of Journalists on Twitter." *Digital Journalism* 3(6): 888-907.

Carl, W. 2008. "The Role of Disclosure in Organized Word-of-Mouth Marketing Programs." *Journal of Marketing Communications* 14(3): 225-241.

Carretero, M., Maíz-Arévalo, C., Ángeles Martínez, M. 2014. "'Hope This Helps!' An Analysis of Expressive Speech Acts in Online Task-Oriented Interaction by University Students." In: Romero-Trillo, J. (ed.) *Yearbook of Corpus Linguistics and Pragmatics 2014: New Empirical and Theoretical Paradigms.* Cham: Springer International Publishing Switzerland, 261-289.

Ceron, A., d'Adda, G. 2016. "E-Campaigning on Twitter: The Effectiveness of Distributive Promises and Negative Campaign in the 2013 Italian Election." *New Media & Society* 18(9): 1935-1955.

Chan, A., Schnurr, S., Zayts, O. 2018. "Exploring Face, Identity and Relationship Management in Disagreements in Business Meetings in Hong Kong." *Journal of Politeness Research* 14(2): 233-260.

Chan, N.L., Guillet, B.D. 2011. "Investigation of Social Media Marketing: How Does the Hotel Industry in Hong Kong Perform in Marketing on Social Media Websites?" *Journal of Travel & Tourism Marketing* 28(4): 345-368.

Chang, A., Hsieh, S.H., Tseng, T.H. 2013. "Online Brand Community Response to Negative Brand Events: The Role of Group eWOM." *Internet Research* 23(4): 486-506.

Chappell, D. 2005. "Opportunities for Negotiation at the Interface of Phone Calls and Service-Counter Interaction." In: Baker, C., Emmison, M., Firth, A. (eds.) *Calling for Help. Language and Social Interaction in Telephone Helplines.* Amsterdam: John Benjamins, 237-256.

Charles, M. 1996. "Business Negotiations: Interdependence Between Discourse and the Business Relationship." *English for Specific Purposes* 15(1): 19-36.

Chatterjee, G. 2001. "Online Reviews. Do Consumers Use Them?" *Advances in Consumer Research* 28: 129-133.

Chaudhry, A. 2011. "Social Media and Compliant Pharmaceutical Industry Promotion: The ASCO 2010 Twitter Experience." *Journal of Medical Marketing* 11(1): 38-48.

Chaudhry, A., Glode, M., Gillman, M., Miller, R. 2012. "Trends in Twitter Use by Physicians at the American Society of Clinical Oncology Annual Meeting, 2010 and 2011." *Journal of Oncology Practice* 8(3): 173-178. Retrieved from: http://jop.ascopubs.org/content/early/2012/04/17/JOP.2011.000483.short (accessed: 14 June 2015).

Chaudhry, I. 2016. "'Not So Black and White': Discussions of Race on Twitter in the Aftermath of #Ferguson and the Shooting Death of Mike Brown." *Cultural Studies Critical Methodologies* 16(3): 296-304.

Cheepen, C. 2000. "Small Talk in Service Dialogues: The Conversational Aspects of Transactional Telephone Talk." In: Coupland, J. (ed.) *Small Talk.* Essex: Pearson, 288-311.

Chen, G.M. 2011. "Tweet This: A Uses and Gratifications Perspective on How Active Twitter Use Gratifies a Need to Connect with Others." *Computers in Human Behavior* 27: 755-762.

Chen, Y.F. 2008. "Herd Behavior in Purchasing Books Online." *Computers in Human Behavior* 24: 1977-1992.

Chen, Y.S., Chen, C.Y., Chang, M.H. 2011. "American and Chinese Complaints: Strategy Use from a Cross-Cultural Perspective." *Intercultural Pragmatics* 8(2): 253-275.

Cheung, M., Luo, C., Sia, C., Chen, H. 2009. "Credibility of Electronic Word-of-Mouth: Informational and Normative Determinants of On-Line Consumer Recommendations." *International Journal of Electronic Commerce* 13(4): 9-38.

Chevalier, J.A., Mayzlin, D. 2006. "The Effect of Word of Mouth on Sales: Online Book Reviews." *Journal of Marketing Research* 43: 345-354.

Chiluwa, I., Ifukor, P. 2015. "'War against our Children': Stance and Evaluation in #BringBackOurGirls Campaign Discourse on Twitter and Facebook." *Discourse & Society* 26(3): 267-296.

Cho, Y., Im, I., Hiltz, R. 2003. "The Impact of E-Services Failures and Customer Complaints on Electronic Commerce Customer Relationship Management." *Journal of Consumer Satisfaction, Dissatisfaction and Complaining Behavior* 16: 106-118.

Chu, S.C., Kim, Y. 2011. "Determinants of Consumer Engagement in Electronic Word-of-Mouth (eWOM) in Social Networking Sites." *International Journal of Advertising* 30: 47-75.

Chu, S.C., Sung, Y. 2015. "Using a Consumer Socialization Framework to Understand Electronic Word-of-Mouth (eWOM) Group Membership among Brand Followers on Twitter." *Electronic Commerce Research and Applications* 14(4): 251-260.

Clark, C. 2009. "'Either You are With Us, or You are With the Terrorists': How UK and US Television News Reported the 2003 Iraq Conflict." In: Morley, J., Bayley, P. (eds.) *Corpus-Assisted Discourse Studies on the Iraq Conflict. Wording the War.* London: Routledge, 165-185.

Clark, C., Drew, P., Pinch, T. 2003. "Managing Prospect Affiliation and Rapport in Real-Life Sales Encounters." *Discourse Studies* 5: 5-31.

Clark, F., Greer, Ph.D., Douglas, A., Ferguson, Ph.D. 2011. "Using Twitter for Promotion and Branding: A Content Analysis of Local Television Twitter Sites." *Journal of Broadcasting & Electronic Media* 55(2): 198-214.

Clyne, M., Norrby, C., Warren, J. 2009. *Language and Human Relations: Styles of Address in Contemporary Language.* Cambridge: Cambridge University Press.

Coesemans, R., De Cock, B. 2017. "Self-Reference by Politicians on Twitter: Strategies to Adapt to 140 Characters." *Journal of Pragmatics* 116: 37-50.

Colliander, J., Dahlén, M., Modig, E. 2015. "Twitter for Two: Investigating the Effects of Dialogue with Customers in Social Media." *International Journal of Advertising* 34(2): 181-194.

Comm, J. 2010. *Twitter Power 2.0. How to Dominate Your Market One Tweet at a Time.* New Jersey: John Wiley & Sons, Inc.

Conlon, D.E., Murray, N.M. 1996. "Customer Perceptions of Corporate Responses to Product Complaints: The Role of Explanations." *Academy of Management Journal* 39: 1040-1056.

Conrad, S., Biber, D. 2003. "Adverbial Marking of Stance in Speech and Writing." In: Hunston, S., Thompson, G. (eds.) *Evaluation in Text. Authorial Stance and the Construction of Discourse.* Oxford: Oxford University Press, 56-73.

Coombs, T.W. 1998. "Analytic Framework for Crisis Situations: Better Responses from a Better Understanding of the Situation." *Journal of Public Relations Research* 10: 177-191.

Coombs, T.W. 2007a. *Ongoing Crisis Communication: Planning, Managing, and Responding.* 2nd ed. Thousand Oaks, California: Sage.

Coombs, T.W. 2007b. "Protecting Organization Reputations During a Crisis: The Development and Application of Situational Crisis Communication Theory." *Corporate Reputation Review* 10(3): 163-176.

Coombs, T.W., Holladay, S.J. 2008. "Comparing Apology to Equivalent Crisis Response Strategies: Clarifying Apology's Role and Value in Crisis Communication." *Public Relations Review* 34: 252-257.

Coupland, J. 2000. "Introduction: Sociolinguistic Perspectives on Small Talk." In: Coupland, J. (ed.) *Small Talk*. Essex: Pearson, 1-25.

Coupland, J. (ed.) 2000. *Small Talk*. London: Longman.

Coupland, N. 2010. "Accommodation Theory." In: Jaspers, J., Östman, J.O., Verschueren, J. (eds.) *Society and Language Use*. Amsterdam: John Benjamins, 21-27.

Cowie, C. 2007. "The Accent of Outsourcing: The Meanings of 'Neutral' in the Indian Call Centres." *World Englishes* 26(3): 316-330.

Coyle, J.R., Smith, T., Platt, G. 2012. "'I'm Here to Help': How Companies' Microblog Responses to Consumer Problems Influence Brand Perceptions." *Journal of Research in Interactive Marketing* 6(1): 27-41.

Cranage, D., Mattila, A. 2005. "Service Recovery and Pre-Emptive Strategies for Service Failure: Both Lead to Customer Satisfaction and Loyalty, But for Different Reasons." *Journal of Hospitality and Leisure Marketing* 13: 161-181.

Crié, D. 2003. "Consumers' Complaint Behavior. Taxonomy, Typology and Determinants: Towards a Unified Ontology." *Journal of Database Marketing and Customer Strategy Management* 11(1): 60-79.

"Crisis Communication." Retrieved from: http://www.businessdictionary.com/definition/crisis-communication.html (accessed: 3 March 2017).

Crystal, D. 2006. *Language and the Internet*. 2nd ed. Cambridge: Cambridge University Press.

Culnan, M.J., McHugh, P.J., Zubillaga, J.I. 2010. "How Large U.S. Companies Can Use Twitter and Other Social Media to Gain Business Value." *MIS Quarterly Executive* 9(4): 243-259.

Cummings, K. 2018. "'Life Savers': Technology and White Masculinities in Twitter-Based Superhero Film Promotion." *Social Media + Society*. Retrieved from: https://doi.org/10.1177/2056305118782677 (accessed: 12 December 2018).

Cunha, E., Magno, G., Comarela, G., Almeida, V., Gonçalves, M.A., Benevenuto, F. 2011. "Analyzing the Dynamic Evolution of Hashtags on Twitter: A Language-Based Approach." *Proceedings of the Workshop on Language in Social Media (LSM 2011)*, 58-65.

Dąbrowska, M. 2013. *Variation in Language: Faces of Facebook English*. Bern: Peter Lang.

Danby, S., Baker, C., Emmison, M. 2005. "Four Observations on Openings in Calls to Kids Help Line." In: Baker, C., Emmison, M., Firth, A. (eds.) *Calling for Help. Language and Social Interaction in Telephone Helplines*. Amsterdam: John Benjamins, 134-151.

Danet, B., Herring, S. (eds.) 2007. *The Multilingual Internet: Language, Culture and Communication Online*. Oxford: Oxford University Press.

Dang-Xuan, L., Stieglitz, S., Wladarsch, J., Neuberger, C. 2013. "An Investigation of Influentials and the Role of Sentiment in Political Communication on Twitter during Election Periods." *Information, Communication & Society* 16(5): 795-825.

Darics, E. 2010. "Politeness in Computer-Mediated Discourse of a Virtual Team." *Journal of Politeness Research* 6: 129-150.

Daugherty, T., Hoffman, E. 2014. "eWOM and the Importance of Capturing Consumer Attention within Social Media." *Journal of Marketing Communications* 20(1-2): 82-102.

Davidow, M. 2000. "The Bottom Line Impact of Organizational Responses to Customer Complaints." *Journal of Hospitality & Tourism Research* 24: 473-490.

Davidow, M. 2003. "Organizational Responses to Customer Complaints: What Works and What Doesn't." *Journal of Service Research* 5: 225-250.

Davidow, M., Dacin, P.A. 1997. "Understanding and Influencing Consumer Complaint Behavior: Improving Organizational Complaint Management." In: Brucks, M., MacInnis, D.J. (eds.) *Advances in Consumer Research* 24. Provo, UT: Association for Consumer Research, 450-456.

Decock, S., Depraetere, I. 2018. "(In)directness and Complaints: A Reassessment." *Journal of Pragmatics* 132: 33-46.

Decock, S., Spiessens, A. 2017. "Customer Complaints and Disagreements in a Multilingual Business Environment. A Discursive-Pragmatic Analysis." *Intercultural Pragmatics* 14(1): 77-115.

Dekay, S.H. 2012. "How Large Companies React to Negative Facebook Comments." *Corporate Communications: An International Journal* 17(3): 289-299.

Dellarocas, C. 2003. "The Digitization of Word of Mouth: Promise and Challenges of Online Feedback Mechanisms." *Management Science* 49(10): 1407-1424.

Depta, K. 2000."Wzorzec gatunkowy skargi." *Stylistyka* 9: 133-145.

Desai, T., Shariff, A., Shariff, A., Kats, M., Fang, X., Christiano, C., Ferris, M. 2012. "Tweeting the Meeting: An In-Depth Analysis of Twitter Activity at Kidney Week 2011." *PLoS ONE* 7(7): e40253.

Deutschmann, M. 2003. *Apologising in British English*. Umeå: Umeå Universitet.

Dimmick, J., Chen, Y., Li, Z. 2004. "Competition Between the Internet and Traditional News Media: The Gratification-Opportunities Niche Dimension." *The Journal of Media Economics* 17: 19-33.

Dorai, S., Webster, C. 2015. "The Role of Nonverbal Communication in Service Encounters." In: Hernández-López, M. de la O., Fernández-Amaya, L. (eds.) *A Multidisciplinary Approach to Service Encounters*. Leiden: Brill, 211-228.

Downey Bartlett, N.J. 2005. "A Double Shot 2% Mocha Latte, Please, with Whip: Service Encounters in Two Coffee Shops and at a Coffee Cart." In: Long, M.H. (ed.) *Second Language Needs Analysis*. New York: Cambridge University Press, 305-343.

Draucker, F., Collister, L. 2015. "Managing Participation through Modal Affordances on Twitter." *Open Library of Humanities* 1(1). Retrieved from: https://olh.openlibhums.org/articles/10.16995/olh.21 (accessed: 24 March 2017).

Dresner, E., Herring, S.C. 2010. "Functions of the Non-Verbal in CMC: Emoticons and Illocutionary Force." *Communication Theory* 20: 249-268.

Dresner, E., Herring, S.C. 2012. "Emoticons and Illocutionary Force." In: Riesenfel, D., Scarafile, G. (eds.) *Philosophical Dialogue: Writings in Honor of Marcelo Dascal*. London: College Publication, 59-70.

Drew, P., Heritage, J. 1992. "Analyzing Talk at Work: An Introduction." In: Drew, P., Heritage, J. (eds.) *Talk at Work: Interaction in Institutional Settings*. Cambridge: Cambridge University Press, 3-65.

Drew, P., Heritage, J. (eds.) 1992. *Talk at Work*. Cambridge: Cambridge University Press.

Drew, P., Heritage, J. 2006. *Conversation Analysis*. London: Sage.

Du Bois, J. 2007. "The Stance Triangle." In: Englebretson, R. (ed.) *Stancetaking in Discourse: Subjectivity, Evaluation, Interaction*. Amsterdam: John Benjamins, 138-182.

Economidou-Kogetsidis, M. 2005. "'Yes, Tell Me Please, What Time is the Midday Flight From Athens Arriving?' Telephone Service Encounters and Politeness." *Intercultural Pragmatics* 2: 253-273.

Economidou-Kogetsidis, M. 2010. "Cross-Cultural and Situational Variation in Requesting Behaviour: Perceptions of Social Situations and Strategic Usage of Request Patterns." *Journal of Pragmatics* 42: 2262-2281.

Edwards, D. 2005. "Moaning, Whinging and Laughing: The Subjective Side of Complaints." *Discourse studies* 7(1): 5-29.

Einwiller, S.A., Steilen, S. 2015. "Handling Complaints on Social Network Sites – An Analysis of Complaints and Complaint Responses on Facebook and Twitter Pages of Large US Companies." *Public Relations Review* 41(2): 195-204.

Einwiller, S.A., Viererbl, B., Himmelreich, S. 2017. "Journalists Coverage of Online Firestorms in German-Language News Media." *Journalism Practice* 11(9): 1178-1197.

Englebretson, R. 2007. "Stancetaking in Discourse. An Introduction." In: Englebretson, R. (ed.) *Stancetaking in Discourse. Subjectivity, Evaluation, Interaction*. Amsterdam: John Benjamins, 1-25.

Englebretson, R. (ed.) 2007. *Stancetaking in Discourse. Subjectivity, Evaluation, Interaction*. Amsterdam: John Benjamins.

English, P. 2016. "Twitter's Diffusion in Sports Journalism: Role Models, Laggards and Followers of the Social Media Innovation." *New Media & Society* 18(3): 484-501.

Erz, A., Marder, B., Osadchaya, E. 2018. "Hashtags: Motivational Drivers, Their Use, and Differences Between Influencers and Followers." *Computers in Human Behavior* 89: 48-60.

Fairclough, N. 1989. *Language and Power*. London: Longman.

Fairclough, N. 1993. "Critical Discourse Analysis and the Marketization of Public Discourse: The Universities." *Discourse & Society* 4(2): 133-168.

Fairclough, N. 1995a. *Critical Discourse Analysis*. Boston: Addison Wesley.

Fairclough, N. 1995b. *Media Discourse*. London: Edward Arnold.

Fairclough, N. 2003. *Analyzing Discourse: Textual Analysis for Social Research*. London: Routledge.

Farina, M. 2018. *Facebook and Conversation Analysis. The Structure and Organization of Comment Threads*. London: Bloomsbury.

Feinberg, R.A., Hokama, L., Kadam, R., Kim, I.S. 2002. "Operational Determinants of Caller Satisfaction in the Banking/Financial Services Call Centre." *International Journal of Bank Marketing* 20(4): 174-180.

Félix-Brasdefer, J.C. 2012. "Pragmatic Variation by Gender in Market Service Encounters in Mexico." In: Félix-Brasdefer, J.C., Koike, D.A. (eds.) *Pragmatic Variation in First and Second Language Contexts: Methodological Issues*. Amsterdam: John Benjamins, 17-49.

Félix-Brasdefer, J.C. 2015. *The Language of Service Encounters: A Pragmatic-Discursive Approach*. Cambridge: Cambridge University Press.

Ferguson, C. 1981. "The Structure and Use of Politeness Formulas." In: Coulmas, F. (ed.) *Conversational Routine*. The Hague: Mouton de Gruyter, 21-35.

Filliettaz, L. 2004. "The Multimodal Negotiation of Service Encounters." In: Le Vine, P., Scollon, R. (eds.) *Discourse and Technology: Multimodal Discourse Analysis.* Washington, DC: Georgetown University Press, 88-100.

Fink, L., Félix-Brasdefer, J.C. 2015. "Pragmalinguistic and Gender Variation in U.S. Café Service Encounters." In: Beeching, K., Woodfield, H. (eds.) *Researching Sociopragmatic Variability: Perspectives from Variational, Interlanguage and Contrastive Pragmatics.* Basingstoke, UK: Palgrave Macmillan, 19-48.

Firth, A., Emmison, M., Baker, C. 2005. "Calling for Help: An Introduction." In: Baker, C., Emmison, M., Firth, A. (eds.) *Calling for Help. Language and Social Interaction in Telephone Helplines.* Amsterdam: John Benjamins, 1-35.

Fischer, E., Reuber, A.R. 2011. "Social Interaction via New Social Media: (How) Can Interactions on Twitter Affect Effectual Thinking and Behavior?" *Journal of Business Venturing* 26(1): 1-18.

Fischer, E., Reuber, A.R. 2014. "Online Entrepreneurial Communication: Mitigating Uncertainty and Increasing Differentiation via Twitter." *Journal of Business Venturing* 29: 565-583.

Floreddu, P.B., Cabiddu, F. 2016. "Social Media Communication Strategies." *Journal of Services Marketing* 20(5): 490-503.

Forey, G., Lockwood, J. 2007. "'I'd Love to Put Someone in Jail for This': An Initial Investigation of English in the Business Processing Outsourcing (BPO) Industry." *English for Specific Purposes* 26(3): 308-326.

Fornell, C., Westbrook, R.A. 1984. "The Vicious Circle of Consumer Complaints." *Journal of Marketing* 48(3): 68-78.

Freed, A.F. 2015. "Institutional Discourse." In: Tracy, K., Sandel, T., Ilie, C. (eds.) *The International Encyclopedia of Language and Social Interaction.* Boston: John Wiley & Sons, 809-826.

Freelon, D., Karpf, D. 2015. "Of Big Birds and Bayonets: Hybrid Twitter Interactivity in the 2012 Presidential Debates." *Information, Communication & Society* 18(4): 390-406.

Friginal, E. 2007. "Outsourced Call Centres and English in the Philippines." *World Englishes* 26(3): 331-345.

Friginal, E. 2008. "Linguistic Variation in the Discourse of Outsourced Call Centres." *Discourse Studies* 10(6): 715-736.

Friginal, E. 2009. *The Language of Outsourced Call Centres.* Amsterdam: John Benjamins.

Gałczyńska, A. 2003. *Akty odmowy we współczesnym języku polskim.* Kielce: Wydawnictwo Akademii Świętokrzyskiej.

Galdieri, C.J., Lucas, J.C., Sisco, T.S. (eds.) 2018. *The Role of Twitter in the 2016 US Election.* London: Palgrave Macmillan.

Gallaugher, J., Ransbotham, S. 2010. "Social Media and Customer Dialog Management at Starbucks." *MIS Quarterly Executive* 9(4): 197-212.

Gavioli, L. 1997. "Book Shop Service Encounters in English and Italian: Notes on the Achievement of Information and Advice." In: Bargiela-Chiappini, F., Harris, S. (eds.) *The Languages of Business. An International Perspective.* Edinburgh: Edinburgh University Press, 136-156.

Gelbrich, K., Roschk, H. 2011. "A Meta-Analysis of Organizational Complaint Handling and Customer Responses." *Journal of Service Research* 14: 24-43.

Georgalou, M. 2018. *Discourse and Identity on Facebook*. London: Bloomsbury.

Giannoni, D.S. 2014. "Comparison of British and Italian Customer-Complaint Forms." *English for Specific Purposes* 34: 48-57.

Giannoulakis, S., Tsapatsoulis, N. 2016. "Evaluating the Descriptive Power of Instagram Hashtags." *Journal of Innovation in Digital Ecosystems* 3: 114-129.

Gillin, P. 2007. *The New Influencers. A Marketer's Guide to the New Social Media*. California, CA: World Dancer Press, Sanger.

Gleason, B. 2013. "#Occupy Wall Street: Exploring Informal Learning About a Social Movement on Twitter." *American Behavioral Scientist* 57(7): 966-982.

Goffman, E. 1967. *Interaction Ritual: Essays on Face-to-Face Behaviour*. New York: Doubleday Anchor Books.

Goffman, E. (ed.) 1971. *Relations in Public: Microstudies of the Public Order*. London: Allen Lane.

Goffman, E. 1981. *Forms of Talk*. Pennsylvania: Pennsylvania University Press.

Golbeck, J., Grimes, J.M., Rogers, A. 2010. "Twitter Use by US Congress." *Journal of the American Society for Science and Technology* 61(8): 612-621.

Goodwin, C., Ross, I. 1989. "Salient Dimensions of Perceived Fairness in Resolution of Service Complaints." *Consumer Satisfaction, Dissatisfaction, and Complaining Behavior* 2: 87-92.

Graham, T., Broersma, M., Hazelhoff, K., van't Haar, G. 2013. "Between Broadcasting Political Messages and Interacting with Voters: The Use of Twitter During the 2010 UK General Election Campaign." *Information, Communication & Society* 16(5): 692-716.

Granberg-Rademacker, J.S., Parsneau, K. 2018. "Tweet You Very Much: An Analysis of Candidate Twitter Usage from the 2016 Iowa Caucus to Super Tuesday." In: Galdieri, C.J., Lucas, J.C., Sisco, T.S. (eds.) *The Role of Twitter in the 2016 US Election*. London: Palgrave Macmillan, 21-44.

Grant, W.J., Moon, B., Grant, J.B. 2010. "Digital Dialogue? Australian Politicians' Use of the Social Network Tool Twitter." *Australian Journal of Political Science* 45(4): 579-604.

Gretzel, U., Yoo, K.H. 2008. "Use and Impact of Online Travel Reviews." In: O'Connor, P., Hopken, W., Gretzel, U. (eds.) *Information and Communication Technologies in Tourism*. New York: Springer, 35-46.

Grice, H.P. 1969. "Utterer's Meaning and Intentions." *The Philosophical Review* 78: 147-177.

Grice, H.P. 1975. "Logic and Conversation." In: Cole, P., Morgan, J. (eds.) *Syntax and Semantics*. Vol. III: *Speech Acts*. New York: Academic Press, 41-58.

Gülnar, B., Balcı, Ş., Çakır, V. 2010. "Motivations of Facebook, YouTube and Similar Web Sites Users." *Bilig* 54: 161-184.

Gumperz, J. 1982. *Discourse Strategies*. Cambridge: Cambridge University Press.

Gutek, B.A. 1999. "The Social Psychology of Service Interactions." *Journal of Social Issues* 55(3): 603-617.

Ha, H.Y. 2006. "An Integrative Model of Consumer Satisfaction in the Context of E-Services." *International Journal of Consumer Studies* 30: 137-149.

Hall, E.J. 1993. "Smiling, Deferring, and Flirting: Doing Gender by Giving 'Good Service.'" *Work and Occupations* 20(4): 452-471.

Halloran, M., Thies, C. 2012. *The Social Media Handbook for Financial Advisors. How to Use LinkedIn, Facebook, and Twitter to Build and Grow Your Business*. New Jersey: John Wiley & Sons, Inc.

Harrington, S., Highfield, T., Bruns, A. 2013. "More Than a Backchannel: Twitter and Television." *Participations: Journal of Audience and Reception Studies* 10(1): 405-409.

Harrison-Walker, L.J. 2001. "E-Complaining: A Content Analysis of an Internet Complaint Forum." *Journal of Services Marketing* 15: 397-412.

Hennig-Thurau, T., Gwinner, K.P., Walsh, G., Gremler, D.D. 2004. "Electronic Word-of-Mouth via Customer-Opinion Platforms: What Motivates Customers to Articulate Themselves on the Internet?" *Journal of Interactive Marketing* 18(1): 38-52.

Hennig-Thurau, T., Malthouse, E.C., Friege, C., Gensler, S., Lobschat, L., Rangaswamy, A., Skiera, B. 2010. "The Impact of New Media on Customer Relationships." *Journal of Service Research* 13(3): 311-330.

Herbert, R.K. 1989. "The Ethnography of English Compliments and Compliment Responses: A Contrastive Sketch." In: Oleksy, W. (ed.) *Contrastive Pragmatics*. Amsterdam: John Benjamins, 3-35.

Heritage, J. 1998. "Oh-Prefaced Responses to Inquiry." *Language in Society* 27: 291-334.

Hermida, A. 2010. "Twittering the News: The Emergence of Ambient Journalism." *Journalism Practice* 4(3): 297-308.

Hernández-López, M. de la O., Fernández-Amaya, L. 2015. "Service Encounters and Communication: Why a Multidisciplinary Approach?" In: Hernández-López, M. de la O, Fernández-Amaya, L. (eds.) *A Multidisciplinary Approach to Service Encounters*. Leiden: Brill, 3-13.

Herring, S.C. 1993. "Gender and Democracy in Computer-Mediated Communication." *Electronic Journal of Communication* 3(2). Retrieved from: http://www.cios.org/www/ejc/v3n293.htm (accessed: 6 April 2015).

Herring, S.C. (ed.) 1996. *Computer-Mediated Communication: Linguistic, Social and Cross-Cultural Perspectives*. Amsterdam: John Benjamins.

Herring, S.C. 1996. "Introduction." In: Herring, S.C. (ed.) *Computer-Mediated Communication: Linguistic, Social and Cross-Cultural Perspectives*. Amsterdam: John Benjamins, 1-10.

Herring, S.C. 1999. "Interactional Coherence in CMC." *Journal of Computer-Mediated Communication* 4(4). Retrieved from: http://www.ascusc.org/jcmc/vol4/issue4/herring.html (accessed: 29 January 2007).

Herring, S.C. 2001. "Computer-Mediated Discourse." In: Schiffrin, D., Tannen, D., Hamilton, H.E. (eds.) *The Handbook of Discourse Analysis*. Oxford: Blackwell, 612-634.

Herring, S.C. 2003. "Gender and Power in Online Communication." In: Holmes, J., Meyerhoff, M. (eds.) *The Handbook of Language and Gender*. Oxford: Blackwell, 202-228.

Herring, S.C. 2004. "Online Communication: Through the Lens of Discourse." In: Consalvo, M., Baym, N., Hunsinger, J., Jensen, K., Logie, J., Murero, M., Shade, L. (eds.) *Internet Research Annual*. Vol. 1. New York: Peter Lang, 65-76.

Herring, S.C., Scheidt, L.A., Bonus, S., Wright, E. 2004. "Bridging the Gap. A Genre Analysis of Weblogs." *Proceedings of the 37ᵗʰ Hawaii International Conference on System Sciences (HICSS-37)*. Los Alamitos: IEEE Computer Society Press. Retrieved from: http://ella.slis.indiana.edu/~herring/herring.scheidt.2004.pdf (accessed: 25 March 2011).

Herring, S.C., Stein, D., Virtanen, T. (eds.) 2013. *Handbook of Pragmatics of Computer-Mediated Communication*. Berlin: Mouton de Gruyter.

Herring, S.C., Stein, D., Virtanen, T. 2013. "Introduction to the Pragmatics of Computer-Mediated Communication." In: Herring, S.C., Stein, D., Virtanen, T. (eds.) *Handbook of Pragmatics of Computer-Mediated Communication*. Berlin: Mouton de Gruyter, 3-31.

Heyd, T., Puschmann, C. 2017. "Hashtagging and the Functional Shift: Adaptation and Appropriation of the #." *Journal of Pragmatics* 116: 51-63.

Hixson, K. 2018. "Candidate Image: When Tweets Trump Tradition." In: Galdieri, C.J., Lucas, J.C., Sisco, T.S. (eds.) *The Role of Twitter in the 2016 US Election*. London: Palgrave Macmillan, 45-62.

Ho, V. 2017a. "Achieving Service Recovery through Responding to Negative Online Reviews." *Discourse & Communication* 11(1): 31-50.

Ho, V. 2017b. "Giving Offence and Making Amends: How Hotel Management Attempts to Manage Rapport with Dissatisfied Customers." *Journal of Pragmatics* 109: 1-11.

Hodgkin, A. 2017. *Following Searle on Twitter. How Words Create Digital Institutions*. Chicago: The University of Chicago Press.

Holmes, J. 1986. "Compliments and Compliment Responses in New Zealand English." *Anthropological Linguistics* 28(4): 485-508.

Holmes, J. 1990. "Apologies in New Zealand English." *Language in Society* 19(2): 155-199.

Holmes, J., Brown, D.F. 1987. "Teachers and Students Learning about Compliments." *TESOL Quarterly* 21: 523-545.

Homburg, Ch., Fürst, A. 2007. "See No Evil, Hear No Evil, Speak No Evil: A Study of Defensive Organizational Behavior towards Customer Complaints." *Journal of the Academy of Marketing Science* 35(4): 523–536.

Honeycutt, C., Herring, S.C. 2009. "Beyond Microblogging: Conversation and Collaboration via Twitter." *Proceedings of the 42nd Hawaii International Conference on System Sciences (HICSS-42) 5-8 Jan. Big Island, HI*, 1-10.

Hood, S., Forey, G. 2008. "The Interpersonal Dynamics of Call-Centre Interactions: Co-Constructing the Rise and Fall of Emotion." *Discourse & Communication* 2(4): 389-409.

Horan, T. 2013. "'Soft' Versus 'Hard' News on Microblogging Networks: Semantic Analysis of Twitter Produsage." *Information, Communication & Society* 16(1): 43-60.

House, J. 1989. "Politeness in English and German: The Functions of Please and Bitte." In: Blum-Kulka, S., House, J., Kasper, G. (eds.) *Cross-Cultural Pragmatics: Requests and Apologies*. Norwood, NJ: Ablex, 96-119.

House, J., Kasper, G. 1981. "Politeness Markers in English and German." In: Coulmas, F. (ed.) *Conversational Routine: Explorations in Standardized Communication Situations and Prepatterned Speech*. New York: Mouton, 157-185.

Houtkoop, H., Jansen, F., Walstock, A. 2005. "Collaborative Problem Description in Help Desk Calls*." In: Baker, C., Emmison, M., Firth, A. (eds.) *Calling for Help. Language and Social Interaction in Telephone Helplines*. Amsterdam: John Benjamins, 64-89.

Huang, J., Thornton, K.M., Efthimiadis, E.N. 2010. "Conversational Tagging in Twitter." *The Proceedings of Hypertext and Hypermedia*. New York, NY: Association for Computing Machinery (ACM), 173-178.

Hunston, S. 1994. "Evaluation and Organization in a Sample of Written Academic Discourse." In: Coulthard, M. (ed.) *Advances in Written Text Analysis*. London: Routledge, 191-218.

Hunston, S. 2007. "Using a Corpus to Investigate Stance Quantitatively and Qualitatively." In: Englebretson, R. (ed.) *Stancetaking in Discourse: Subjectivity, Evaluation, Interaction*. Amsterdam: John Benjamins, 27-48.

Hunston, S. 2011. *Corpus Approaches to Evaluation. Phraseology and Evaluative Language*. London: Routledge.

Hunston, S., Thompson, G. (eds.) 2003. *Evaluation in Text. Authorial Stance and the Construction of Discourse*. Oxford: Oxford University Press.

Hutchby, I., Wooffitt, R. 2008. *Conversation Analysis*. London: Polity.

Hyland, K. 1998. "Exploring Corporate Rhetoric: Metadiscourse in the CEO's Letter." *The Journal of Business Communication* 35(2): 224-245.

Hymes, D. 1969. "Sociolinguistics and the Ethnography of Speaking." In: Ardener, E. (ed.) *Social Anthropology and Language*. London: Tavistock Publications, 47-93.

Ivorra-Perez, F.M. 2015. "The Impact of Cultural Dimensions on the Engagement Markers of Spanish, British and US Toy Selling Websites." In: Hernández-López, M. de la O, Fernández-Amaya, L. (eds.) *A Multidisciplinary Approach to Service Encounters*. Leiden: Brill, 141-163.

Jackson, N., Lilleker, D. 2011. "Microblogging, Constituency Service and Impression Management: UK MPs and the Use of Twitter." *The Journal of Legislative Studies* 17(1): 86-105.

Jacoby, J., Jaccard, J.J. 1981. "The Sources, Meaning and Validity of Customer Comment Behavior: A Psychological Analysis." *Journal of Retailing* 57(3): 4-24.

Jagodziński, P. 2013. "Impoliteness Strategies in a British Airline Call Centre: A Pragmatic Analysis of Customer Service Interactions." Doctoral thesis, Adam Mickiewicz University, Poznań.

Jagodziński, P., Archer, D. 2018. "Co-Creating Customer Experience through Call Centre Interaction: Interactional Achievement and Professional Face." *Journal of Politeness Research* 14(2): 179-199.

Jakosz, M. 2016. *Wartościowanie w internetowych komentarzach do artykułów prasowych dotyczących stosunków niemiecko-polskich. Próba analizy pragmalingwistycznej*. Katowice: Wydawnictwo Uniwersytetu Śląskiego.

Jakubowska, E. 1999. *Cross-Cultural Dimensions of Politeness in the Case of Polish and English*. Katowice: Wydawnictwo Uniwersytetu Śląskiego.

Jansen, B., Zhang, M., Sobel, K., Chowdhury, A. 2009. "Twitter Power: Tweets as Electronic Word of Mouth." *Journal of the American Society for Information Science* 60(11): 2169-2188.

Java, A., Song, X., Finin, T., Tseng, B. 2007. "Why We Twitter: Understanding Microblogging Usage and Communities." *Joint 9th WEBKDD and 1st SNA-KDD Workshop, San Jose, CA*. Retrieved from: http://aisl.umbc.edu/resources/369.pdf (accessed: 15 January 2015).

Jaworski, A., Galasiński, D. 2002. "The Verbal Construction of Non-Verbal Behaviour: British Press Reports of President Clinton's Grand Jury Testimony Video." *Discourse & Society* 13: 629-649.

Jefferson, G., Lee, J. 1981. "The Rejection of Advice: Managing the Problematic Convergence of 'Troubles-Telling' and a 'Service Encounter.'" *Journal of Pragmatics* 5: 399-422.

Joos, M. 1959. "The Isolation of Styles." *Georgetown University Monograph Series on Language and Linguistics* 12: 107-113.

Jucker, A.H., Ziv, Y. 1998. *Discourse Markers. Descriptions and Theory.* Amsterdam: John Benjamins Publishing.

Jungherr, A. 2015. *Analyzing Political Communication with Digital Trace Data. The Role of Twitter Messages in Social Science Research.* Cham: Springer International Publishing Switzerland.

Jungherr, A. 2016. "Twitter Use in Election Campaigns: A Systematic Literature Review." *Journal of Information Technology & Politics* 13(1): 72-91.

Kaplan, M.A., Haenlein, M. 2010. "Users of the World, Unite! The Challenges and Opportunities of Social Media." *Business Horizons* 53: 59-68.

Kasper, G., Blum-Kulka, S. 1993. *Interlanguage Pragmatics.* New York: Oxford University Press.

Kaszewski, K. 2009. "'Niestety nie ma takiej możliwości,' czyli jak przekazać klientowi złe wieści." In: Kaszewski, K., Ptaszek, G. (eds.) *„W czym mogę pomóc?" Zachowania komunikacyjnojęzykowe konsultantów i klientów call center.* Warszawa: Semper, 53-86.

Kaszewski, K. 2014. "Co niezadowolony klient pisze o sprzedawcy? Analiza komentarzy negatywnych w serwisie Allegro.pl." *Poradnik Językowy* 1: 81-90.

Kaszewski, K., Ptaszek, G. (eds.) 2009. *„W czym mogę pomóc?" Zachowania komunikacyjnojęzykowe konsultantów i klientów call center.* Warszawa: Semper.

Katz, E., Lazarsfeld, P. 1955. *Personal Influence: The Part Played by People in the Flow of Mass Communication.* Glencoe, UK: The Free Press.

Kehrberg, A. 2015. "'I Love You, Please Notice Me': The Hierarchical Rhetoric of Twitter Fandom." *Celebrity Studies* 6(1): 85-99.

Keller, E. 2007. "Unleashing the Power of Word of Mouth: Creating Brand Advocacy to Drive Growth." *Journal of Advertising Research* 47(4): 448-452.

Kenney, R., Akita, K. 2012. "The Epistemology of Retweeting and the Ethics of Trust." *Journal of Mass Media Ethics* 27(1): 68-70.

Kerbrat-Orecchioni, C. 2005. "Politeness in France: How to Buy Bread Politely." In: Hickey, L., Stewart, M. (eds.) *Politeness in Europe.* Clevedon: Multilingual Matters, 29-57.

Kerbrat-Orecchioni, C. 2006. "Politeness in Small Shops in France." *Journal of Politeness Research* 2(1): 79-103.

Kharroub, T., Bas, O. 2016. "Social Media and Protests: An Examination of Twitter Images of the 2011 Egyptian Revolution." *New Media & Society* 18(9): 1973-1992.

Ki, E.J., Nekmat, E. 2014. "Situational Crisis Communication and Interactivity: Usage and Effectiveness of Facebook for Crisis Management by Fortune 500 Companies." *Computers in Human Behavior* 35: 140-147.

Kiełkiewicz-Janowiak, A. 2013. "Brytyjczycy." In: Marcjanik, M. (ed.) *Jak zwracają się do siebie Europejczycy.* Warszawa: Wydawnictwo Uniwersytetu Warszawskiego, 187-204.

Kim, J., Song, H. 2016. "Celebrity's Self-Disclosure on Twitter and Parasocial Relationships: A Mediating Role of Social Presence." *Computers in Human Behavior* 62: 570-577.

Kinzey, R. 2009. "Managing Your Reputation in the Social Media World." *The Business Journal*. Retrieved from: http://www.bizjournals.com/triad/stories/2009/07/27/smallb2.html?page=all (accessed: 20 April 2015).

Knox, G., Oestvan, R. 2014. "Customer Complaints and Recovery Effectiveness: A Customer Base Approach." *Journal of Marketing* 78(5): 42-57.

Ko, H., Cho, C.H., Roberts, M.S. 2005. "Internet Uses and Gratifications: A Structural Equation Model of Interactive Advertising." *Journal of Advertising* 34: 57-70.

Kozicka-Borysowska, Ż. 2009. *Akt mowy przeproszenia. Studium pragmalingwistyczne.* Szczecin: Wydawnictwo Print Group.

Kraan, W. 2005. "The Metaphoric Use of Space in Expert-Lay Interaction about Computing Systems." In: Baker, C., Emmison, M., Firth, A. (eds.) *Calling for Help. Language and Social Interaction in Telephone Helplines.* Amsterdam: John Benjamins, 91-105.

Kreis, R. 2017. "#Refugeesnotwelcome: Anti-Refugee Discourse on Twitter." *Discourse & Communication* 11(5): 498-514.

Kreiss, D. 2016. "Seizing the Moment: The Presidential Campaigns' Use of Twitter During the 2012 Electoral Cycle." *New Media & Society* 18(8): 1473-1490.

Krüger, N., Stieglitz, S., Pothof, T. 2012. "Brand Communication in Twiter – A Case Study on Adidas." *PACIS 2012 Proceedings.* Paper 161. Retrieved from: http://aisel.aisnet.org/pacis2012/161 (accessed: 9 April 2015).

Kuiper, K., Flindall, M. 2000. "Social Rituals, Formulaic Speech and Small Talk at the Supermarket Checkout." In: Coupland, J. (ed.) *Small Talk.* London: Longman, 183-207.

Kumar, V., Mirchandani, R. 2012. "Winning with Data: Social Media-Increasing the ROI of Social Media Marketing." *MIT Sloan Management Review* 54(1): 55-61.

Kwak, H., Lee, C., Park, H., Moon, S. 2010. "What is Twitter, a Social Network or a News Media?" *WWW' 10: Proceedings of the 19th International Conference on World Wide Web.* New York, NY: ACM, 591-600.

Kwon, E.S., Sung, Y. 2011. "Follow Me! Global Marketers' Twitter Use." *Journal of Interactive Advertising* 12(1): 4-16.

Landqvist, H. 2005. "Constructing and Negotiating Advice in Calls to a Poison Information Centre." In: Baker, C., Emmison, M., Firth, A. (eds.) *Calling for Help. Language and Social Interaction in Telephone Helplines.* Amsterdam: John Benjamins, 207-234.

Langlotz, A., Locher, M.A. 2012. "Ways of Communicating Emotional Stance in Online Disagreements." *Journal of Pragmatics* 44: 1591-1606.

Laroche, M., Habibi, M.R., Richard, M.O., Sankaranarayanan, R. 2012. "The Effects of Social Media Based Brand Communities on Brand Community Markers, Value Creation Practices, Brand Trust and Brand Loyalty." *Computers in Human Behavior* 28: 1755-1767.

LaRose, R., Eastin, M.S. 2004. "A Social Cognitive Theory of Internet Uses and Gratifications: Toward a New Model of Media Attendance." *Journal of Broadcasting & Electronic Media* 48: 358-377.

Larson, K., Watson, R.T. 2011. "The Value of Social Media: Toward Measuring Social Media Strategies." *Proceedings of the International Conference on Information Systems (ICIS) 2011*, 1-18. Retrieved from: https://aisel.aisnet.org/icis2011 (accessed: 19 June 2015).

Larsson, A.O., Kalsnes, B., Christensen, C. 2017. "Elite Interaction: Public Service Broadcasters' Use of Twitter During National Elections in Norway and Sweden." *Journalism Practice* 11(9): 1137-1157.

Larsson, A.O., Moe, H. 2012. "Studying Political Microblogging: Twitter Users in the 2010 Swedish Election Campaign." *New Media & Society* 14(5): 729-747.

Laskowska, E. 2000. "Językowe środki wartościujące w funkcji nakłaniającej (na przykładzie wypowiedzi na sesjach Rady Miejskiej Bydgoszczy)." In: Michalewski, K. (ed.) *Regulacyjna funkcja tekstów*. Łódź: Wydawnictwo Uniwersytetu Łódzkiego, 342-348.

Lee, C., Chau, D. 2018. "Language as Pride, Love, and Hate: Archiving Emotions through Multilingual Instagram Hashtags." *Discourse, Context & Media* 22: 21-29.

Lee, C.C., Hu, C. 2005. "Analyzing Hotel Customers' E-Complaints From an Internet Complaint Forum." *Journal of Travel and Tourism Marketing* 17(2/3): 167-181.

Lee, C.K.M. 2011. "Micro-Blogging and Status Updates on Facebook: Texts and Practices." In: Thurlow, C., Mroczek, K. (eds.) *Digital Discourse: Language in the New Media*. New York: Oxford University Press, 110-130.

Lee, E.J., Oh, S.Y. 2012. "To Personalize or Depersonalize? When and How Politicians' Peronalized Tweets Affect the Public's Reactions." *Journal of Communication* 62: 932-949.

Lee, J., Park, D.H., Han, I. 2008. "The Effect of Negative Online Consumer Reviews on Product Attitude: An Information Processing View." *Electronic Commerce Research and Applications* 7: 341-352.

Lee, J.Y., Sundar, S.S. 2013. "To Tweet or to Retweet? That is the Question for Health Professionals on Twitter." *Health Communication* 28(5): 509-524.

Lee, M., Youn, S. 2009. "Electronic Word of Mouth (Ewom). How Ewom Platforms Influence Consumer Product Judgment." *International Journal of Advertising* 28: 473-499.

Leppänen, V. 2005. "Callers' Presentations of Problems in Telephone Calls to Swedish Primary Care." In: Baker, C., Emmison, M., Firth, A. (eds.) *Calling for Help. Language and Social Interaction in Telephone Helplines*. Amsterdam: John Benjamins, 177-205.

Lerner, G.H. 2003. "Selecting Next Speaker: The Context-Sensitive Operation of a Context-Free Organization." *Language in Society* 32(2): 177-201.

Letierce, J., Passant, A., Decker, S., Breslin, J.G. 2010. "Understanding How Twitter is Used to Spread Scientific Messages." *Proceedings of the Web Science Conference 2010*. Retrieved from: http://journal.webscience.org/314/2/websci10_submission_79.pdf (accessed: 29 September 2013).

Levy, S.E., Duan, W., Boo, S. 2013. "An Analysis of One-Star Online Reviews and Responses in the Washington, D.C., Lodging Market." *Cornell Hospitality Quarterly* 54: 49-63.

Lewandowska-Tomaszczyk, B. 2016. "Negative Emotions: Conflict & Cross-Linguistic Contrasts in Online Commenting Discourse." *Kwartalnik Neofilologiczny* LXIII(1): 66-83.

Lewandowska-Tomaszczyk, B. 2017. "Incivility and Confrontation in Online Conflict Discourses." *Lodz Papers in Pragmatics* 13(2): 347-367.

Li, Z., Li, C. 2014. "Twitter as a Social Actor." *Computers in Human Behavior* 39(C): 187-196.

Liao, H. 2007. "Do It Right This Time: The Role of Employee Service Recovery Performance in Customer-Perceived Justice and Customer Loyalty after Service Failures." *Journal of Applied Psychology* 92: 475-489.

Lillqvist, E., Louhiala-Salminen, L. 2014. "Facing Facebook: Impression Management Strategies in Company–Consumer Interactions." *Journal of Business and Technical Communication* 28(1): 3-30.

Lillqvist, E., Louhiala-Salminen, L., Kankaanranta, A. 2016. "Power Relations in Social Media Discourse: Dialogization and Monologization on Corporate Facebook Pages." *Discourse, Context & Media* 12: 68-76.

Lin, J.S., Peña, J. 2013. "Are You Following Me? A Content Analysis of TV Networks' Brand Communication on Twitter." *Journal of Interactive Advertising* 12(1): 17-29.

Linvill, D.L., McGee, S.E., Hicks, L. 2015. "Colleges' and Universities' Use of Twitter: A Content Analysis." *Public Relations Review* 38: 636-638.

Litvin, S.W., Goldsmith, R.E., Pan, B. 2008. "Electronic Word-of-Mouth in Hospitality and Tourism Management." *Tourism Management* 29(3): 458-468.

Liu, Z., Liu, L., Li, H. 2012. "Determinants of Information Retweeting in Microblogging." *Internet Research* 22(4): 443-466.

Lombardo, L. 2009. "Positioning and Stance in TV News Reporting of the 2003 Iraq War: The Anchor on CBS and the News Presenter on BBC." In: Morley, J., Bayley, P. (eds.) *Corpus-Assisted Discourse Studies on the Iraq Conflict. Wording the War.* London: Routledge, 141-164.

Lomborg, S. 2014. *Social Media, Social Genres. Making Sense of the Ordinary.* London: Routledge.

Lotan, G., Graeff, E., Ananny, M., Gaffney, D., Pearce, I., boyd, d. 2011. "The Arab Spring. The Revolutions Were Tweeted: Information Flows during the 2011 Tunisian and Egyptian Revolutions." *International Journal of Communication* 5: 1375-1405.

Loth, S., Huth, K., Ruiter de, J.P. 2015. "Seeking Attention: Testing a Model of Initiating Service Interactions." In: Hernández-López, M. de la O, Fernández-Amaya, L. (eds.) *A Multidisciplinary Approach to Service Encounters.* Leiden: Brill, 229-247.

Lovejoy, K., Saxton, G.D. 2012. "Information, Community, and Action: How Nonprofit Organizations Use Social Media*." *Journal of Computer-Mediated Communication* 17: 337-353.

Lovett, M., Peres, R., Shachar, R. 2013. "On Brands and Word-of-Mouth." *Journal of Marketing Research* 50(4): 427-444.

Lubecka, A. 1993. *Forms of Address in English, French and Polish: A Sociolinguistic Approach.* Kraków: Sumptibus Universitatis Iagellonicae.

Lubecka, A. 2000. *Requests, Invitations, Apologies and Compliments in American English and Polish. A Cross-Cultural Communication Perspective.* Kraków: Księgarnia Akademicka.

Lutzky, U., Gee, M. 2018. "'I Just Found Your Blog.' The Pragmatics of Initiating Comments on Blog Posts." *Journal of Pragmatics* 129: 173-184.

Maíz-Arévalo, C. 2014. "Expressing Disagreement in English as a Lingua Franca: Whose Pragmatic Rules?" *Intercultural Pragmatics* 11(2): 199-224.

Maiz-Arévalo, C. 2015. "Jocular Mockery in Computer-Mediated Communication: A Contrastive Study of a Spanish and English Facebook Community." *Journal of Politeness Research* 11(2): 289-327.

Malik, M.M., Pfeffer, J.A. 2016. "Macroscopic Analysis of News Content in Twitter." *Digital Journalism* 4(8): 955-979.

Malinowski, B. 1972 [1923]. "Phatic Communion." In: Laver, J., Hutcheson, S. (eds.) *Communication in Face-to-Face Interaction*. Harmondsworth, Middlesex: Penguin, 146-152.

Mamet, P. 2005. *Język w służbie menedżerów – deklaracja misji przedsiębiorstwa*. Katowice: Wydawnictwo Uniwersytetu Śląskiego.

Manes, J., Wolfson, N. 1981. "The Compliment Formula." In: Coulmas, F. (ed.) *Conversational Routine*. New York: Mouton, 115-132.

Manzanaro, L., Valor, C., Paredes-Gázquez, J.D. 2018. "Retweet If You Please! Do News Factors Explain Engagement?" *Journal of Marketing Communications* 24(4): 375-392.

Maragh, R.S. 2016. "'Our Struggles Are Unequal': Black Women's Affective Labor Between Television and Twitter." *Journal of Communication Inquiry* 40(4): 351-369.

Marquez Reiter, R. 1997. "Politeness Phenomena in British English and Uruguayan Spanish: The Case of Requests." *Miscelánea: A Journal of English and American Studies* 18: 159-167.

Marquez Reiter, R. 2000. *Linguistic Politeness in Britain and Uruguay. A Contrastive Study of Requests and Apologies*. Amsterdam: John Benjamins.

Marquez Reiter, R. 2002. "A Contrastive Study of Conventional Indirectness in Spanish: Evidence from Uruguayan and Peninsular Spanish." *Pragmatics* 12(2): 135-151.

Marquez Reiter, R. 2003. "Pragmatic Variation in Spanish: External Request Modification in Uruguayan and Peninsular Spanish." In: Núñez-Cedeño, R., López, L., Cameron, R. (eds.) *A Romance Perspective on Language Knowledge and Use*. Amsterdam: John Benjamins, 167-180.

Marquez Reiter, R. 2005. "Complaint Calls to a Caregiver Service Company: The Case of Desahogo." *Intercultural Pragmatics* 2(4): 481-513.

Marquez Reiter, R. 2006. "Interactional Closeness in Service Calls to Montevidean Carer Service Company." *Research on Language and Social Interaction* 39(1): 7-39.

Marquez Reiter, R. 2008. "Intra-Cultural Variation: Explanations in Service Calls to Two Montevidean Service Providers." *Journal of Politeness Research* 4(1): 1-29.

Marquez Reiter, R. 2009. "How to Get Rid of a Telemarketing Agent: Face-Work Strategies in an Intercultural Service Call." In: Lorenzo-Dus, N. (ed.) *Spanish at Work Analyzing Institutional Discourse across the Spanish-Speaking World*. London: Palgrave Macmillan, 208-226.

Marquez Reiter, R., Fulcher, G., Rainey, I. 2005. "A Comparative Study of Certainty and Conventional Indirectness: Evidence from British English and Peninsular Spanish." *Applied Linguistics* 26(1): 1-31.

Marquez Reiter, R., Luke, K.K. 2010. "Telephone Conversations Openings across Languages, Cultures and Settings." In: Trosborg, A. (ed.) *Pragmatics across Languages and Cultures (Handbook of Pragmatics)*. Berlin: Mouton de Gruyter, 103-138.

Marquez Reiter, R., Orthaber, S., Kádár, D.Z. 2015. "Disattending Customer Dissatisfaction on Facebook: A Case Study of a Slovenian Public Transport Company." In: Christopher, E. (ed.) *International Management and Intercultural Communication*. London: Palgrave Macmillan, 108-126.

Marquez Reiter, R., Placencia, M.E. 2004. "Displaying Closeness and Respectful Distance in Montevidean and Quinteno Service Encounters." In: Marquez Reiter, R.,

Placencia, M.E. (eds.) *Current Trends in the Pragmatics of Spanish*. Amsterdam: John Benjamins, 121-155.

Martin, J.R., White, P.R.R. 2005. *The Language of Evaluation: Appraisal in English*. New York: Palgrave Macmillan.

Marwick, A., boyd, d. 2011a. "'I Tweet Honestly, I Tweet Passionately': Twitter Users, Context Collapse, and the Imagined Audience." *New Media & Society* 13(1): 114-133.

Marwick, A., boyd, d. 2011b. "To See and Be Seen: Celebrity Practice on Twitter." *Convergence: The International Journal of Research into New Media Technologies* 17(2): 139-158.

Matley, D. 2018a. "'Let's See How Many of You Mother Fuckers Unfollow Me For This': The Pragmatic Function of the Hashtag #Sorrynotsorry in Non-Apologetic Instagram Posts." *Journal of Pragmatics* 133: 66-78.

Matley, D. 2018b. "This is NOT a #Humblebrag, This is Just a #Brag: The Pragmatics of Self-Praise, Hashtags and Politeness in Instagram Posts." *Discourse, Context & Media* 22: 30-38.

Matzat, U., Snijders, C. 2012. "Rebuilding Trust in Online Shops on Consumer Review Sites: Sellers' Responses to User-Generated Complaints." *Journal of Computer-Mediated Communication* 18: 62-79.

Mauri, A.G., Minazzi, R. 2013. "Web Reviews Influence on Expectation and Purchasing Intentions of Potential Hotel Customers." *International Journal of Hospitality Management* 34: 99-107.

McCarthy, M. 2000. "Mutually Captive Audiences: Small Talk and the Genre of Close-Contact Service Encounters." In: Coupland, J. (ed.) *Small Talk*. Harlow: Pearson Education, 84-109.

McColl-Kennedy, J.R., Sparks, B.A. 2003. "Application of Fairness Theory to Service Failures and Recovery." *Journal of Services Research* 5: 251-266.

McKeown, J., Zhang, Q. 2015. "Socio-Pragmatic Influence on Opening Salutation and Closing Valediction of British Workplace Email." *Journal of Pragmatics* 85: 92-107.

McWilliam, G. 2000. "Building Stronger Brands through Online Communities." *Sloan Management Review* 41(3): 43-54.

Meinl, M. 2010. "Electronic Complaints: An Empirical Study on British English and German Complaints On Ebay." Doctoral thesis, Rheinische Friedrich-Wilhelms-Universität Bonn. Retrieved from: http://hss.ulb.uni-bonn.de/2010/2122/2122.pdf (accessed: 26 January 2015).

Merritt, M. 1976. "On Questions Following Questions in Service Encounters." *Language in Society* 5(3): 315-357.

Michel, S., Bowen, D., Johnston, R. 2009. "Why Service Recovery Fails: Tensions among Customer, Employee, and Process Perspectives." *Journal of Service Management* 20: 253-273.

Miller, V. 2008. "New Media, Networking and Phatic Culture." *Convergence: The International Journal of Research into New Media Technologies* 14(4): 387-400.

Mitchell, T.F. 1957/1975. "The Language of Buying and Selling in Cyrenaica." *Hesperis* 44: 31-71. Reprinted as "The Language of Buying and Selling in Cyrenaica: A Situational Statement." In: Mitchell, T.F. (ed.) *Principles of Firthian Linguistics*. London: Longman, 167-200.

Molder te, H. 2005. "'I Just Want to Hear Somebody Right Now.' Managing Identities on a Telephone Helpline." In: Baker, C., Emmison, M., Firth, A. (eds.) *Calling for Help. Language and Social Interaction in Telephone Helplines*. Amsterdam: John Benjamins, 153-173.

Monzoni, C.M. 2008. "Introducing Direct Complaints through Questions: The Interaction Achievement of 'Pre-Sequences'?" *Discourse Studies* 10(1): 73-87.

Moon, S.J., Hadley, P. 2014. "Routinizing a New Technology in the Newsroom: Twitter as a News Source in Mainstream Media." *Journal of Broadcasting & Electronic Media* 58(2): 289-305.

Mourão, R.R. 2015. "The Boys on the Timeline: Political Journalists' Use of Twitter for Building Interpretive Communities." *Journalism* 16(8): 1107-1123.

Murphy, B., Neu, J. 1996. "My Grade's Too Low: The Speech Act Set of Complaining." In: Gass, S.M., Neu, J. (eds.) *Speech Acts across Cultures*. Berlin: Mouton de Gruyter, 191-216.

Murtagh, G. 2005. "Some Initial Reflections on Conversational Structures for Instruction Giving." In: Baker, C., Emmison, M., Firth, A. (eds.) *Calling for Help. Language and Social Interaction in Telephone Helplines*. Amsterdam: John Benjamins, 287-307.

Murthy, D. 2011. "Twitter: Microphone for the Masses?" *Media, Culture & Society* 33(5): 779-789.

Murthy, D. 2013. *Twitter. Social Communication in the Twitter Age*. Cambridge: Polity Press.

Myers, G. 2010. *The Discourse of Blogs and Wikis*. London: Continuum.

Myers, G. 2015. "Social Media and Professional Practice in Medial Twitter." In: Gotti, M., Maci, S., Sala, M. (eds.) *Insights into Medical Communication*. Bern: Peter Lang, 51-69.

Myers-Scotton, C. 2009. "Code-Switching." In: Coupland, N., Jaworski, A. (eds.) *The New Sociolinguistics Reader*. Basingstoke: Palgrave Macmillan, 473-489.

Naaman, M., Boase, J., Lai, C. 2010. "Is it Really about Me? Message Content in Social Awareness Streams." *CSCW' 10 Proceedings of the 2010 ACM Conference on Computer Supported Cooperative Work*, 189-192.

Neurauter-Kessels, M. 2011. "Im/polite Reader Responses in British Online News Sites." *Journal of Politeness Research* 7(2): 187-214.

Newman, R., Chang, V., Walters, R.J., Wills, G.B. 2016. "Web 2.0 – The Past and the Future." *International Journal of Information Management* 36: 591-598.

Nitins, T., Burgess, J. 2014. "Twitter, Brands, and User Engagement." In: Weller, K., Bruns, A., Burgess, J., Mahrt, M., Puschmann, C. (eds.) *Twitter and Society*. New York: Peter Lang, 293-304.

Norrick, N.R. 1978. "Expressive Illocutionary Acts." *Journal of Pragmatics* 2(3): 277-291.

Norrick, N.R. 1993. *Conversational Joking: Humor in Everyday Talk*. Bloomington, IN: Indiana University Press.

Ochs, E. (ed.) 1989. *The Pragmatics of Affect*. Special Issue of *Text* 9(1).

Ochs, E., Schegloff, E., Thompson, S. (eds.) 1996. *Interaction and Grammar*. Cambridge: Cambridge University Press.

Ochs, E., Schieffelin, B. 1989. "Language Has a Heart." *Text* 9(1): 7-25.

Ogiermann, E. 2009a. *On Apologising in Negative and Positive Politeness Cultures*. Amsterdam: John Benjamins.

Ogiermann, E. 2009b. "Politeness and In-Directness across Cultures: A Comparison of English, German, Polish and Russian Requests." *Journal of Politeness Research* 5: 189-216.

Ogiermann, E. 2012. "About Polish Politeness." In: Ruiz de Zarobe, L., Ruiz de Zarobe, Y. (eds.) *Linguistic Insights*. Vol. 132: *Speech Acts and Politeness across Languages and Cultures*. Bern: Peter Lang, 27-52.

Ogiermann, E. 2015. "Apology Discourse." In: Tracy, K. (ed.) *The International Encyclopedia of Language and Social Interaction*. Chichester: John Wiley & Sons, 1-6.

Ogiermann, E., Suszczyńska, M. 2011. "On Im/politeness behind the Iron Curtain." In: Bargiela-Chiappini, F., Kadar, D.Z. (eds.) *Politeness across Cultures*. London: Palgrave Macmillan, 194-215.

Olshtain, E. 1989. "Apologies across Languages." In: Blum-Kulka, S., House, J., Kasper, G. (eds.) *Cross-Cultural Pragmatics: Requests and Apologies*. Norwood, NJ: Ablex, 155-173.

Olshtain, E., Cohen, A.D. 1983. "Apology: A Speech Act Set." In: Wolfson, N., Judd, E. (eds.) *Sociolinguistics and Language Acquisition*. Rowley, MA: Newbury House Publishers, Inc., 18-35.

Olshtain, E., Weinbach, L. 1987. "Complaints: A Study of Speech Act Behavior among Native and Non Native Speakers of Hebrew." In: Vershueren, J., Bertuccelli-Papi, M. (eds.) *The Pragmatic Perspective: Selected Papers from the 1985 International Pragmatics Conference*. Amsterdam: John Benjamins, 195-208.

Olshtain, E., Weinbach, L. 1993. "Interlanguage Features of the Speech Act of Complaining." In: Kasper, G., Blum-Kulka, S. (eds.) *Interlanguage Pragmatics*. New York: Oxford University Press, 108-137.

Orchard, L.J., Fullwood, C., Galbraith, N., Morris, N. 2014. "Individual Differences as Predictors of Social Networking." *Journal of Computer-Mediated Communication* 19(3): 388-402.

O'Reilly, T. 2005. "What is Web 2.0? Pattern Recognition." Retrieved from: https://www.oreilly.com/pub/a/web2/archive/what-is-web-20.html (accessed: 19 January 2019).

Orthaber, S., Marquez Reiter, R. 2011. "'Talk to the Hand.' Complaints to a Public Transport Company." *Journal of Pragmatics* 43: 3860-3876.

Orthaber, S., Marquez Reiter, R. 2014. "'Thanks For Nothing' – Impoliteness in Service Calls." In: Ruhi, S., Aksan, Y. (eds.) *Exploring Impoliteness in Specialized and Generalized Corpora: Converging Methodologies and Analytic Procedures*. Newcastle upon Tyne: Cambridge Scholars Publishing, 11-39.

Page, R. 2012. *Stories and Social Media: Identities and Interaction*. London: Routledge.

Page, R. 2014. "Saying 'Sorry': Corporate Apologies on Twitter." *Journal of Pragmatics* 62: 30-45.

Pałka, P. 2009. *Strategie dyskursywne w rozmowie handlowej*. Katowice: Śląsk.

Palmer, S. 2013. "Characterisation of the Use of Twitter by Australian Universities." *Journal of Higher Education Policy and Management* 35(4): 333-344.

Palmer, A., Koenig-Lewis, N. 2009. "An Experiential, Social Network-Based Approach to Direct Marketing." *Direct Marketing: An International Journal* 3(3): 162-176.

Pallotti, G., Varcasia, C. 2008. "Service Telephone Call Openings: A Comparative Study on Five European Languages." *Journal of Intercultural Communication* 17: 1-29.

Pancer, E., Poole, M. 2016. "The Popularity and Virality of Political Social Media: Hashtags, Mentions, and Links Predict Likes and Retweets of 2016 U.S. Presidential Nominees' Tweets." *Social Influence* 11(4): 259-270.

Park, D.H., Lee, J. 2009. "eWOM Overload and its Effect on Consumer Behavioral Intention Depending on Consumer Involvement." *Electronic Commerce Research and Applications* 7(4): 386-398.

Park, H., Reber, B.H., Chon, M.G. 2016. "Tweeting as Health Communication: Health Organizations' Use of Twitter for Health Promotion and Public Engagement." *Journal of Health Communication* 21(2): 188-198.

Park, H., Rodger, S., Stemmle, J. 2013. "Analyzing Health Organizations' Use of Twitter for Promoting Health Literacy." *Journal of Health Communication* 18(4): 410-425.

Park, N., Kee, K.F., Valenzuela, S. 2009. "Being Immersed in Social Networking Environment: Facebook Groups, Uses and Gratifications, and Social Outcomes." *CyberPsychology & Behavior* 12(6): 729-733.

Parmelee, J. 2013. "Political Journalists and Twitter: Influences on Norms and Practices." *Journal of Media Practice* 14(4): 291-305.

Pfeffer, J., Zorbach, T., Carley, K.M. 2014. "Understanding Online Firestorms: Negative Word-of-Mouth Dynamics in Social Media Networks." *Journal of Marketing Communications* 20: 117-128.

Phelps, J.E., Lewis, R., Mobilio, L., Perry, D., Raman, N. 2004. "Viral Marketing or Electronic Word-of-Mouth Advertising: Examining Consumer Responses and Motivations to Pass Along Email." *Journal of Advertising Research* 44(4): 333-348.

Phua, J., Jin, S.V., Kim, J. 2017a. "Gratifications of Using Facebook, Twitter, Instagram, or Snapchat to Follow Brands: The Moderating Effect of Social Comparison, Trust, Tie Strength, and Network Homophily on Brand Identification, Brand Engagement, Brand Commitment, and Membership Intention." *Telematics and Informatics* 34(1): 412-424.

Phua, J., Jin, S.V., Kim, J. 2017b. "Uses and Gratifications of Social Networking Sites for Bridging and Bonding Social Capital: A Comparison of Facebook, Twitter, Instagram, and Snapchat." *Computers in Human Behavior* 72: 115-122.

Pihlaja, S. 2016. *Antagonism on YouTube. Metaphor in Online Discourse*. London: Bloomsbury.

Placencia, M.E. 2004. "Rapport-Building Activities in Corner Shop Interactions." *Journal of Sociolinguistics* 8(2): 215-245.

Placencia, M.E. 2005. "Pragmatic Variation in Corner Store Interactions in Quito and Madrid." *Hispania* 88(3): 583-598.

Placencia, M.E. 2008. "Requests in Corner Shop Transactions in Ecuadorian Andean and Coastal Spanish." In: Schneider, K.P., Barron, A. (eds.) *Variational Pragmatics*. Amsterdam: John Benjamins, 307-332.

Placencia, M.E. 2015. "Address Forms and Relational Work in E-Commerce: The Case of Service Encounter Interactions in Mercadolibre Ecuador." In: Hernández-López, M. de la O, Fernández-Amaya, L. (eds.) *A Multidisciplinary Approach to Service Encounters*. Leiden: Brill, 37-64.

Placencia, M.E., Lower, A. 2013. "Your Kids are Stinking Cute. Complimenting Behaviour on Facebook among Family and Friends." *Intercultural Pragmatics* 10(4): 617-646.

Placencia, M.E., Mancera Rueda, A. 2011. "'Vaya, ¡qué chungo!' Rapport-Building Talk in Service Encounters: The Case of Bars in Seville at Breakfast Time." In: Lorenzo-Dus, N. (ed.) *Spanish at Work*. London: Palgrave Macmillan, 192-207.

Pomerantz, A. 1987. "Compliment Responses: Notes on the Co-Operation of Multiple Constraints." In: Schenkein, J. (ed.) *Studies in the Organization of Conversational Interaction*. New York: Elsevier, 79-112.

Poster, W. 2007. "Who's on the Ling? Indian Call Centre Agents Pose as Americans for U.S.-Outsourced Firms." *Industrial Relations* 46(2): 271-304.

Pozzi, F.A., Fersini, E., Messina, E., Liu, B. 2016. *Sentiment Analysis in Social Networks*. London: Elsevier.

Ptaszek, G. 2008. "'Klient nasz pan' – językowe wykładniki grzeczności i uprzejmości konsultantów call center w rozmowie telefonicznej z klientami." In: Podracki, J., Wolańska, E. (eds.) *Język w mediach elektronicznych*. Warszawa: Semper, 105-112.

Ptaszek, G. 2009a. "'Ale my gadamy o Zosi, która mieszka w Australii' – językowe sposoby wyrażania niezadowolenia przez klientów." In: Kaszewski, K., Ptaszek, G. (eds.) *„W czym mogę pomóc?" Zachowania komunikacyjnojęzykowe konsultantów i klientów call center*. Warszawa: Semper, 87-95.

Ptaszek, G. 2009b. "Telefoniczna rozmowa handlowa." In: Kaszewski, K., Ptaszek, G. (eds.) *„W czym mogę pomóc?" Zachowania komunikacyjnojęzykowe konsultantów i klientów call center*. Warszawa: Semper, 11-17.

Pudlinski, C. 2005. "The Mitigation of Advice. Interactional Dilemmas of Peers on a Telephone Support Service." In: Baker, C., Emmison, M., Firth, A. (eds.) *Calling for Help. Language and Social Interaction in Telephone Helplines*. Amsterdam: John Benjamins, 109-131.

Puschmann, C. 2015. "The Form and Function of Quoting in Digital Media." *Discourse, Context & Media* 7: 28-36.

Puzynina, J. 1992. *Język wartości*. Warszawa: Wydawnictwo Naukowe PWN.

Puzynina, J. 1997. *Słowo – wartość – kultura*. Lublin: Towarzystwo Naukowe Katolickiego Uniwersytetu Lubelskiego.

Puzynina, J. 2013. *Wartości i wartościowanie w perspektywie językoznawstwa*. Kraków: Polska Akademia Umiejętności.

Quan-Haase, A., Young, A.L. 2010. "Uses and Gratifications of Social Media: A Comparison of Facebook and Instant Messaging." *Bulletin of Science, Technology & Society* 30: 350-361.

Rambukanna, N. (ed.) 2015. *Hashtag Publics: The Power and Politics of Discursive Networks*. New York: Peter Lang.

Ramírez-Cruz, H. 2017. "¡No Manches, Güey! Service Encounters in a Hispanic American Intercultural Communication Setting." *Journal of Pragmatics* 108: 28-47.

Rapp, A., Beitelspacher, L.S., Grewal, D., Hughes, D.E. 2013. "Understanding Social Media Effects across Seller, Retailer, and Consumer Interactions." *Journal of the Academy of Marketing Science* 41(5): 547-566.

Rendle-Short, J. 2007. "'Catherine, You're Wasting your Time': Address Terms within the Australian Political Interview." *Journal of Pragmatics* 39(9): 1503-1525.

Resnik, A.J., Harmon, R.R. 1983. "Consumer Complaints and Managerial Response: A Holistic Approach." *Journal of Marketing* 47(1): 86-97.

Riegner, C. 2007. "Word of Mouth on the Web: The Impact of Web 2.0 on Consumer Purchase Decisions." *Journal of Advertising Research* 47: 436-447.

Roberts, C., Sarangi, S. 1999. "Hybridity in Gatekeeping Discourse: Issues of Practical Relevance for the Researcher." In: Sarangi, S., Roberts, C. (eds.) *Talk, Work, and Institutional Order*. Berlin: Mouton de Gruyter, 473-504.

Rogers, R. 2014. "Foreword: Debanalising Twitter: The Transformation of an Object of Study." In: Weller, K., Bruns, A., Burgess, J., Mahrt, M., Puschmann, C. (eds.) *Twitter and Society*. New York: Peter Lang, ix-xxvi.

Romenti, S., Murtarelli, G., Valentini, C. 2014. "Organizations' Conversations in Social Media: Applying Dialogue Strategies in Times of Crises." *Corporate Communications: An International Journal* 19(1): 10-33.

Roshan, M., Warren, M., Carr, R. 2016. "Understanding the Use of Social Media by Organisations For Crisis Communication." *Computers in Human Behavior* 63: 350-361.

Ross, C., Terras, M., Warwick, C., Welsh, A. 2011. "Enabled Backchannel: Conference Twitter Use by Digital Humanists." *Journal of Documentation* 67(2): 214-237.

Rothenbuhler, E. 1998. *Ritual Communication: From Everyday Conversation to Mediated Ceremony*. London: Sage.

Rybalko, S., Seltzer, T. 2010. "Dialogic Communication in 140 Characters or Less: How Fortune 500 Companies Engage Stakeholders Using Twitter." *Public Relations Review* 36(4): 336-341.

Sacks, H., Schegloff, E., Jefferson, G. 1974. "A Simplest Systematics for the Organization of Turn-Taking for Conversation." *Language* 50: 697-735.

Safko, L., Brake, D.K. 2009. *The Social Media Bible: Tactics, Tools, and Strategies for Business Success*. Hoboken, NJ: Wiley.

Sashi, C.M. 2012. "Customer Engagement, Buyer-Seller Relationships, and Social Media." *Management Decision* 50(2): 253-272.

"Say Hello to Customer 3.0." 2013. Accenture. Retrieved from: http://www.accenture.com/SiteCollectionDocuments/Accenture-Customer-3.0-POV-Final-v2.pdf (accessed: 28 March 2017).

Scarborough, W.J. 2018. "Feminist Twitter and Gender Attitudes: Opportunities and Limitations to Using Twitter in the Study of Public Opinion." *Socius: Sociological Research for a Dynamic World*. Retrieved from: https://doi.org/10.1177/2378023118780760 (accessed: 8 December 2018).

Schegloff, E.A. 1968. "Sequencing in Conversational Openings." *American Anthropologist* 70: 1075-1095.

Schegloff, E.A. 1972. "Sequencing in Conversational Openings." In: Gumperz, J.J., Hymes, D. (eds.) *Directions in Sociolinguistics: The Ethnography of Communication*. New York: Holt, Rinehartand Winston, 346-380.

Schegloff, E.A. 2007. *Sequence Organization in Interaction: A Primer in Conversation Analysis*. Cambridge: Cambridge University Press.

Schegloff, E.A., Sacks, H. 1973. "Opening up Closings." *Semiotica* 7: 289-327.

Schiffrin, D. 1987. *Discourse Markers*. Cambridge: Cambridge University Press.

Schmidt, J. 2014. "Twitter and the Rise of Personal Publics." In: Weller, K., Bruns, A., Burgess, J., Mahrt, M., Puschmann, C. (eds.) *Twitter and Society*. New York: Peter Lang, 3-15.

Schneiker, A. 2018. "Telling the Story of the Superhero and the Anti-Politician as President: Donald Trump's Branding on Twitter." *Political Studies Review*. Retrieved from: https://doi.org/10.1177/1478929918807712 (accessed: 10 December 2018).

Scollon, R., Scollon, S. 1983. "Face in Interethnic Communication." In: Richards, J.C., Schmidt, R.W. (eds.) *Language and Communication*. London: Longman, 156-188.

Scollon, R., Scollon, S. 1995. *Intercultural Communication: A Discourse Approach*. Oxford: Blackwell.

Seargeant, P., Tagg, C. (eds.) 2014. *The Language of Social Media. Identity and Community on the Internet*. London: Palgrave Macmillan.

Searle, J. 1969. *Speech Acts. An Essay in the Philosophy of Language*. Cambridge: Cambridge University Press.

Sen, S., Lerman, D. 2007. "Why Are You Telling Me This? An Examination into Negative Consumer Reviews on the Web." *Journal of Interactive Marketing* 21(4): 76-94.

"Sentiment Analysis." Retrieved from: https://www.techopedia.com/definition/29695/sentiment-analysis (accessed: 18 January 2019).

Shane, T. 2018. "The Semiotics of Authenticity: Indexicality in Donald Trump's Tweets." *Social Media + Society*. Retrieved from: https://doi.org/10.1177/2056305118800315 (accessed: 10 December 2018).

Shermak, J. 2018. "Scoring Live Tweets on the Beat: Examining Twitter Engagement in Sports Newspaper Beat Reporters' Live Coverage." *Digital Journalism* 6(1): 118-136.

Shin, W., Pang, A., Kim, H.J. 2015. "Building Relationships through Integrated Online Media: Global Organizations' Use of Brand Web Sites, Facebook, and Twitter." *Journal of Business and Technical Communication* 29(2): 184-220.

Shively, R.L. 2011. "L2 Pragmatic Development in Study Abroad: A Longitudinal Study of Spanish Service Encounters." *Journal of Pragmatics* 43(6): 1818-1835.

Shmargad, Y. 2018. "Twitter Influencers in the 2016 US Congressional Races." *Journal of Political Marketing*. Retrieved from: https://doi.org/10.1080/15377857.2018.1513385 (accessed: 8 December 2018).

Siapera, E., Boudourides, M., Lenis, S., Suiter, J. 2018. "Refugees and Network Publics on Twitter: Networked Framing, Affect, and Capture." *Social Media + Society*. Retrieved from: https://doi.org/10.1177/2056305118764437 (accessed: 14 June 2018).

Sifianou, M. 2013. "The Impact of Globalization on Politeness and Impoliteness." *Journal of Pragmatics* 55: 86-102.

Simon, F.M. 2018. "What Determines a Journalist's Popularity on Twitter?: A Case Study of Behaviour and Self-Presentation." *Journalism Studies*. Retrieved from: https://doi.org/10.1080/1461670X.2018.1500491 (accessed: 14 December 2018).

Simons, H.W. 1986. *Persuasion: Understanding, Practice, and Analysis*. New York: McGraw-Hill.

Singh, J. 1988. "Consumer Complaint Intentions and Behavior: Definitional and Taxonomical Issues." *Journal of Marketing* 52: 93-107.

Singh, J., Howell, R.D. 1984. "Customer Complaining Behavior: A Review and Prospectus." In: Hunt, H.K., Day, R.C. (eds.) *Customer Satisfaction, Dissatisfaction and Complaining Behavior*. Bloomington, IN: Indiana University, 41-49.

Singh, V., Jain, A., Choraria, S. 2016. "Exploring the Role of Complaint Handling among Complaining Consumers." *Vision* 20(4): 331-344.

Skovholt, K., Grønning, A., Kankaanranta, A. 2014. "The Communicative Functions of Emoticons in Workplace E-Mails: :-)" *Journal of Computer-Mediated Communication* 19: 780-797.

Smith, A., Bolton, R., Wagner, J. 1999. "A Model of Customer Satisfaction with Service Encounters Involving Failure and Recovery." *Journal of Marketing Research* 36: 356-372.

Smith, A., Fischer, A., Yongjian, C. 2012. "How Does Brand-Related User-Generated Content Differ across YouTube, Facebook, and Twitter?" *Journal of Interactive Marketing* 26(2): 102-113.

Smól, J. 2010. "Językowe sposoby wyrażania negatywnych emocji w komentarzach użytkowników serwisu aukcyjnego Allegro." *Poradnik Językowy* 5: 51-61.

Sparks, B.A. 2001. "Managing Service Failure through Recovery." In: Kandampully, J., Mok, C., Sparks, B.A. (eds.) *Service Quality Management in Hospitality, Tourism and Leisure*. New York: Haworth, 193-219.

Sparks, B.A., Bradley, G.L. 2017. "A 'Triple A' Typology of Responding to Negative Consumer-Generated Online Reviews." *Journal of Hospitality & Tourism Research* 41(6): 719-745.

Sparks, B.A., Browning, V. 2010. "Complaining in Cyberspace: The Motives and Forms of Hotel Guests' Complaints Online." *Journal of Hospitality Marketing & Management* 19(7): 797-818.

Sparks, B.A., Browning, V. 2011. "The Impact of Online Reviews on Hotel Booking Intentions and Perception of Trust." *Tourism Management* 32: 1310-1323.

Sparks, B.A., Fredline, L. 2007. "Providing an Explanation for Service Failure: Context, Content, and Customer Responses." *Journal of Hospitality & Tourism Research* 31(2): 241-260.

Stieglitz, S., Krüger, N. 2014. "Public Enterprise-Related Communication and its Impact on Social Media Issue Management." In: Weller, K., Bruns, A., Burgess, J., Mahrt, M., Puschmann, C. (eds.) *Twitter and Society*. New York: Peter Lang, 281-292.

Strauss, J., Frost, R. 2009. *E-Marketing*. New York: Pearson Prentice Hall.

Stubbs, M. 1983. *Discourse Analysis: The Sociolinguistic Analysis of Natural Language*. Oxford: Blackwell.

Suh, B., Hong, L., Pirolli, P., Chi, E.H. 2010. "Want to be Retweeted? Large Scale Analytics on Factors Impacting Retweet." *2010 IEEE Second International Conference on Social Computing, Minneapolis*, 177-184.

Suszczyńska, M. 1999. "Apologizing in English, Polish and Hungarian: Different Languages, Different Strategies." *Journal of Pragmatics* 31(8): 1053-1065.

Svinhufvud, K. 2018. "Waiting for the Customer: Multimodal Analysis of Waiting in Service Encounters." *Journal of Pragmatics* 129: 48-75.

Swani, K., Brown, B.P., Milne, G.R. 2014. "Should Tweets Differ for B2B and B2C? An Analysis of Fortune 500 Companies' Twitter Communications." *Industrial Marketing Management* 43: 873-881.

Swani, K., Milne, G.R., Brown, B.P. 2013a. "Spreading the Word through Likes on Facebook: Evaluating the Message Strategy Effectiveness of Fortune 500 Companies." *Journal of Research in Interactive Marketing* 7(4): 269-294.

Swani, K., Milne, G.R., Cromer, C., Brown, B.P. 2013b. "Fortune 500 Companies' Use of Twitter Communications: A Comparison between Product and Service Tweets." *International Journal of Integrated Marketing Communications* 5(2): 47-56.

Tagg, C. 2012. *Discourse of Text Messaging.* London: Continuum.

Tagg, C. 2015. *Exploring Digital Communication. Language in Action.* London: Routledge.

Tannen, D., Trester, A. (eds.) 2013. *Discourse 2.0: Language and New Media.* Washington, DC: Georgetown University Press.

Tax, S.S., Brown, S.W. 1998. "Recovering and Learning from Service Failure." *Sloan Management Review* 40(1): 75-88.

Tax, S.S., Brown, S.W., Chandrashekaran, M. 1998. "Customer Evaluations of Service Complaint Experiences: Implications for Relationship Marketing." *Journal of Marketing* 62(2): 60-76.

Taylor, D.G., Lewin, J.E., Strutton, D. 2011. "Friends, Fans, and Followers: Do Ads Work on Social Networks? How Gender and Age Shape Receptivity." *Journal of Advertising Research* 51(1): 258-275.

Taylor, J. 2015. "Need a Coffee: Pragmalinguistic Variation of Starbucks Service Encounters." *IULC Working Papers* 15(1): 33-61.

Taylor, P., Bain, P. 2005. "'India Calling to the Far Away Towns': The Call Centre Labour Process and Globalization." *Work, Employment and Society* 19(2): 261-282.

Tereszkiewicz, A. 2015a. "Skarga na Twitterze (sposoby wyrażania skarg przez klientów firm telekomunikacyjnych)." *Poradnik Językowy* 9: 28-40.

Tereszkiewicz, A. 2015b. "Zachowania grzecznościowe w interakcji handlowej na Twitterze." *Media-Kultura-Komunikacja Społeczna* 11(4): 65-80.

Tereszkiewicz, A. 2016. "Ministerstwa na Twitterze. Strategie reagowania na negatywne komentarze użytkowników na profilach wybranych ministerstw." *Studia Medioznawcze* 2(65): 39-50.

Tereszkiewicz, A. 2017a. "Komunikacja z klientem na Twitterze – analiza wybranych aktów mowy w interakcji handlowej online." *Studia Medioznawcze* 1(68): 75-85.

Tereszkiewicz, A. 2017b. "Przykro nam to słyszeć :(Reakcje firm telekomunikacyjnych na skargi i zażalenia klientów publikowane w serwisie Twitter." *Poradnik Językowy* 3: 17-29.

Tereszkiewicz, A. 2018. "Handling Positive Evaluation in Customer Encounters on Twitter." *Media i Społeczeństwo* 8: 194-205.

Tereszkiewicz, A. forthcoming-a. "Rejecting Consumer Complaints in Customer Encounters on Twitter – The Case of English and Polish Brand Communication." *Journal of Politeness Research.*

Tereszkiewicz, A. forthcoming-b. "Responding to Customer Complaints on English and Polish Corporate Profiles on Twitter." *Pragmatics and Society.*

Tereszkiewicz, A. forthcoming-c. "The Language of English and Polish Corporate Tweets – A Corpus Analysis." *Kwartalnik Neofilologiczny.*

Thelwall, M., Buckley, K., Paltoglou, G. 2011. "Sentiment in Twitter Events." *Journal of the American Society for Information Science and Technology* 62: 406-418.

Thornborrow, J. 2015. *The Discourse of Public Participation Media. From Talk Show to Twitter*. London: Routledge.

Thurlow, C. 2013. "Fakebook: Synthetic Media, Pseudo-Sociality and the Rhetorics of Web 2.0." In: Tannen, D., Trester, A. (eds.) *Discourse 2.0: Language and New Media*. Washington, DC: Georgetown University Press, 225-248.

Thurlow, C., Mroczek, K. (eds.) 2011. *Digital Discourse: Language in the New Media*. New York: Oxford University Press.

"Top 100 Twitter Users by Followers." Retrieved from: https://socialblade.com/twitter/top/100/followers (accessed: 19 January 2019).

Torode, B. 2005. "Institutionality at Issue. The Helpline Call as a 'Language Game.'" In: Baker, C., Emmison, M., Firth, A. (eds.) *Calling for Help. Language and Social Interaction in Telephone Helplines*. Amsterdam: John Benjamins, 257-283.

Torras, M.C., Gafaranga, J. 2002. "Social Identities and Language Alternation in Non-Formal Institutional Bilingual Talk: Trilingual Service Encounters in Barcelona." *Language in Society* 31: 527-548.

Traverso, V. 2006. "Aspects of Polite Behaviour in French and Syrian Service Encounters: A Data-Based Comparative Study." *Journal of Politeness Research* 2: 105-122.

Trosborg, A. 1995. *Interlanguage Pragmatics: Requests, Complaints and Apologies*. Berlin: Mouton de Gruyter.

Trosborg, A., Shaw, P. 1998. "'Sorry Does Not Pay My Bills': Customer Complaints in a Cross Cultural Setting." *Hermes Journal of Linguistics* 21: 67-94.

Trottier, D., Fuchs, C. (eds.) 2015. *Social Media, Politics and the State. Protests, Revolutions, Riots, Crime and Policing in the Age of Facebook, Twitter and YouTube*. London: Routledge.

Tsimonis, G., Dimitriadis, S. 2014. "Brand Strategies in Social Media." *Marketing Intelligence & Planning* 32(3): 328-344.

Tsur, O., Rappoport, A. 2012. "What's in a Hashtag?: Content Based Prediction of the Spread of Ideas in Microblogging Communities." *Proceedings of the Fifth ACM International Conference on Web Search and Data Mining*, 643-652.

Tumasjan, A., Sprenger, T.O., Sandner, P.G., Welpe, I.M. 2010. "Predicting Elections with Twitter: What 140 Characters Reveal about Political Sentiment." In: Hearst, M., Cohen, W., Gosling, S. (eds.) *ICWSM 2010: Proceedings of the 4th International AAAI Conference on Weblogs and Social Media, Association for the Advancement of Artificial Intelligence (AAAI), Menlo Park*, 178-185.

"Twitter – Statistics & Facts." Retrieved from: https://www.statista.com/topics/737/twitter (accessed: 19 January 2019).

"Twitter by the Numbers: Stats, Demographics & Fun Facts." Retrieved from: https://www.omnicoreagency.com/twitter-statistics (accessed: 19 January 2019).

Van Mulken, M., Meerder, W. 2005. "Are You Being Served? A Genre Analysis of American and Dutch Company Replies to Customer Services." *English for Specific Purposes* 24: 93-109.

Vander Wal, T. 2007. "Folksonomy Coinage and Definition." Retrieved from: http://vanderwal.net/folksonomy.html (accessed: 12 February 2015).

Vanderveken, D., MacQueen, K. 1990. "Semantic Analysis of English Performative Verbs." In: Vanderveken, D. (ed.) *Meaning and Speech Acts*. Vol. 1: *Principles of Language Use*. Cambridge: Cambridge University Press, 166-219.

Van Norel, N.D., Kommers, P.A.M., Van Hoof, J.J., Verhoeven, J.W.M. 2014. "Damaged Corporate Reputation: Can Celebrity Tweets Repair It?" *Computers in Human Behavior* 36: 308-315.

Varcasia, C. 2013. *Business and Service Telephone Conversations. An Investigation of British English, German and Italian Encounters*. London: Palgrave Macmillan.

Vásquez, C. 2011. "Complaints Online: The Case of TripAdvisor." *Journal of Pragmatics* 43: 1707-1717.

Vásquez, C. 2012. "Narrativity and Involvement in Online Consumer Reviews. The Case of TripAdvisor." *Narrative Inquiry* 22(1): 105-121.

Vásquez, C. 2014. *The Discourse of Online Consumer Reviews*. London: Bloomsbury.

Vásquez, C. 2015. "'Don't Even Get Me Started...': Interactive Metadiscourse in Online Consumer Reviews." In: Darics, E. (ed.) *Digital Business Discourse*. Hampshire: Palgrave Macmillan, 19-39.

Vasterman, P. (ed.) 2018. *From Media Hype to Twitter Storm. News Explosions and Their Impact on Issues, Crises, and Public Opinion*. Amsterdam: Amsterdam University Press.

Ventola, E. 1987. *The Structure of Social Interaction: A Systemic Approach to the Semiotics of Service Encounters*. London: Frances Pinter.

Ventola, E. 2005. "Revisiting Service Encounters Genre – Some Reflections." *Folia Linguistica* 39(1-2): 19-43.

Verweij, P. 2012. "Twitter Links Between Politicians and Journalists." *Journalism Practice* 6(5-6): 680-691.

Vis, F. 2013. "Twitter as a Reporting Tool for Breaking News. Journalists Tweeting the 2011 UK Riots." *Digital Journalism* 1(1): 27-47.

Vollmer, C., Precourt, G. 2008. *Always On: Advertising, Marketing, and Media in an Era of Consumer Control*. New York: McGraw-Hill.

Vollmer, H., Olshtain, E. 1989. "The Language of Apologies in German." In: Blum-Kulka, S., House, J., Kasper, G. (eds.) *Cross-Cultural Pragmatics: Requests and Apologies*. Norwood, NJ: Ablex, 196-218.

Wallace, D., Walker, J., Lopez, T., Jones, M. 2011. "Do Word of Mouth and Advertising Messages on Social Networks Influence the Purchasing Behavior of College Students?" *Journal of Applied Business Research* 25: 101-109.

Walther, J.B., Jang, J. 2012. "Communication Processes in Participatory Websites." *Journal of Computer-Mediated Communication* 18: 2-15.

Wang, A., Chen, T., Kan, M.Y. 2012. "Re-Tweeting From a Linguistic Perspective." *LSM 12 Proceedings of the Second Workshop on Language in Social Media. Montréal, Association of Computational Linguistics*, 46-55.

"Web 1.0." Retrieved from: https://www.techopedia.com/definition/27960/web-10 (accessed: 18 January 2019).

Wei, W., Miao, L., Huang, Z. 2013. "Customer Engagement Behaviors and Hotel Responses." *International Journal of Hospitality Management* 33: 316-330.

Weinberg, T. 2009. *The New Community Rules: Marketing on the Social Web*. Sebastopol, CA: O'Reilly Media, Inc.

Weller, K., Bruns, A., Burgess, J., Mahrt, M., Puschmann, C. (eds.) 2014. *Twitter and Society*. New York: Peter Lang.

Weller, K., Bruns, A., Burgess, J., Mahrt, M., Puschmann, C. 2014. "Twitter and Society: An Introduction." In: Weller, K., Bruns, A., Burgess, J., Mahrt, M., Puschmann, C. (eds.) *Twitter and Society*. New York: Peter Lang, xxix-xxxviii.

Whalen, J., Zimmerman, D.H. 2005. "Working a Call. Multiparty Management and Interactional Infrastructure in Calls for Help." In: Baker, C., Emmison, M., Firth, A. (eds.) *Calling for Help. Language and Social Interaction in Telephone Helplines*. Amsterdam: John Benjamins, 309-345.

Whiting, A., Williams, D. 2013. "Why People Use Social Media: A Uses and Gratifications Approach." *Qualitative Market Research: An International Journal* 16(4): 362-369.

Wieczorek, U. 1999. *Wartościowanie, perswazja, język*. Kraków: Wydawnictwo Naukowe Księgarnia Akademicka.

Wiersema, F. 2013. "The B2B Agenda: The Current State of B2B Marketing and a Look Ahead." *Industrial Marketing Management* 42(4): 470-488.

Wierzbicka, A. 1983. "Genry mowy." In: Dobrzyńska, T. (ed.) *Tekst i zdanie. Zbiór studiów*. Wrocław: Zakład Narodowy im. Ossolińskich, 125-137.

Wierzbicka, A. 1985. "Different Cultures, Different Languages, Different Speech Acts. Polish vs. English." *Journal of Pragmatics* 9(2-3): 145-178.

Wierzbicka, A. 1999. *Emotions across Languages and Cultures. Diversity and Universals*. Cambridge: Cambridge University Press.

Wierzbicka, A. 2003. *Cross-Cultural Pragmatics. The Semantics of Human Interaction*. Berlin: Mouton de Gruyter.

Wierzchowska, A. 2009. "'Ja pani wysłuchałem, teraz pani wysłucha mnie' – Sposoby przejmowania kontroli w rozmowie call center." In: Kaszewski, K., Ptaszek, G. (eds.) *„W czym mogę pomóc?" Zachowania komunikacyjnojęzykowe konsultantów i klientów call center*. Warszawa: Semper, 113-135.

Wilson, P.A., Lewandowska-Tomaszczyk, B. 2014. "Affective Robotics: Modelling and Testing Cultural Prototypes." *Cognitive Computation* 6(2): 1-2.

Wilson, P. A., Lewandowska-Tomaszczyk, B., Njiya, Y. 2013. "Happiness and Contentment in English and Polish." In: Fontaine, J., Scherer, K.R., Soriano, C. (eds.) *Components of Emotional Meaning: A Sourcebook*. Oxford: Oxford University Press, 477-481.

Wirtz, J., Chew, P. 2002. "The Effects of Incentives, Deal Proneness, Satisfaction and Tie Strength on Word-of-Mouth Behaviour." *International Journal of Service Industry Management* 13: 141-162.

Wirtz, J., Mattila, A.S. 2004. "Consumer Responses to Compensation, Speed of Recovery and Apology After a Service Failure." *International Journal of Service Industry Management* 15: 150-166.

Wolfson, N. 1981. "Compliments in Cross-Cultural Perspective." *TESOL Quarterly* 15(2): 117-124.

Wood, N., Burkhalter, J.N. 2014. "Tweet This, Not That: A Comparison Between Brand Promotions in Microblogging Environments Using Celebrity and Company-Generated Tweets." *Journal of Marketing Communications* 20(1-2): 129-146.

Wray, A. 2002. *Formulaic Language and the Lexicon*. Cambridge: Cambridge University Press.

Wyrwas, K. 2000a. "Struktura skargi mówionej." *Stylistyka* 9: 373-388.

Wyrwas, K. 2000b. "Wzorzec gatunkowy skargi i jego realizacje (na przykładzie tekstów literackich oraz skarg do instytucji)." In: Ostaszewska, D. (ed.) *Gatunki mowy i ich ewolucja*. Vol. 1: *Mowy piękno wielorakie*. Katowice: Wydawnictwo Uniwersytetu Śląskiego, 118-135.

Wyrwas, K. 2002. *Skarga jako gatunek mowy*. Katowice: Wydawnictwo Uniwersytetu Śląskiego.

Yan, Y., Zhang, W. 2018. "Gossip at One's Fingertips: Predictors of Celebrity News on Twitter." *Journalism*. Retrieved from: https://doi.org/10.1177/1464884918791349 (accessed: 18 December 2018).

Yang, L., Sun, T., Zhang, M., Mei, Q. 2012. "We Know What @You #Tag: Does the Dual Role Affect Hashtag Adoption?" *Proceedings of the 21st int'l Conference on World Wide Web, WWW'12, New York*, 261-270.

Yates, A.B. 2015. "Pragmatic Variation in Service Encounters in Buenos Aires, Argentina." *IULC Working Papers* 15(1): 128-158.

Ye, L., Ki, E.J. 2017. "Organizational Crisis Communication on Facebook: A Study of BP's Deepwater Horizon Oil Spill." *Corporate Communications: An International Journal* 22(1): 80-92.

Yule, G. 1996. *Pragmatics*. Oxford: Oxford University Press.

Yus, F. 2011. *Cyberpragmatics. Internet-Mediated Communication in Context*. Amsterdam: John Benjamins.

Zappavigna, M. 2011. "Ambient Affiliation: A Linguistic Perspective on Twitter." *New Media & Society* 13(5): 788-806.

Zappavigna, M. 2012. *Discourse of Twitter and Social Media. How We Use Language to Create Affiliation on the Web*. London: Continuum.

Zappavigna, M. 2014a. "Coffeetweets: Bonding Around the Bean on Twitter." In: Seargeant, P., Tagg, C. (eds.) *The Language of Social Media: Communication and Community on the Internet*. London: Palgrave Macmillan, 139-160.

Zappavigna, M. 2014b. "Enacting Identity in Microblogging through Ambient Affiliation." *Discourse & Communication* 8(2): 209-228.

Zappavigna, M. 2015. "Searchable Talk: The Linguistic Functions of Hashtags." *Social Semiotics* 25(3): 274-291.

Zappavigna, M. 2018. *Searchable Talk. Hashtags and Social Media Metadiscourse*. London: Bloomsbury.

Zarella, D. 2010. *The Social Media Marketing Book*. Sebastopol, CA: O'Reilly Media, Inc.

Zdunkiewicz, D. 1989. "Teoria implikatur Grice'a a język wartości." *Poradnik Językowy* 8: 519-527.

Zemke, R., Connellan, T. 2001. *E-Service. 24 Ways to Keep Your Customers When the Competition Is Just a Click Away*. New York: MACOM.

Zhang, J., Daugherty, T. 2009. "Third-Person Effect and Online Social Networking: Implications for Viral Marketing, Word-of-Mouth Brand Communications, and Consumer Behavior in User-Generated Context." *American Journal of Business* 24(2): 53-63.

Zhang, J., Daugherty, T. 2010. "Third-Person Effect Comparison Between US and Chinese Social Networking Website Users: Implications for Online Marketing and Word-of-Mouth Communication." *International Journal of Electronic Marketing and Retailing* 3(3): 293-315.

Zhang, M., Jansen, B., Chowdhury, A. 2011. "Business Engagement on Twitter: A Path Analysis." *Electronic Markets* 21: 161-175.

Zhang, Y., Vásquez, C. 2014. "Hotels' Responses to Online Reviews: Managing Consumer Dissatisfaction." *Discourse, Context & Media* 6: 54-64.

Zheng, T., Youn, H., Kincaid, C.S. 2009. "An Analysis of Customers' E-Complaints for Luxury Resort Properties." *Journal of Hospitality Marketing & Management* 18(7): 718-729.

Zimmerman, D. 1984. "Talk and Its Occasions: The Case of Calling the Police." In: Schiffrin, D. (ed.) *Meaning, Form, and Use in Context: Linguistic Applications, Georgetown University Roundtable on Languages and Linguistics*. Washington, DC: Georgetown University Press, 210-228.

Copy Editor
Karolina Wąsowska

Proofreader
Helena Piecuch

Typesetter
Marian Hanik

Jagiellonian University Press
Editorial Offices: ul. Michałowskiego 9/2, 31-126 Kraków
Phone: +48 12 663 23 80, +48 12 663 23 82, Fax: +48 12 663 23 83